Feminist Poetics of the Sacred

AMERICAN ACADEMY OF RELIGION
CULTURAL CRITICISM SERIES

SERIES EDITOR
Bjorn Krondorfer, St. Mary's College of Maryland

A Publication Series of
The American Academy of Religion and
Oxford University Press

Anti-Judaism in Feminist Religious Writings
Katharina von Kellenbach

The Great White Flood
Racism in Australia
Anne Pattel-Gray

On Deconstructing Life-Worlds
Buddhism, Christianity, Culture
Robert Magliola

Cultural Otherness
Correspondence with Richard Rorty, Second Edition
Anindita Niyogi Balslev

Cross Cultural Conversation
(Initiation)
Edited by Anindita Niyogi Balslev

Imag(in)ing Otherness
Filmic Visions of Living Together
Edited by S. Brent Plate and David Jasper

AMERICAN ACADEMY OF RELIGION

Feminist Poetics
of the Sacred

Creative Suspicions

EDITED BY
Frances Devlin-Glass
Lyn McCredden

OXFORD
UNIVERSITY PRESS
2001

OXFORD
UNIVERSITY PRESS

Oxford   New York
Athens   Auckland   Bangkok   Bogotá   Buenos Aires   Calcutta
Cape Town   Chennai   Dar es Salaam   Delhi   Florence   Hong Kong   Istanbul
Karachi   Kuala Lumpur   Madrid   Melbourne   Mexico City   Mumbai   Nairobi
Paris   São Paulo   Shanghai   Singapore   Taipei   Tokyo   Toronto   Warsaw

and associated companies in
Berlin   Ibadan

Copyright © 2001 by The American Academy of Religion

Published by Oxford University Press, Inc.,
198 Madison Avenue, New York, New York 10016

Oxford is a registered trademark of Oxford University Press

Library of Congress Cataloging-in-Publication Data
Feminist poetics of the sacred : Creative suspicions / edited by
Frances Devlin-Glass and Lyn McCredden.
p. cm.—(American Academy of Religion cultural criticism series)
Includes bibliographical references and index.
ISBN 0-19-514468-6; 0-19-514469-4 (pbk.)
1. Women and religion.   2. Feminist literary criticism.   3. Religious literature—History
and criticism.   I. Devlin-Glass, Frances.   II. McCredden, Lyn.   III. Series.
BL458 .C74 2001
200.82—dc21   00-063698

9   8   7   6   5   4   3   2   1
Printed in the United States of America
on acid-free paper

This volume is dedicated to the memory of Deborah Doxtator, a Mohawk woman, who had she lived would have been the youngest contributor to this collection. It is also dedicated to the many women who have encouraged and inspired with their prophetic courage, taking risks in the field of feminist spiritualities. To be active in this endeavor is to risk much in an often patriarchal, secular, and racist world.

Acknowledgments

There are many scholars whose intellectual leadership in the field of feminist spiritualities we wish to acknowledge: Frances Devlin-Glass wishes to thank Johanna Stuckey, who has been a continuing and generous powerhouse of knowledge about contemporary and ancient women's religious beliefs and practices. Johanna's intellectual curiosity was sparked decades before it was fashionable for feminists to rethink the sacred. She, and many other women, have been wonderfully supported (as has Frances) by the Center for Feminist Research at York, Ontario, Canada, especially by Nancy Mandell and Naomi Black, and by a male feminist scholar, Jordan Paper.

Lyn McCredden acknowledges the impact of the Australian Movement for the Ordination of Women, which throughout the 1980s struggled to articulate a vision of women as equal partners in the Christian church. Many of the women in this movement continue to bear the wounds of this struggle. She would also like to thank the Faculty of the Churches of Christ Theological College in Australia for the example of their tenacious commitment to a critical, gender-conscious, and grounded education in theological studies.

The editors would like to acknowledge the financial assistance of the Australian Women's Research Centre (Deakin University); the inspiration of many of the contributors to the 1997 Feminism and Spiritualities

Conference; the helpful staff of Deakin University Library and the Uniting Faculty of Theology Library (University of Melbourne); and the professional courtesy of the series editor, Professor Björn Krondorfer.

We thank the following publishers/holders of copyright for permission to reprint material: Dangeroo Press, Hale & Iremonger, Hyland House, and Dr. John E. Stanton. Extracts from "No More Boomerang," "Aboriginal Charter of Rights," and "Time is Running Out" by Oodgeroo of the tribe Noonuccal (formerly known as Kath Walker) from *My People*, third edition, Jacaranda Press, © 1990, reprinted by permission of John Wiley & Sons, Austrialia.

The editors thank all those women who have helped to form their passion for things of the spirit in very down-to-earth ways: Clare, Pat, Angela, Mary, Gwen, Marilyn, Ann, Doris, Wendy, Dorothy, Vicki, Victoria, Veronica. Finally, loving thanks to our families: Bride, Nicholas, Daniel, Terry, and Bob.

Contents

Contributors

Clare Bradford (Ph.D., Sydney University) is an Associate Professor at Deakin University in Melbourne, Australia, where she teaches literary studies and children's literature. She has published four books, and most recently has edited *Writing the Australian Child* (University of Western Australia Press, 1996), a study of children's literature. Her main research interests are in colonial and postcolonial literatures for children, picture books, and English medieval literature.

Amila Butorovic (Ph.D., McGill University) is an Assistant Professor in the Humanities Division, York University, Ontario, Canada. She teaches courses on Islamic religious tradition, Islamic literatures, and Islamic mysticism. Her research addresses two main issues: one, links among literature, Islam, and identity and two, Islamic literatures in interregional and intercultural contexts.

Stephen Curkpatrick (Ph.D., Flinders University) is an ordained Churches of Christ minister and lectures in New Testament studies and theology in the Evangelical Theological Association, an associated teaching institution of the Melbourne College of Divinity. His research interests are hermeneutics and language in theology, the parabolic and aphoristic in biblical tradition. More recently, he has been exploring alternative genres in theological education and communication.

Frances Devlin-Glass (Ph.D., Australian National University) is an Associate Professor in Literature and Women's Studies in the School of Literary and Communication Studies at Deakin University (Melbourne Campus). Her research is in Irish and Australian studies and feminist literature and theory. Her publications include *The Annotated Such is Life* (1991), and *"Flying in Between": Feminism and Literature Since Franken-stein* (1994), and she is currently working with senior women from an Aboriginal community on a website about Aboriginal myth and meaning-making.

Mary Dove (M.A., Ph.D. Cambridge) is a Lecturer in English, specializing in medieval studies, in the School of English and American Studies at the University of Sussex, United Kingdom. She has published several works on medieval interpretation of the Bible and is currently investigating the Wycliffite Old Testament.

Diane Fahey is a much-honored Australian poet, whose work is preoccupied with feminist retellings of Greek myth and fairy tales, with art and landscape, and, increasingly, ecological themes. Her books include *Voices from the Honeycomb* (Brisbane: Jacaranda, 1986), *Metamorphoses* and *Turning the Hourglass* (Sydney: Dangeroo, 1988 and 1990, respectively), *Mayflies in Amber* (Sydney: Angus and Robertson, 1993) and *The Body in Time* (Melbourne: Spinifex, 1995).

Dorothy A. Lee (Ph.D.) is Professor of New Testament in the United Faculty of Theology, Melbourne. She has published books and articles in the area of biblical theology (especially the Gospel of John), feminist theology and hermeneutics, and spirituality.

Lyn McCredden (Ph.D., Melbourne University) teaches literature at Deakin University, Melbourne, Australia. She is the author of two critical works, *James McAuley* (1992) and, with Rose Lucas, *Bridgings: Readings in Australian Women's Poetry* (1996).

Anne Pattel-Gray (Ph.D., D.D., FAIM) is Professor of Mission and Ecumenics at the United Theological College, Bangalore, India. Until recently, she was Director of Indigenous Communications Research (Asia-Pacific) of the World Association for Christian Communication; previously, she was Executive Secretary of the Aboriginal and Islander

Commission of the National Council of Churches in Australia. She is the author of *The Great White Flood: Racism in Australia* (Atlanta: Scholars Press, 1998), and editor of *Tiddas Talking Business* (Delhi: ISPCK, 2000).

Kate Rigby (Ph.D., Melbourne University) is a Senior Lecturer at Monash University and teaches in the areas of German studies, religious studies, and comparative literature and cultural studies. Her primary research interests lie in the interface of ecology, philosophy, literature, and religion. She is the author of *Transgressions of the Feminine. Tragedy, Enlightenment and the Figure of Woman in Classical German Drama* (Heidelberg: C. Winter, 1996) and, together with Silke Beinssen-Hesse, *Out of the Shadows. Contemporary German Feminist Theory* (Melbourne University Press, 1996) and has also published several articles in the areas of ecological aesthetics, "spirit of place," and ecofeminism.

Johanna H. Stuckey (Ph.D., Yale University) is University Professor Emerita, Humanities Division (in Women's Studies and Religious Studies Programmes), Faculty of Arts, York University (Ontario, Canada). She teaches ancient Goddess worship, feminist theology, and female spirituality at York University and the School of Continuing Studies of the University of Toronto. In her research, she uses the disciplines of women's studies and religious studies, as well as ritual studies, history, anthropology, literary criticism, and archaeology. She is working on a book tentatively entitled *Goddesses and Dying Gods in the Ancient Eastern Mediterranean*. She has recently published *Feminist Spirituality: An Introduction to Feminist Theology in Judaism, Christianity, Islam and Feminist Goddess Worship* (Centre for Feminist Research, York University, Toronto, Canada, 1998).

Feminist Poetics of the Sacred

Inside and Outside the Traditions

The Changing Shapes of Feminist Spiritualities

Frances Devlin-Glass and Lyn McCredden

For many contemporary women, their relationships to the institutions and traditions of religious faith are constructed on shifting ground. While some place themselves "outside" the institution, and often outside any orthodox understandings of their faith, others identify themselves to varying degrees as "inside." This metaphor—inside/outside—may be used as a means of self-definition that begins from a critical, discriminating acknowledgment of the power of religion and its institutions; conversely, the metaphor may be used by those in power within the religious establishments to marginalise such women. For the writers in this book, metaphors are never "mere" language but are sources of both creativity and suspicion. It may be helpful to think of oneself "outside" orthodoxy when the consequent insights and experiences yield new and challenging possibilities, even when such gains may be experienced through a great deal of pain. But when such metaphors are wielded as categorizing truths, with no sense of their transience on the one hand and of their tendency to rigidify on the other, they become weapons.

The essays in this book enable readers to ask questions about the kinds of power wielded by the organized monotheistic religions of Judaism, Christianity, and Islam. What forms of violence—psychic and spiritual, physical and political—have been experienced by women, that they attest to such ambivalent relations with religion? And how do the affiliations of women with different traditions and forms of spirituality—focused on indigeneity, goddess worship, alternative female voices, re-writings of canonical thinking, environmentalism—speak to women both "inside" and "outside" the traditions?

This book draws on the thought, experiences and scholarship of a range of women (and one man) who place themselves at various points across this spectrum, this shifting ground of inside/outside. Many are literary academics by profession, some are religious studies scholars, some theologians, some poets. Some place themselves as working within the religious establishments of their faith, some stand at a distance. Others would want to roam in territory well beyond the walls of ortho-doxy. But all have a keen interest in questions of female spirituality. Many attest, in different ways, to the violence done to women by or-ganized religions, if not the untenability of such organizations, and to what they see as the radical impoverishment of religious systems through such patriarchal violence. For French psychoanalyst and fem-inist philosopher Luce Irigaray, discussing relations within patriarchy, the effects of such violence are total, reaching both those excluded and those wielding the power to exclude:

> Everywhere you shut me in. Always you assign a place to me. Even outside the frame that I form with you. . . . You set limits even to events that could happen with others. . . . You mark out boundaries, draw lines, surround, enclose. Excising, cutting out. What is your fear? That you might lose your property. What re-mains is an empty frame. You cling to it, dead. (Irigaray 1992: 24–5)

Irigaray's notion of the frame—frame of the house, the home, the shared image—is a human one, formed of you *and* me. It is movable and expansive, but therefore it can also be moved to exclude, to shut in, to limit. Such boundary-marking is read as part of patriarchy's ex-ercise of power, a power connected to ownership and a deploying of identity politics that must know itself *as against* the other and fails to embrace what "could happen with others." The writers in this book are alive, through poststructuralist, feminist, and theological thought, to the "other," not out of fear and a desire to exclude. Their subject is often this "other"—the Aboriginal, the victim of sexual and wider patriarchal abuse, the strong, rebellious woman, nature, the heretic—as they strive to understand how the gargantuan and rigidifying structures of religion may work to obliterate otherness, even sometimes in the name of love for that other. It is often the very act of seeking community, the desire to belong and to experience mutuality, that can turn into defensiveness, fear, and exclusivity: "Our *differential* identification with families, with cultures, and with nations—the fact that we feel a part of some groups rather than others—creates the divisions between 'us' and 'them,' between self and other" (Manderson 1997:96).

This insight, reached in a recent debate about race relations in Australia, is two-edged. It may seem to be advocating a bland homogeneity or, worse, an obliteration of difference. But it is interested in the quality of identification—"*differential* identification"—that feels, out of fear, or ignorance, the need to obliterate the other family, or culture or nation, in order to experience and celebrate its own selfhood. This understanding and experience of being "inside" shows all the traits of brittleness and boundary-riding, a preoccupation with the offenses against the self, and is shaped by self-righteousness. Theorist Julia Kristeva, writing of Old Testament Judaism specifically but also more generally in relation to religious identity, writes:

> The one and the other are two aspects, semantic and logical, of the imposition of a *strategy of identity*, which is, in all strictness, that of monotheism. The semes that clothe the process of separation . . . are the inseparable lining of its logical representation aiming to guarantee the place and law of the One God. In other words, the place *and* law of the One do not exist without a *series of separations* that are oral, corporeal, or even more generally material. (Kristeva 1982:94)

To be "within" this desire for the One True God, according to Kristeva, is necessarily to conform to the "strategy of identity" that guarantees by exclusion, separation, and monolithic thinking. Further, the powerful delineation of the exclusions and separations of Judaic monotheism, with its strict ritual laws concerning food, relationships, and worship, is also applied by Kristeva to later Christian forms of identification, which do not, she argues, eradicate such strategies but *internalize* them in the form of conscience and guilt, complete with their regime of metaphors for standing guard: moral/immoral, righteous/sinful, saved/damned, rebellious/justified:

> [T]he New Testament will propose a subtle elaboration of the splitting that contemporary analytic listening discovers in so-called split subjects: the boundary between inside and outside. Before any relation to an other is set up, and as if underlying it, it is the

building of that archaic space, the topological demarcation of the preconditions of a subjectivity, *qua* difference between a sub-ject and an ab-ject . . . that takes over from earlier Levitical abominations. "Kill and eat," says God to an astonished Peter at Joppa (Acts 10:9–16). But that permission, far from being a liberalization, will lead the subject who complies with it to seek no longer his defilement but the error within his own thoughts and speech. (Kristeva 1982:117)

So, is the religious subject—and perhaps particularly the monotheist—necessarily a split subject, caught in the thrall of difference and condemned to shuttle back and forward, in and out, of her beliefs and their logical consequences? Is the religious subject always finally condemned to abjection, bound to seek purity while confessing impurity, seeking transcendence *because* mortality is experienced as so burdening? Many of these questions are of course closely analogous to those being asked by a wide range of feminists, both secular and religious, over the past thirty years in their relationship to patriarchy and to the symbolic. For many interpreters of the Acts 10 passage read the story of Peter's dream—of a sheet descending from heaven, filled with "every kind of animal and reptile and bird you could think of and a voice commanding 'Go to it, Peter—kill and eat' "—as announcing a new order of freedom from the old Jewish rules and rituals of eating. However, Kristeva is at pains in her essay "Qui Tollis Peccata Mundi" to argue that no such freedom—from guilt, from abjection, from fragmentary subjectivity—is possible as a religious subject. Whether experienced through external religious rituals or through internalizing of the truths, and foods, of the faith, for Kristeva the religious subject cannot escape abjection. As far as Christianity goes, "One of the insights of Christianity, and not the least one, is to have gathered in a single move perversion and beauty as the lining and cloth of one and the same economy" (1982:125).

However, there continue to be many questions raised by feminists, and religious feminists, about ways of thinking and being *beyond* or *in spite of*, or *after* patriarchal religion, and in full recognition of the (hopefully moveable) limitations of the symbolic order. The struggles of feminist spirituality over the past decades, and indeed throughout the centuries, are necessarily joined to those of the wider feminist movement.

The contributors to this book use a range of tools that have been developed and honed over the past three decades of feminist thinking and activism. Such tools have enabled the feminist search for an *inclusive* understanding and experience of belonging and difference. They provide ways of constructing and reviewing the kinds of spiritual identification and selfhood that enable not mere *tolerance* of difference but an open embrace, a being washed by such difference. Their development has a vital, heterogeneous, and ongoing history.

New Histories, New Epistemologies

When in the mid-1980s Clare B. Fischer revised her first bibliography of feminist writings in theology for publication under the title *Of Spirituality: A Feminist Perspective* (1995), it was with a sense that she was documenting a rapidly expanding field of scholarly research and that she was "a cartographer of new terrain" (1995: vii). The brief she gave herself was commendably comprehensive: to list both scholarly and more general resources; to be catholic in her representation of feminisms and spiritual traditions; to pay attention to theory as well as praxis, heterodoxy as well as orthodoxy, the mainstream and ex-centric traditions, male as well as female writers, thealogy and theology. This edition of essays shares these aims. She was aware, as we are, that spirituality and notions of sacredness may be understood within single disciplinary discourses but that the most exciting work often happens as a result of the dynamic interaction between disciplinary discourses. The history of late-nineteenth-century and twentieth-century disciplinary formation (and the increasing specialization that was and is its corollary) and the challenge to that history represented by postmodern and poststructuralist methodologies constitute for us an opportunity. This book celebrates those opportunities by putting narratologist into conversation with religious studies scholar, by crossing traditions examining particular iconographies, by seeking out muted traditions (especially those rendered dumb by the patriarchal and colonial experience) and inviting them to speak. This book represents a cross-section of the ways women scholars and thinkers are debating issues of how to practise and think about the sacred.

What kinds of conversations and debates are occurring as a result of three decades of self-conscious feminist literary critical methodologies in relation to narratives of the sacred? Where are three decades of reclamation, revising and re-visioning, and deconstruction, in both the mainstream and in marginalized and repressed traditions, leading us at the end of the twentieth century? Many women, even those committed to life within patriarchal institutions, have resisted and revisioned men's definitions of them and their forms of spirituality. The list is a long one: Schüssler Fiorenza includes Mary of Magdala, Prisca, Proba, Hildegard, Teresa of Avila, Sojourner Truth, Christine de Pizan, and Elizabeth Cady

Stanton, among others (1992a: 20; see also Schüssler Fiorenza 1992b [1983]: part 1). The heroic and sometimes subversive nature of that resistance has been documented compellingly in the scholarly synthesizing work of Gerda Lerner (1986, 1993). Several of the essays in this book (Butorovic, Dove, Bradford) stand as testimony to the phenomenon of women's resistance, and this in eras when feminism as a movement or a philosophy did not yet have a presence. In the case of Bradford's Margery, we are invited to admire the wit and daring of her performance in self-defense against the charge of Lollardy and not to underestimate its brinkmanship: it was a life-and-death struggle, indeed a heroic one. An implication this essay does not foreground but that deserves comment is that this successful defense was achieved by a woman who was technically illiterate but who clearly knew the protocols and strategies of ecclesiastical court debate. To read of Margery's outwitting of the mayor and the steward of Leicester is to be reminded that although the patriarchal machine depended heavily for its entrenchment of privilege on excluding women from literacy and making them marginal in the formation of the symbol system (Lerner 1986:57, 200), lack of writing skills was not necessarily an impediment to the successful enactment of feminist spiritual subjectivity. One can, however, only lament the fact that the survival of Margery Kempe's memoirs (even given her struggles with inadequate scribes) is the exception rather than the rule. The women's spirituality tradition would indeed be much enriched had more such memoirs survived, or had Islamic mystics like Rabiʿa al-ʿAdawiyya, Fatima of Nishapur, Rabiʿa of Syria, Umm Hayyan, Umm Ayman, or Fatima Umm Ali been literate or enjoyed the services of scribes as did Margery.

Early second-wave feminists' attempts at constructing a female tradition of spirituality have been in themselves an energizing process. Whether envisaged as parallel to the mainstream, resistant to it but committed to renewing it (Schüssler Fiorenza 1992b [1983], Meyers 1988; Mernissi 1991, 1993, Plaskow 1990, and more debatably Ruether 1983, 1992, 1998), as outside it (Goldenberg 1979; Preston 1982, Gimbutas 1991; Eller 1993), as filling in the gaps of mainstream traditions (Frymer-Kensky 1992), or as separatist (Daly 1978, 1985), the debates about such traditions' very existence and form have been essential and will presumably be ongoing. Visibility is in itself a radical achievement. What such enterprises clearly demonstrate is women's sense of exclusion from institutional and cultural traditions that claim to define the sacred. These women's desires to reclaim, to systematize and theorize, to shape and renew the myths and symbols that are central to their experience of the sacred provide an important impetus for this collection.

In the West, among the historians of women's religious traditions were many who set their faces determinedly against the mainstream Judeo-Christian tradition (Davis 1971, Stone 1984, Condren 1989, Eisler 1987, Sjöö and Mor 1987, Matthews 1991), which they saw as having systematically demeaned women in their own eyes (Eller 1993:210–1) and robbed them of a place in discourses of the sacred. They focused on pre-Judeo-Christian traditions, sometimes finding their source-country, their spiritual homeland in the most remote reaches of pre-history, in traditions of which the only remains are archaeological (Gimbutas 1991). In looking for symbols in a time-frame beyond and outside mainstream religion, they took their lead from, challenged, and in a sense feminized, the work of the great comparative mythographers of the late nineteenth and early twentieth centuries, in particular James Frazer and Robert Graves (Stone 1976; Eisler 1987, Read 1989; Larrington 1992; Eller 1993; Christ 1997; for Frazer's and Graves's androcentrism, see Christ 1997:80–6). Like them, they questioned the hegemonic status and claims of the mainstream Western religious tradition and their patriarchal biases (e.g., James Frazer's focus on dying gods at the expense of their consorts, and Robert Graves's pathologization of the Great White Goddess). Not only did they look to the ancient past, they also paid attention to contemporary, non-Western cultures, those newly being described (not to say constructed by and for the West) via the disciplines of anthropology, philology, and archaeology (Martin & Voorhies 1975; Sanday 1981). In these land-based indigenous and ancient cultures, the quest often took the form of an earth-centered spirituality, as the essays herein by Rigby and McCredden demonstrate.

Watertight Compartments and New Porosities

In the last two decades, there have been some dramatic rencontres between traditions historically hostile to each other. In a most intriguing development of the 80s and early 90s, two seemingly watertight compartments, the mainstream Christian and the "pagan," sometimes acquired a new porosity in the work of such Christian mainstreamers as Ruether (1983, 1992) and Schüssler Fiorenza (1992a, b[1983]). The latter insists, in ways that explicitly recuperate goddess cults and see them as constitutive of both Judaism and Christianity via wisdom theology (1992b [1983]: 132–3), that "the earliest Christian theology is sophialogy" (1992b [1983]: 134). Schüssler Fiorenza argues that Jesus "probably understood himself as the prophet and child of Sophia," whom she characterizes thus:

> Divine Sophia is Israel's God in the language and *Gestalt* of the goddess. Sophia is called sister, wife, mother, beloved, and teacher. She is the leader on the way, the preacher in Israel, the taskmaster and creator God. She seeks people, finds them on the road, invites them to dinner. She offers life, rest, knowledge, and salvation to those who accept her. She dwells in Israel and officiates in the sanctuary. She send[s] prophets and apostles and makes those who accept her "friends of God." "She is but one but yet can do everything, herself unchanging. She makes all things new"(Wis 7:27). (1992a: 133)

Similarly, Rosemary Radford Ruether insists on a God/ess, an iconography for the sacred that is beyond gender. Interestingly, she uses what she claims is a "classical Christian [theological]" argument that to represent God as a bearded male is tantamount to idolatry and that all language for God is analogical (1983:66–8), including metaphors like that of God as mother/father. Such a maneuver not only revivifies some undervalued (that is, by male exegetes) Biblical traditions but it also occurs within the context of informed scholarship about male monotheism's rupture with "all previous human consciousness" and with traditions in which paired images of gods and goddesses were normative (Ruether 1983:53).

A further example of these rencontres between traditions is the greater ease (which such "authorities" as Ruether help to make legitimate) scholars appear to experience in accommodating intertextual understandings from once antithetical traditions. Dorothy Lee's reading, in this edition, of Revelation 12 depends on her understanding of it as a triumphalist reworking of earlier mythological intertexts, in particular of the violent account in the Akkadian *Enuma Elish* of the dismemberment of Tiamat by Marduk but also of the Isis and Leto myths of ancient Egypt and Rome (in which mother deities are assailed by monsters) and of the Hebrew Leviathan. In this case, the maneuver of introducing material from an antithetical tradition is mobilized as a redemptive hermeneutic in which the heavenly woman, despite her travail, is sovereign and powerful over vandalism and death. The polyvalency of this myth might also suggest that a dissonant postcolonial critique of the iconography of dominance enacted in the image of the queenly woman could also be mounted. What could be argued is that

Lee's intertextual maneuver, in gathering into its semiotic the preexisting mythology, itself constitutes an appropriative and *triumphalist* maneuver, or could it be described as a liberatory gesture designed to rebuild links between traditions that were sundered?

What must be pointed out about many recuperations of cultures that predate or stand outside the mainstream monotheisms is that they take the form of rhetorical and sometimes ahistorical pseudohistories, more akin to what Stuckey would term "foundation myths" than grounded, politicized histories (of the sort that Cady, Ronan, & Taussig [1986] attempt for the Wisdom tradition [see especially chapter 5] or Meyers [1988] more generally for the early Biblical tradition in Israel). To a large extent, the decontextualized use of sacred myths that such scholars contest is a legacy of generations of myth- and narrative-universalizers (the followers of Jung, Frazer, Joseph Campbell, Eric Neumann, and the structuralists), who would reduce cultural, historical, and geographical particularities to archetypes and to a minimum of plots. Such universalizing practices remain an important, energizing, and debatable tradition within feminist spiritualities. While these traditions continue to have their followers and supporters, the major thrust of the essays in this collection is to insist on the political nature of storying about the sacred, its historical and cultural specificity and historical contingency. It is, for example, important to locate the work of Oodgeroo Noonuccal at its particular moment in time, as McCredden does, if its prophetic voice, directed as it is simultaneously at two audiences, is to be given the credence it deserves. This collection offers implicitly and explicitly a critique of universalizing claims of traditional scholarship, not only but especially in relation to the perspectives of women of color, colonized women, and women from non-Western cultures.

Reclaiming and Resignifying

Of those who survey and critique the work of the Goddess worshipers, many of whom have been active in the work of reclamation of lost female deities, Stuckey (1998:126–48) is more tolerant of their enterprise than many scholars would be (for example, Townsend 1990), arguing that practitioners of women's spirituality are doing a particular cultural job—to wit, the rediscovery of lost knowledge, the generation of new knowledge to serve as the basis for a new religion, and the creation of foundational myths for a new religion. The sacred stories they reclaim are commonly used in rituals, which have among their purposes individual and societal transformation. Furthermore, rather than be content with nostalgic and romantic recuperations of a past golden era or a present that has somehow evaded the problems of late capitalism (as does some New Age "scholarship"), this collection hopes to establish that the debates that ensue when histories and discourses are confronted with scholarly rigor and in the light of historical and archaeological findings can be powerfully energizing.

Feminists have become skilled at reading for "traces" of older mythologies and at reading texts as palimpsests. This has been most striking in the field of scriptural analysis in the work of Bal (1987, 1988), Schüssler Fiorenza (1984, 1992a), Russell (1985), and of course, the pioneer of feminist biblical exegesis, Phyllis Trible (1978, 1984), and the legions of feminist exegetes who continue to follow them. Other works have restored the Sophia tradition (Pagels 1990 [1979]; Cady, Ronan, & Taussig 1985, and Good 1987) and reread the female deities of the pre-Celtic and Celtic traditions (Bowen 1975, Tymoczko 1985, 1985–86; Condren 1989, Clark 1991, Findon 1997).

One of the key strategies used by gynocritics has been to expose the ways the resignification of both symbols and narratives has served to implement patriarchal agendas (Pomeroy 1975, Daly 1978, duBois 1988:43, Condren 1989). Such knowledge is important and empowering because it suggests that if the narratives that construct the sacred can be modified, then they can be made to resignify in ways that celebrate women's investment as women in the sacred. In two essays in this book, we see the process of resignification at work in a demotionary direction. When the Inanna myth was first published in 1983 as *Inanna Queen of Heaven and Earth* by the doyen of Sumerology, Samuel Noah Kramer, and Diane Wolkstein, a feminist storyteller, there was (muted) cause for celebration because for the first time in the history of transmission of ancient narratives, this new translation of work that had been in circulation in fragments was given a fuller shape and the benefit of a feminist filter. Stuckey's account here acts as a corrective to the kinds of readings we are offered of the Huluppu Tree story by reminding us, implicitly, of the extent to which Sumer was a patriarchal society by the time these stories and hymns were committed to cuneiform. In her reading of the myth, she is critical of humanist interpretations (including those of Kramer [1967 (1963), 1969, 1972], Jacobsen [1976] and Frymer-Kensky [1992]), which often serve to patronize, moralize, or euhemerize this deity. In the place of such readings, she offers an account that romanticizing feminists might find unpalatable because it points to Inanna's implication in her own demotion. Gerda Lerner's theorized and hypothetical history, *The Creation of Patriarchy* (1986), suggests that the processes of demotion of goddesses, and of women, was multifactorial, uneven across cultures, gradual (occurring over a period of two and a half millennia), and participated in, unwittingly, by women. Despite Stuckey's dark, historically informed reading of what is often read by feminists as a woman-friendly episode, Stuckey reports being empowered by the narrative. The task of tradition-building has been criticized by some on the grounds that a rereading and reconstruction of women's history and of historical and literary epistemologies does not have a clear relevance for modern feminists in their struggle against sexism in religious thinking and that living conditions at the beginning of the third millennium are vastly different from those pertaining in ancient cultures (Rutledge 1996:29). However, it is clear that women do find such historical revisionism empowering and that the process needs to be done in such a way as to problematize the notion of authoritative histories and to raise consciousness of the dangers of ideologically driven, wish-fulfilling depatriarchalization of history.

As with Inanna, the myth system that Devlin-Glass analyzes is seen to be similarly patriarchalized, revealing only glimpses, but powerful ones, of a role for women in marriage and in warfare, which accord status and, under rare circumstances, a measure of autonomy and respect. This reading of the Ulster Cycle suggests that the pathologized heterosexual relationships come about as a result of male failure to honor contracts and of unnatural hubris. Here the suggestion is that the myth required massaging and patriarchalizing because it was transmitted by Christian monks with a vested interest in literary misogyny as a form of social control. Furthermore, there is in this essay an attempt to track several other and subsequent agendas by which the myths served the purposes of nationalism and of Irish claims to literary seriousness.

The Theoretical Turn—Poststructuralism and the Sacred

The postmodern era has seen increasingly corrosive attacks, driven often by suspicion of master narratives and metanarratives (Lyotard 1984, Jameson 1991), on the power of social institutions (religious, state, education, and legal systems) and on the concepts and ideals that underpin liberal humanism, Derrida's "transcendental signifiers." What makes the poststructuralist turn such a powerful methodology for feminists, compared with liberal humanist critique, is its acknowledgment, and dismantling, of institutionalized systemic domination built into the

language we use and the ways we think, into the foundationalist discourses by which we organize our lives. As a reading technology and
an analytical methodology, it foregrounds metacognitive processes, and
in doing so constitutes a radical tool. It engages in and enables a critique
of the premises of Western philosophy and of disciplinary knowledges
and does so in a way that announces its ideological self-interest. Finally,
as we hope to demonstrate, it ideally issues in a politics: that of "transform[ing] the intellectual bases of culture" (Buchanan 1987:435). Three
main bodies of feminist theory inform the poststructuralist methodologies at work in this collection: deconstruction, postcolonialism, and
new historicism. And, focusing all of them, a politicized feminism.

Because of deconstruction's concern with "writing" and "text," it is
highly relevant not only to mainstream biblical hermeneutics but also
to textual constructions of female deities. It is with surprise that some
commentators note that as a reading methodology deconstruction has
been slower to take root in biblical hermeneutics than in literary studies
(Moore 1992:2; Bible and Culture Collective 1995:13), though many
feminist biblical exegetes can be seen to be forerunners (Schüssler Fiorenza and Bal in particular). Rutledge (1996:65) explains the standoff
between literary and biblical studies that predated the last decade as a
defense of "Sacred Literature" against "the creeping tide of secular
(post)modernism in literary studies" (deemed "heretical"). He sees the
recent engagement within biblical studies with deconstructive and postmodern reading technologies and theory as closely akin to the processes
of midrash and so not at all an alien tradition. For him, it is similar in
its playfulness, its conviction that interpretation is vested in the community of readers, and its promotion of an openness to change (1996:
172). In particular, Rutledge is strongly supportive of feminist deconstructive activity that might bring to bear a radical critique of the ruling
patriarchal logic of the text, a voicing and legitimizing of voices from
the margins, a radical unsettling of "truth-claims" (1996:177–9). The
act of critical reading itself, without the guarantee of authoritative
truth, may very well constitute "spirituality."

Although some feminists are critical of deconstructionists' preoccupation with textuality, it can be argued that texts, understood in the broadest sense as discourses of any kind (i.e., rituals, forms of worship) that
encode ideology and represent the imaginary (and desired) relationship
of individuals and collective groups to their real conditions of existence.
In fact, a more compelling drive for textual analysis and production may

arise from the need to bring the imaginary and the real into closer alignment. Insofar as communities and individuals accord texts status and deem them "holy," and continue to read and expound on them, they constitute a potentially dynamic site for the elaboration of new and, hopefully, women-inclusive uses, both textual and political. In the Derridean scheme, meaning cannot be fixed. Rather, it is endlessly deferred, and women and women-friendly men can and do employ this indeterminacy for their own purposes (see Moore 1994:chapter 2). Stephen Curkpatrick, in a move owing a debt to Derrida and Foucault, dramatizes in his chapter an historian, Helen, who is aware of the partialities of history, its interpretive and exclusionary functions, its hegemonic drive, and its litter of "traces and fragments." Traces such as can be unearthed in (the fictional) *Hermes' Conceit* await the analyses of later scholars. He demonstrates his female protagonist's need for such an inclusive history and wittily dramatizes in her male antagonist the incomprehension and well-meaning bafflement that block a fuller version of history, expunging what is deemed ideologically impure from the archives. Curkpatrick's imagined but sacred text–based reading of the biblical Resurrection story as itself constituting an example of a diversity of witness stories is energizing in itself as a piece of exegesis. It is conducted partly through a fictional dialogue about a fictional journal and partly through his scholarly footnotes, which give witness to how he theoretically positions himself as an exegete. This chapter is also a practical (though fictional) instance of the fallibilities of the traditional historical method. What even the conservative antagonist, the pastor, is prepared to confess to are the "nonchalant discrepancies of the Gospel tradition itself." For Curkpatrick, though, such discrepancies constitute portals through which to discover a new reading.

In part I, "The Politics and Poetics of the Sacred," the contributors focus on earthed spiritualities, in particular indigenous Australian questions of sacredness and the land and ecofeminist approaches to the sacred. The colonialist heritage of Aboriginal Australians is the context in which Pattel-Gray and McCredden seek to explore the contributions of Aboriginal voices to Australian spiritualities. For mainstream secular Australia, as for other modern nations, the claims of indigenous ties to the land are proving to be a major and unsettling challenge in both political and religious arenas. Such challenges increasingly emerge from indigenous women's claims to specifically female spiritualities and practices. In a parallel series of claims and maneuvers, ecofeminists are also claiming the land as a source of spiritual knowledge and regeneration.

Their apocalyptic as well as empirical approaches, in interesting ways, work through scientific and spiritual discourses that only a few generations ago were considered antithetical.

Part II, "Interrogating 'Matriarchy,' " offers politicized scholarship of texts that have long been the preserve of male scholars. Both Stuckey and Devlin-Glass contest the notion of "matriarchy" so beloved of wish-fulfillment feminists who look utopically to the past in the hopes of finding a prepatriarchal state. Rather than fully fledged prepatriarchal Edens, these essays offer accounts of myths that bear only traces and fragments of older female-focused ways of valuing women. This is not to say that such mythological archaeology does not offer suggestive ways of rereading the present and the future. Each author would argue that scrutinizing the gradual processes of patriarchalization of such myths is itself politically useful and empowering for contemporary feminists.

The essays of part III, "Interrogating Patriarchy," converge from several different directions on patriarchal texts and interpretations. They each demonstrate ways of resisting those processes of patriarchalization and of radically reinterpreting the past. For Bradford and Butorovic, the texts they recuperate offer unexpected examples of medieval women challenging the overwhelmingly patriarchal systems in which they successfully (but at some risk to themselves) operated. Dove and Lee, working from within mainstream biblical hermeneutics, offer significant feminist rereadings of scriptural texts. Each author brings into dialogue with biblical traditions a broader range of literary and textual methodologies, consciously transgressing sacred/secular boundaries.

The whole collection explicitly offers diverse literary and generic approaches to questions of feminism and the sacred. For all the contributors, language is not merely an aesthetic or secondary tool but has been understood as implicitly political and historically contingent. As literary scholars drawing on a wide range of interdisciplinary studies, we foreground textuality and interpretation as central sites in the articulation of culture, whether these texts are the land, the body, or sacred scriptures. Fahey's and Curkpatrick's writerly contributions stand out as different from standard academic modes of discourse and serve to diversify this book's range of genres. Using poetry and fiction techniques, supplemented in Curkpatrick's case by footnotes, they construct an active, contemporary poetics of spirituality. Fahey, a poet with a strong reputation in Australia, as a poet and feminist is here given space to write about the processes of her feminist poetics. Readers of this book are given an opportunity to read her powerful and often disorienting rewritings of Greek mythology reconstructed within a contemporary gender politics. Fahey's work, spanning the decade 1988–1998, serves as a map of the shifts in feminist poetics in the postfeminist era, in resisting female victimhood and considering masculine as well as feminine subjectivities. Curkpatrick's experimental essay, with its interplay between fictional text and scholarly footnotes, enables a rich conversation to take place. This conversation works at multiple levels: between student and teacher; woman and man; lived belief and scholarly tradition; and between masculinist, conservative scholarship and new forms of postmodern enquiry. The essay constitutes an invitation to embrace uncertainty as a constituent element of belief and to acknowledge the necessity for continual reinscription of the traditional and canonical.

Finally, this book does not seek to present a homogeneous group of practitioners defining the field of "feminist spirituality." Rather, it draws together a diverse group of writers and disciplines—literary academics, theologians, textual and religious studies scholars and poets—who explore this field both creatively and suspiciously. In fact, in the field of feminist spirituality, and in a world that too often sets up rigid, fortified, and merely institutional definitions of "the one truth," it might be argued that creativity and suspicion must necessarily move together. Feminism and its rich history has provided many of the intellectual tools for this group of writers. A desire to reach beyond the legion intolerances of truth-mongering and systemic injustice and to find new, liberating, and livable possibilities for spirituality—for women *and* men—is what motivates the essays of this book.

References

Bal, Mieke. 1987. *Lethal Love: Feminist Literary Readings of Biblical Love Stories*. Bloomington: Indiana University Press.

———. 1988. *Murder and Difference: Gender, Genre and Scholarship*. Bloomington: Indiana University Press.

Bible and Culture Collective, The. 1995. *The Postmodern Bible*. New Haven: Yale University Press.

Bowen, Charles. 1975. Great-Bladdered Medb: Mythology and Invention in the *Táin bó Cualinge*. Eire-Ireland 10 (4): 14–34.

Buchanan, Constance. 1987. Women's Studies in Religion. In Mircea Eliade (ed.), *The Encyclopaedia of Religion* (New York: Macmillan): vol. 15, 433–40.

Cady, Susan, Marian Ronan, and Hal Taussig. 1986. *Sophia, The Future of Feminist Spirituality*. San Francisco: Harper and Row.

Christ, Carol. 1997. *Rebirth of the Goddess: Finding Meaning in Feminist Spirituality*. Reading, Mass.: Addison-Wesley.

Clark, Rosalind. 1991. *The Great Queens: Irish Goddesses from the Morrígan to Cathleen Ní Houlihan*. Gerrards Cross, England: Colin Smythe.

Condren, Mary. 1989. *The Serpent and the Goddess: Women, Religion and Power in Celtic Ireland*. San Francisco: Harper and Row.

Daly, Mary. 1978. *Gyn/Ecology: The Metaethics of Radical Feminism*. Boston: Beacon Press.

———. 1985. *Beyond God the Father*. Boston: Beacon Press.

Davis, Elizabeth Gould. 1971. *The First Sex*. Baltimore: Penguin.

duBois, Page. 1988. *Sowing the Body: Psychoanalysis and Ancient Representations of Women*. Chicago: University of Chicago Press.

Eisler, Riane 1987. *The Chalice and the Blade*. San Francisco: Harper and Row.

Eller, Cynthia. 1993. *Living in the Lap of the Goddess: The Feminist Spirituality Movement in America*. New York: Crossroad.

Findon, Joanne. 1997. *A Woman's Words: Emer and Female Speech in the Ulster Cycle*. Toronto: University of Toronto Press.

Fischer, Clare B. 1995. *Of Spirituality: A Feminist Perspective*. ATLA Bibliography Series, no. 35. Lanham, Md.: American Theological Library Association.

Frymer-Kensky, Tikva. 1992. *In the Wake of the Goddesses: Women, Culture, and the Biblical Transformation of Pagan Myth*. New York: Free Press.

Gimbutas, Marija. 1991. *The Civilization of the Goddess: The World of Old Europe*. San Francisco: Harper.

Goldenberg, Naomi. 1979. *Changing of the Gods: Feminism and the End of Traditional Religions*. Boston: Beacon Press.

Good, Deirdre J. 1987. *Reconstructing the Tradition of Sophia in Gnostic Literature*. Alpharetta, Ga.: Scholars Press.

Hurtado, Larry W. (ed.). 1990. *Goddesses in Religions and Modern Debate*. Atlanta: Scholars Press.

Irigaray, Luce. 1992. *Elemental Passions*. Trans. Joanne Collie and Judith Still. New York: Routledge.

Jacobsen, Thorkild. 1976. *The Treasures of Darkness: A History of Mesopotamian Religion*. New Haven: Yale University.

Jameson, Fredric. 1991. *Postmodernism, or, The Cultural Logic of Late Capitalism*. Durham, N.C.: Duke University Press.

Kramer, Samuel Noah. 1967 [1963]. *The Sumerians: Their History, Culture, and Character*. Chicago: University of Chicago Press.

———. 1969. *The Sacred Marriage Rite: Aspects of Faith, Myth, and Ritual in Ancient Sumer*. Bloomington: University of Indiana Press.

———. 1972. *Sumerian Mythology*. Philadelphia: University of Pennsylvania Press.

Kristeva, Julia. 1982. *Powers of Horror: An Essay on Abjection*. Trans. Leon S. Roudiez. New York: Columbia University Press.

Larrington, Carolyne (ed.). 1992. *The Feminist Companion to Mythology*. London: Pandora Press.

Lerner, Gerda. 1986. *The Creation of Patriarchy*. New York: Oxford University Press.

———. 1993. *The Creation of Feminist Consciousness: From the Middle Ages to Eighteen-Seventy*. New York: Oxford University Press.

Lyotard, Jean-François. 1984. *The Postmodern Condition: A Report on Knowledge*. Minneapolis: University of Minnesota Press.

McCance, Dawne. 1990. Understandings of "The Goddess" in Contemporary Feminist Scholarship. In Hurtado 1990:165–79.

Manderson, Desmond. 1997. Guilt, Shame and Reconciliation. *Quadrant* 41 (July–August): 96–9.

Martin, M. Kay, and Barbara Voorhies. 1975. *Female of the Species*. New York: Columbia University Press.

Matthews, Caitlín. 1992. *Sophia Goddess of Wisdom: The Divine Feminine from Black Goddess to World Soul*. London: Aquarian.

Mernissi, Fatima. 1991. *Women and Islam: An Historical and Theological Enquiry*. Oxford: Blackwell.

———. 1993. *The Forgotten Queens of Islam*. Minneapolis: University of Minnesota Press.

Meyers, Carol. 1988. *Discovering Eve: Ancient Israelite Women in Context*. New York: Oxford University Press.

Moore, Stephen D. 1994. *Poststucturalism and the New Testament*. Minneapolis: Fortress Press.

Moore, Stephen D., and David Jobling (eds.). 1992. *Poststructuralism as Exegesis. Semeia* 54.

Pagels, Elaine. 1990 [1979]. *The Gnostic Gospels*. New York: Random House.

Perera, Sylvia Brinton. 1981. *Descent to the Goddess; A Way of Initiation for Women*. Toronto: Inner City.

Plaskow, Judith. 1990. *Standing Again at Sinai: Judaism from a Feminist Perspective*. San Francisco: Harper and Row.

Pomeroy, Sarah B. 1975. *Goddesses, Whores, Wives and Slaves:Women in Classical Antiquity*. New York: Schocken Books.

Preston, J. J. 1982. *Mother Worship: Theme and Variations*. Chapel Hill: University of North Carolina Press.

Pritchard, James B. (ed.). 1969. *Ancient Near Eastern Texts Relating to the Old Testament*. 3rd ed. with supplement. Princeton: Princeton University Press.

Read, Donna. 1989. *Goddess Remembered* [a film]. Studio D, National Film Board of Canada.

Ruether, Rosemary Radford. 1983. *Sexism and God-Talk: Towards a Feminist Theology*. London: SCM Press.

———. 1992. *Gaia and God: An Ecofeminist Theology of Earth Healing*. San Francisco: Harper Collins.

———. 1998. *Women and Redemption: A Theological History*. Minneapolis: Fortress Press.

Russell, Letty M. 1985. *Feminist Interpretation of the Bible*. Oxford: Blackwell.

Rutledge, David. 1996. *Reading Marginally: Feminism, Deconstruction and the Bible*. Leiden: E. J. Brill.

Sanday, Peggy Reeves. 1981. *Female Power and Male Dominance: On the Origins of Sexual Inequality*. Cambridge, England: Cambridge University Press.

Schüssler Fiorenza, Elizabeth. 1984. *Bread Not Stone: The Challenge of Feminist Biblical Interpretation*. Boston: Beacon Press.

———. 1992a. *But SHE Said: Feminist Practices of Biblical Interpretation*. Boston: Beacon Press.

————. 1992b [1983]. *In Memory of Her: A Feminist Theological Reconstruction of Christian Origins*. New York: Crossroad.

Schüssler Fiorenza, Elizabeth (ed.). 1993. *Searching the Scriptures: A Feminist Introduction*. New York: Crossroad.

Sjöö, Monica, and Barbara Mor. 1987. *The Great Cosmic Mother: Rediscovering the Religion of the Earth*. San Francisco: Harper and Row.

Stone, Merlin. 1976. *When God Was a Woman*. New York: Harvest.

————. 1984. *Ancient Mirrors of Womanhood: A Treasury of Goddess and Heroine Lore from Around the World*. Boston: Beacon Press.

Stuckey, Johanna H. 1998. *Feminist Spirituality: An Introduction to Feminist Theology in Judaism, Christianity, Islam and Feminist Goddess Worship*. Toronto: Centre for Feminist Research, York University.

Townsend, Joan B. 1990. The Goddess: Fact, Fallacy and Revitalization Movement. In Hurtado 1990:180–204.

Trible, Phyllis. 1978. *God and the Rhetoric of Sexuality*. Philadelphia: Fortress Press.

————. 1984. *Texts of Terror: Literary-Feminist Readings of Biblical Narratives*. Philadelphia: Fortress Press.

Tymoczko, Maria. 1985. Unity and Duality: A Theoretical Perspective on the Ambivalence of Celtic Goddesses. In Paul Jefferiss and William J. Mahon (eds.), *Proceedings of the Harvard Celtic Colloquium* 5:22–37.

————. 1985–86. Animal Imagery in *Loinges MacnUislenn*. *Studia Celtica*. 20–21:145–66.

Wolkstein, Diane, and Samuel Noah Kramer. 1983. *Inanna, Queen of Heaven and Earth*. New York: Harper and Row.

Part One

The Politics and Poetics of the Sacred

The Goddess Returns

Ecofeminist Reconfigurations of Gender, Nature, and the Sacred

Kate Rigby

It is now nearly twenty years since Carol Christ presented her arguments as to "why women need the Goddess" in her famous keynote address to the first major academic conference on the "reemergence of the Goddess" held at the University of California, Santa Cruz, in spring 1978. A more experientially oriented festival celebrating the new feminist spirituality movement had taken place in Boston two years previously. In the recollection of one participant, this "Gynenergetic Experience," as it was termed, involved "incantations, dreams, moon meditations, exhibits and films on blood mysteries, workshops on feminist interpretations of the Tarot, women's hidden history, goddess worship, Amazons, the martyrdom of the witches, [and] discussions of the relationship between spirituality and politics, women and ecology" (Roszak 1995:291). Inspired by feminist research into ancient nature religions incorporating powerful female deities[1] and motivated by the search for a nonpatriarchal and earth-centered mode of spiritual expression, a great many more women (and a good many men) appear to have embraced "the Goddess" since then. Drawing selectively and eclectically on numerous sources, including Greek, Celtic, and Germanic mythology, modern Wicca, and, more recently, certain indigenous traditions,[2] feminist spirituality groups celebrating the figure of the Goddess have sprung up throughout the English-speaking world and in

parts of continental Europe (especially Holland and Germany), wherever
the women's movement has generated a strong grass-roots feminist
counterculture.[3] English-language publications in the area of feminist
spirituality presently number well over nine hundred (Carsen 1992).
Needless to say, it is now also possible to access the Goddess in cyber-
space.[4]

In the United States, where religious discourses have traditionally
played an important role in public life, the feminist spirituality movement seems to be particularly strong and diverse (Eller 1993), and the
Goddess has even acquired a certain academic respectability there. Although few of the major writers on and practitioners of non-Judeo-
Christian feminist spirituality currently hold permanent positions at any
mainstream American universities (quite possibly by choice in most
cases), their work is frequently published alongside that of highly regarded academically based feminist theologians and ecofeminists.[5] The
situation is rather different in Australia, however, where the hegemony
of secular rationalist and, more recently, poststructuralist modes of feminist critique has hitherto tended to marginalize any sympathetic discussion of spirituality. In my view, this is unfortunate, as it entrenches
the divide between "high" feminist theory and grass-roots feminist
counterculture to the impoverishment of both. While it is certainly true
that the feminist spirituality movement could do with an infusion of
critical sociopolitical analysis and a heightened awareness of the etiol-
ogy and implications of the discourses on woman, nature, and the sacred in which it participates, it may well be that academic feminist
thinking could benefit in turn from a certain spiritual deepening. At the
very least, I would argue (with Theodore Roszak) that although some
might be tempted to scoff at certain manifestations of feminist spirituality, it would be making a grave mistake not to take seriously the real
psychological and social needs underlying these manifestations—needs
that are not going to be satisfied by yet more rationalist critiques from
on high, however theoretically sophisticated.[6]

Why might women need the Goddess? Let us return, first, to Carol
Christ. Her initial argument for the feminist transformation of religious
imagery is one that many feminists would accede to—that is, "[b]ecause
religion has such a compelling hold on the deep psyches of so many
people, feminists cannot afford to leave it in the hands of the fathers"
(Christ 1979:274). Christ follows anthropologist Clifford Geertz in her
analysis of the psychological and social function of religious symbols
in producing particular attitudes or "moods" in the people of a given
culture; moods that in turn generate certain "motivations" with regard
to the social and political arrangements within which these people live.

According to Geertz, such moods and motivations are generally directed toward ensuring acquiescence in the prevailing order of things. Religion, in other words, tends to have a socially conservative function— or as Marx put it, famously, "religion is the opiate of the people." Within patriarchal societies, religious symbolism has been seen by feminist critics to reinforce male dominance. In the highly influential assessment of Simone de Beauvoir (1953) and Mary Daly (1974), both of whom Christ cites here, this is especially the case with the monotheistic religions of Judaism, Islam, and Christianity, which are centered on the exclusive worship of a transcendent God, conventionally figured as male. These religions have traditionally created "moods" and "motivations" that "keep women in a state of psychological dependence on men and male authority, while at the same time legitimating the political and social authority of fathers and sons in the institutions of society" (Christ 1979: 275).

While doubtless rather overgeneralized, this critique of patriarchal religion is one most feminists would accept. Christ's next move, however, is considerably more controversial. For de Beauvoir, and indeed the majority of liberal and socialist feminists standing within the enlightenment tradition of Western rationalism, all religious beliefs are simply delusory, to be cast aside with the rest of the baggage of patriarchal tradition. Other feminists, by contrast, for whom religion has remained a source of revelation and inspiration, have embarked on the project of critically reconstructing the traditions they have inherited, perceiving in them not only an oppressive legacy but also emancipatory possibilities and even, in some cases, traces of the prepatriarchal religions they are believed to have displaced.[7] Christ, however, is skeptical both of the capacity of enlightened critique to entirely dislodge those images of male divinity and female dependence that have become so deeply embedded in the individual psyche and in our culture generally, and of the adequacy of feminist endeavors to transform these images purely from within the religious traditions that generated or perpetuated them. Instead, she argues, these symbol systems "must be replaced." Here, for Christ and many others, is where the Goddess comes in.

Arising from and undergirding the concerns of the women's movement, Goddess symbolism, Christ suggests, is emerging as a new matrix of moods and motivations countering those generated by what Daly calls "father religion" in a number of psychologically and politically significant ways. According to Christ, the Goddess functions as a "symbolic acknowledgment of the legitimacy of female power as a beneficent and independent power" (1979 276), as well as affirming the "female body and the life cycle expressed in it" (279), together with "women's bonds and heritage" (285). The Goddess, in other words, provided an appropriate and indeed necessary metaphysical grounding for the new culture that was taking shape as women struggled to overcome patriarchal structures of domination both within themselves and in society at large.

In addition to indicating how the Goddess might be good for feminism, Christ makes a further claim for Goddess symbolism that is of particular interest from an ecofeminist perspective: namely, that the revaluation of the female body "would help to overcome the spirit–flesh, mind–body dualisms of Western culture" and, in so doing, would create a mood of reverence towards not only human bodies, but also the body of the earth (291). More generally, it is apparent from Christ's account that Goddess spirituality is not simply a feminized version of monotheistic transcendentalism—God, as it were, in drag. While Christ concedes that for some women, the Goddess is "out there," suggesting belief in some kind of unitary and at least partially transcendent divine Creatrix, the Goddess is always also seen to be immanent within the physical universe as a whole and in each of its individuated entities. Indeed, for many, the Goddess is only a metaphor, personifying that animating and life-generating energy that flows through and interconnects all things. The symbolism of the Goddess thus returns an aura of the sacred to the world of matter, and as such would appear to shape a spirituality that is not only feminist but also ecological in orientation, undermining the binary oppositions inscribed within patriarchal monotheism (and, as others have pointed out, Western rationalism) that have for so long contrived to make us strangers to ourselves and the earth.

This affirmation of the immanence of the divine in the world, in individual bodies and in nature generally, is a striking feature not only of Goddess spirituality and feminist Wicca but also of much feminist theology. Why should this be so? What are the connections between women and nature, feminism and ecology, that seem to predispose feminist spiritualities of many kinds toward this sanctification of matter and celebration of embodiment? Ecofeminists have developed a number of different approaches to this question. In the following section, I will outline some of the main ways ecofeminist theorists have sought to reconfigure the relationship of women and nature, before returning to a more critical consideration of the place of the Goddess in the project of ecofeminist transformation. Here I would also like to raise some more general questions about feminism, ecology and the sacred, including the difficult issue of the relationship between politics and spirituality. The final section of this essay moves beyond the Goddess to acknowledge the tremendous diversification of ecofeminist spiritualities over the past decade, as women (and men) in many parts of the world endeavor to reenvision their religious traditions in ways that affirm human earthliness, while also empowering us to challenge those structures of social domination in which a multiplicity of oppressions (notably, on the basis of race and class, as well as gender) have been inscribed.

Woman and Nature: Ecofeminist Reconfigurations

The term "écofeminisme" was first coined in 1974 by radical French feminist Françoise D'Eaubonne. Identifying the underlying cause for the current ecological crisis compounded of overpopulation, overconsumption, and pollution in the age-old patriarchal oppression of women, D'Eaubonne called on feminists to wed their cause to that of the environment and lead the way into a postpatriarchal, genuinely "humanist" and ecologically sustainable future (D'Eaubonne 1994). The conceptual underpinnings of ecofeminism were further developed in the mid-1970s by Ynestra King at the Institute of Social Ecology in Vermont. Ecofeminism subsequently blossomed into a social movement in the wake of a number of environmental disasters, including the chemical spill at Seveso, in 1976; the meltdown at Three Mile Island Reactor Unit 2, which prompted the first "Women and Life on Earth Conference" in Amherst, Massachusetts, in March 1980 and the subsequent Women's Pentagon Action to protest nuclear war and weapons development; the toxic gas spill in Bhopal, India, in 1984; and the Chernobyl nuclear catastrophe in the Ukraine in 1986.[8] Although I am not aware of any formal ecofeminist networks in Australia like the Women and Life on Earth networks in the United States and United Kingdom,[9] feminists have long been active in the antinuclear and environment movements in Australia too, and several Australian philosophers and political theorists, including Val Plumwood, Freya Mathews, Ariel Kay Salleh, and Canadian-born Patsy Hallen, have made a significant contribution to the development of ecofeminist thought since the mid-1980s.[10]

Today, as Freya Mathews has observed, "ecofeminism is by no means a position or a theory, but simply a fairly wide open field of enquiry" (1994b: 62).[11] What nonetheless distinguishes ecofeminist thinking from an environmentally concerned feminism or, conversely, a profeminist environmentalism, are the substantive connections it discloses between the patriarchal domination of women (and other socially oppressed groups) and the industrial exploitation of the earth. In making these connections, ecofeminism necessarily reaffirms to some extent that link between women and nature that liberal and socialist feminists, from Simone de Beauvoir onward, had been at pains to sever. According to de Beauvoir's powerful critique (1953), the association of woman and nature was a key element in patriarchal ideology that served to legitimate women's exclusion from the public sphere and their confinement to the realm of "mere" reproduction, centered on the home. Full equality, for de Beauvoir, was premised on women's liberation from this emersion in reproduction and indeed from their own sexed bodies, for it was women's capacity to give birth that underlay both the feminine imaging of nature and the biologistic reduction of woman to womb. If biology was no longer to be women's destiny, Shulamith Firestone concluded twenty years later (1970), then child-rearing must be socialized and reproduction technologized: only when conception and gestation could be routinely carried out under the sterile conditions of the laboratory would women be truly emancipated from the womb and free to participate as equals in the socialist-feminist utopia of the future. For women (and indeed men) whose feminism had been forged on the anvil of this rationalist egalitarian tradition—whether or not they subscribed fully to Firestone's extreme technosocialist optimism—the positive revaluation of the connection between women and nature within ecofeminism looked like a politically dangerous fallback into the mirror of patriarchal projection, which could only play into the hands of those reactionary forces who would like to see women once more in their "proper place."

While the risk of a reactionary reinscription of the woman–nature connection is forever hovering ominously over the ecofeminist project, I do not believe that this necessitates a retreat into what Val Plumwood terms the feminism of "uncritical equality" (1993). In Plumwood's analysis, egalitarian feminism of this kind is blind to the ways the patriarchal "master model" of the human has been formed in the context of gender, class, race, and species domination: to be human, on this model, is to be cast in opposition to nature and its cognate terms (the feminine, the body, the "primitive," etc.) (1993:22). It is this model of the human that has underpinned the flawed, because ultimately self-defeating, project of the domination of nature, which has assumed a particularly virulent form in Western industrial modernity and which now threatens the ecological basis of all human life on this planet (not to mention that of millions of other species, in addition to those that have already been lost).[12] For women (and other colonized peoples) to now uncritically assimilate themselves to this model of the human might mean to forego the opportunity to affirm or develop a different kind of self-conception incorporating a different relation to nature. While the affirmation of a "community of fate" between women and nature has certainly proven dangerous in the past (notably in the eugenically oriented

Nazi cult of motherhood), today an even graver danger is presented by
the failure to acknowledge the community of fate that exists between
humanity and the earth (Beinssen-Hesse and Rigby 1996:100). In seeking to redress this failure, ecofeminists have argued, the perspectives of
women, among others who have been similarly marginalized in relation
to the master model of the human and have suffered disproportionately
from the results of ecological destruction, might prove particularly valuable.

At the risk of oversimplifying a by now extensive and varied body of
research and reflection, it is possible to delineate two main approaches
to the ecofeminist reconfiguration of the woman–nature connection:
whereas one foregrounds the body and its cultural inscriptions (as in
cultural ecofeminism), the other focuses on social positioning and discursive structures as the basis for women's different relation to nature
(as in social, socialist, and poststructuralist ecofeminism).[13] While cultural ecofeminists are often accused of "essentialism," as distinct from
the "constructivist" view of the woman-nature nexus espoused by most
social(ist) and poststructuralist ecofeminists, it should be pointed out
that very few of the former have ever claimed that women's "closeness
to nature" is biologically determined.[14] Susan Griffin's influential early
work *Women and Nature* (1978), a key text of cultural ecofeminism,
explicitly identifies the assimilation of women to nature as a culturally
specific patriarchal construct.[15] Indeed, as Gloria Fenan Orenstein has
recently observed, Griffin's book is "an early critique of essentialism"
that "historicizes and contextualizes in detail the parallel oppression of
women and nature" (Orenstein 1990:20). *Women and Nature* is, however, a work not only of critique but also of affirmation—this is why it
has been so inspirational for some and so problematic for others. Having
shared a common history of oppression with nature, in the course of
which we were largely excluded from the Western male project of mastery and transcendence, thus remaining closer to the realm of embodiment and immanence, women were now, Griffin suggests, in a privileged position to *speak for* nature in the context of pursuing their own
social emancipation.

Reversing the common evaluation of the woman-nature connection,
Griffin effectively redefines the feminist project as an emancipation *with*
nature, rather than *from* it, as in the dominant Enlightenment tradition.
This was a truly radical move and one that remains fundamental to
any deeper ecofeminist transformation of culture and society. However,
the cultural feminist celebration of women's alleged closeness to nature,
while not necessarily biologically determinist, is certainly problematic
from a contemporary perspective. First, there is a tendency here to sim-

ply reverse the value judgments attaching to the dualistically opposed terms of *man* and *woman, culture* and *nature, reason* and *emotion* without questioning either the content of these terms or the structure of dualism itself. Plumwood refers to this approach as the "feminism of uncritical reversal" (1993:31).[16] To the extent that patriarchal constructions of the feminine are not adequately distinguished from the actual historical experience of women, they tend to return to haunt the ecofeminist vision of a liberated "female nature." This is possibly exacerbated by the highly poetic style of much cultural feminist writing, including Griffin's, which is directed toward developing a nonratiocentric, or in poststructuralist parlance, nonphallogocentric form of discourse. It may well be that the "revolution in thought" (Christ 1990:62) embodied by the new ecofeminist paradigm requires new modes of writing. But it is important that salient distinctions and critical insights do not get lost in the process.[17]

Second, there is a tendency within cultural feminism to generalize from the experience of some women, interpreted in a certain way, to the experience of all women. This effaces significant differences between women, arising, for example, from race, class, or culture, as well as masking the complicity of many women in the domination of nature (and of socially subordinate women and men). Underlying this tendency to universalize is the radical feminist prioritization of the patriarchal oppression of women as the root cause of all other structures of domination. Many cultural feminists have sought support for this view in research on that epochal shift that appears to have taken place in the Mediterranean region around 3000 B.C.E. from a matrilineal, matrifocal, seemingly peaceful, relatively egalitarian, earth goddess-worshiping culture to a patriarchal warrior society characterized by new tools, weapons, heirarchies, and sky gods. As Rosemary Radford Ruether has observed, cultural feminists have tended to interpret the archeological evidence for this transition on the mythical model of the Fall, whereby the subjection of women to male domination, often said to have been brought about by "invading Indo-Germanic horsemen," is seen to have led simultaneously to the masculinization of culture and the institution of a more aggressive and exploitative relationship to the land and other peoples (Ruether 1992:147–155). Within this account, prepatriarchal culture tends to be idealized in terms reminiscent of nineteenth-century theories of "matriarchy," which were in turn strongly influenced by a Romantic view of woman as universally nurturing and pacific.[18] The notion of a "Fall into patriarchy" has doubtless been valuable as an enabling myth for many women, holding out the hope that since things were different once, they can be so again. However, it has also generated a certain kind of feminist "bad faith." This takes the form not only of universalizations concerning "patriarchy," viewed monolithically, and "women's experience," viewed homogeneously, but also the notion that women have retained certain psychological or cultural links to this era of primordial harmony with nature that have been lost to men. Suppressing complicity, cultural ecofeminists have been reluctant to confront the extent to which women, too, have been deformed by patriarchy. Prioritizing sexism, they have also overlooked the complex socioeconomic factors underlying the current ecological crisis and intersecting with patriarchal structures of domination in ways that do not impact on all women in the same manner or to the same degree.[19]

For a closer analysis of the interstructuration of the domination of women and nature with other forms of oppression in specific historical contexts, it is necessary to turn from cultural to social(ist) ecofeminist analyses, which draw attention to the fact that although the association of woman and nature is ancient and widespread across many cultures, it assumes a particular form in the context of Western modernity. For Carolyn Merchant (1980), for example, the key factors here are the "scientific revolution" of the seventeenth century and, in connection with this, the rise of capitalism. As Adorno and Horkheimer had observed as early as 1944 in their powerful critique of the "dialectic of enlightenment," the "chaste and lawful marriage between the mind of man and the nature of things" proclaimed by Francis Bacon was fundamentally patriarchal (Adorno & Horkheimer 1989:4). The discourse of modern science breaks decisively with earlier constructions of nature as nurturing mother, commanding respect and restraint, or alternatively as fundamentally chaotic and lawless, in imaging its object of inquiry as both rationally knowable and ideally subject to masculine control, whether as docile "wife" or recalcitrant "witch" who must be forced to give up her secrets "in the grip and under the pressure of art" (Lloyd 1984:11). As Merchant and others have suggested, it is no coincidence that this scientific view of nature emerges at the height of the witch hunts, which led to the demonization of women's traditional knowledge, as well as contributing to the destruction of the subsistence culture of the village, in which women, as midwives and healers, as well as producers of food and many other household necessities, had a respected place.[20] Somewhat ironically, it is around the time when women begin to cede their traditional authority in the area of reproduction to male-dominated medical science that their social identity becomes more narrowly focused on the role of mother. Central to this was the expansion of capitalist industrialization, facilitated by the more effective technological exploitation of a now thoroughly disenchanted

nature. For this necessitated the relocation of production away from the
home, which in turn brought about a redefinition of work solely as
money-earning activity and a shift in the status of women from that
of economic partners to dependents (and in the case of lower-class
women, a cheap source of labor for the new manufactories).[21]

It is important to note that this kind of critique of mechanistic science and capitalism does not necessarily imply a hostility to science and
modernity per se. Social(ist) ecofeminists might well agree with Karen
Green's observation, in response to Merchant, that capitalism also
brought "an increase in free-time for middle-class women, an improvement in their level of education, increased involvement with literature
and politics, and the subsequent battle for the right to vote" (Green
1994:123). However, they would also point out that these advantages
for a minority were premised most immediately on the exploitation of
the labor of lower-class women to service the needs of the household
(as in the professional success of many middle-class women today); and,
more generally, on the maintenance of a socioeconomic system that
was—and remains—socially unjust and ecologically unsustainable.
From this perspective, there is no possibility of getting out of history;
but neither is there any chance of overcoming the domination of
women and nature in the context of a growth economy dependent on
the exploitation of both as resources. Nor do ecofeminists of any per-
suasion suggest that we can or should simply ditch modern science; but
most argue strongly for a different kind of scientific practice—one
grounded either in "a feeling for the organism," fostering empathic attention to the "object" of knowledge as a subject in its own right (Keller
1983) or, alternatively, in a wider sense of objectivity, which acknowledges both the embodied embeddedness of the subject of knowledge in
time and place and the independent agency of the other (Haraway
1991); a science, above all, that is capable of seeing things in context,
as profoundly interconnected, and that is oriented, as far as possible,
toward the flourishing of all life on earth, human and otherwise.

In recent years, ecofeminist thinking has been greatly enriched by
the voices of women of color and Third World women. Dolores S. Williams, for example, discloses the connections between the abuse and
exploitation of African-American women's bodies, which were used as
breeding machines by slave owners in America's South, and the exploitation and degradation of the land in the plantations on which the
slaves were made to work (Williams 1993); while Vandana Shiva calls
attention to the hardships suffered by Third World women as a result
of "development" projects modeled on the ideology and practices of
Western capitalist industrialization (Shiva 1989). Because women are

largely responsible for providing basic subsistence in areas such as rural India, it is they who are most immediately affected when commercial logging deprives them of readily accessible firewood and fodder, industrial effluents pollute their sources of fresh water, the introduction of industrial agricultural practices (chemical fertilizers, pesticides, dams, etc.) degrade their soil and the pressure to produce cash crops reduces the amount of land available for providing food. Moreover, it is women and their children who have suffered most from the introduction of Western reproductive technologies, such as potentially harmful contraceptives, sterilization, and breast-milk substitutes. Here the connections between women and nature emerge from the character of women's work in reproducing the material basis for everyday life; and it is out of their struggle to maintain this material basis that many third-world women have been drawn into ecological activism, whether in defense of their forest livelihood, as in the case of the Chipko or "tree-hugging" peasant women of India's Doon Valley, or in research institutes, such as Shiva's Foundation for Science and Ecology, exploring alternative models of development that could better meet peoples' needs in a genuinely sustainable way.

Shiva has collaborated closely over a number of years with German feminist sociologist Maria Mies, who argues that the "subsistence perspective" of Third World women can also point the way toward a more radical ecofeminist transformation in the industrialized world (Mies & Shiva 1993). A similar position is also taken by Mary Mellor (1997) and Ariel Salleh (1997), who call for a revaluation of the concern with embodiment and embeddedness implicit in the kinds of reproductive work that still commonly fall to women, whatever else women might do, with the socially constructed sexual division of labor. Salleh argues further that, because of their marginalized position as unpaid subsistence workers, women now constitute the "hidden subject of History/ Nature" (1997:3), who, together with other marginalized groups (notably indigenous peoples), are presently well placed to further the cause of radical ecological transformation. Whereas Mellor looks to the creation of a "feminist, green socialism" (1997:195), Salleh, like Mies and Shiva, favors the (re)emergence of "self-sufficient, decentralized relations of production, where men and women work together in reciprocity with external nature" (1997:180). Although serious doubt has been shed on the practicability of a global return to subsistence, as advocated by Mies and Shiva (e.g., Eckersley 1994; Braidotti et al. 1994:93–5), it is clear that if the earth's limited "resources" are to be shared more equitably, a drastic reduction in consumption levels in industrialized nations is essential. The question remains, however, how this is to be

achieved, and whether Western women's ecorevolutionary agency is as
assured as Salleh assumes, given that, despite their relatively high level
of environmental concern,[22] most women in countries like Australia
remain locked into consumer culture, even—or perhaps especially—in
the midst of their caring labors.

To the extent that ecofeminists do not seek to shore up the conventional sexual division of labor or to reaffirm traditional gender dualisms—and the majority do not—their project is in a sense a paradoxical
one: namely, to critically affirm women's historically and socially constituted different relation to nature as a source of insight in the context
of ecological transformation, while simultaneously working, as feminists, to dismantle those structures of domination in which this difference is grounded. Women are called to walk a tightrope, constantly on
their guard against falling one way, into an uncritical identification with
a revalued but still dualistically defined "femininity" and "nature," or
the other, into an equally dualistic disavowal of embodiment and embeddedness. Critically affirming "female identity," in Plumwood's view,
involves recognizing this as "an important if problematic tradition
which requires critical reconstruction, a potential source of strength as
well as a problem, and a ground of both continuity and difference with
traditional ideals" (1993:64). Thus, for example, some feminists have
argued that women's traditional monopoly on caring for young children
has imbued them with a more relational sense of self—as little girls we
learn to model our identity on the basis of similarity to and continuity
with the (M)other,[23] while as mothers, women (ideally) learn that their
child's well-being is inextricably bound up with their own. This more
relational sense of self, it has been suggested, could form the basis for
a new ecological ethics of care (e.g., Curtin 1991). However, if ecology
is not to be seen exclusively as "women's business," then the contribution of men must also be affirmed and encouraged; and if men are
also to develop this more ecological kind of relational self, then the logic
of this analysis suggests that they must become more involved in par-
enting. Moreover, since "care" is so closely tied to a particular ideology
of maternal femininity, some ecofeminists have argued instead for an
ethics of partnership (Merchant 1992:188, 1996:209–224) or mutuality
(Plumwood 1993:156–), in which the "earth other" is recognized as "a
Centre of agency or having its origin and place like mine in the community of the earth, but as a different Centre of agency, which limits
mine" (Plumwood 1993:159).

The counterpart of this restoration of agency or telos to nonhuman
nature is the reincorporation of "nature" as body into subjectivity and
as emotion into reason. Here too, women's association with bodiliness,

both in cultural representation and in practice (e.g., as menstruants, birth-givers, and carers for the bodies of children, the aged, and the sick), and with the so-called reason of the heart, suggests that female identities might provide a model for a more embodied sense of self and a more inclusive understanding of reason. However, for women to simply celebrate their (patriarchally) proclaimed corporeality and emotiveness will get them nowhere. For the aim of ecofeminist transformation cannot be to reify existing differences between the sexes but must be to facilitate the relocation of women (and other subordinated groups) into culture, as well as nature, and of men into nature as well as culture, while simultaneously contributing to the redefinition and reattunement of culture and nature. To the extent that critical ecofeminism succeeds in this tricky tightrope dance, it can indeed claim to be a "third wave or stage of feminism moving beyond the conventional divisions in feminist theory" (Plumwood 1993:39).

Feminism, Ecology and the Goddess

The (re)turn to the Goddess advocated by Christ and others in the late 1970s arises from the radical cultural feminist insight that legislative changes brought about by political action directed toward ensuring equality of opportunity to women, while doubtless necessary, would not in themselves bring about the desired dissolution of patriarchal attitudes and social structures. This view is shared by social(ist) feminists, who argue that the full emancipation of women, or any other oppressed group, cannot be realized under capitalism. Whereas socialist feminists prioritize the restructuring of socioeconomic relations, however, the former look to the transformation of perceptions and beliefs through the creation of alternative cultural practices and identities. These differences have a direct parallel in the ecology movement in the split between the resource management approach, oriented toward less destructive uses of "natural assets" within the current system; social(ist) ecology, which seeks the end of social structures of domination as a prerequisite for a reharmonization of culture and nature; and deep ecology, which calls for a more fundamental transformation in our understanding of ourselves and our place in nature.

Not surprisingly, the intersection of feminism and ecology has replicated these divisions, with materialist ecofeminists accusing spiritual ecofeminists of a retreat into the merely personal and, worse, of reactionary antimodernism and neo-Romantic irrationalism (which, in a German context in particular, always carries an imputation of fascistic

tendencies).[24] In recent years, however, some ecofeminists, on both sides
of the divide, have sought to move beyond this false opposition of politics and spirituality.[25] As Ynestra King has observed, the often ill-
informed hostility of materialist feminists to feminist spirituality is
grounded in the old Marxist base–superstructure dualism that must
itself "be overcome before we can have a dialectical, or genuinely ecological, feminism" (King 1990:115). Similarly, Susan Griffin has recently
drawn attention to the dialectical codetermination of ideas and socioeconomic relations, such that it is no longer possible to say which has
come first—or which should be targeted as the privileged site for strategies of change (Griffin 1995:119). From this perspective, and in view
of the urgency of our current global crisis, in which social injustice is
intimately intertwined with ecological devastation, it seems imperative
that women work simultaneously on all fronts—legal and political, social and economic, cultural and psychological. Inevitably, this will entail
some division of labor and some differences in approach; but if the work
of transformation is to have any chance of success, we need to cultivate
an attitude of collaboration and mutual respect (including respect for
differences) rather than divisiveness and mutual hostility.

While it is certainly true that religion and spirituality can and do
often serve a compensatory function, deflecting attention and energy
away from political engagement, this is not necessarily the case, as, for
example, the inspirational and politically radicalizing role of liberation
theology in Latin America clearly indicates. In the case of Goddess spirituality, it should be stressed that some forms of contemporary Goddess
worship are neither feminist nor ecological in orientation. However, spiritual ecofeminism—unlike the more consumerist and individualist end
of New Age spirituality, to which it is sometimes falsely assimilated[26]— is
resolutely worldly and self-consciously political, while simultaneously
redefining the terrain and methodology of political activism.[27] While
ritual plays an important role in ecofeminist Goddess spirituality and is
understood to have its own political charge, it is not necessarily seen as
sufficient in itself. In Spretnak's analysis, the value of practices such as
meditation or ritual celebration within any ecological spirituality is primarily to enable the participants to experience inwardly the ecological
insight "that we live in a participatory universe—that each of us, each
minute part of us, is a node within a vast network of creative dynamics"
(Spretnak 1991:22). Spretnak's account of contemporary ecospiritualities reveals an underlying kinship between religion and ecology to the
extent that both are concerned with connectedness. Whereas, however,
traditional religious practices, especially in the West, have prioritized
the connection to a transcendent divinity and limited communion to

the fellowship of the faith, ecospiritual practices teach of a wider and more worldly kind of "interbeing,"[28] affirming our bond to the earth, our interconnectedness with all earth others, human and otherwise, and our common origins in the dynamic process of cosmic unfolding. It is through this spiritual experience of interanimation that women are to be sustained in our endeavors to create a just and sustainable future for all.

Within ecofeminist Goddess spirituality, the conscious alignment of the self with nature is practiced in the form of seasonal, solar, and lunar celebrations and rites of passage, which affirm our bodily particularity, and attendant needs and desires, as the material locus of our earthliness and interconnectedness with others and, as such, as profoundly hierophanic, revealing the divine within the mundanity of our mortal flesh.[29] As a radically immanental religion, whereby each and every individual entity, human and otherwise, is valued equally as such a manifestation of the divine with its own "Centre" and telos, ecofeminist Goddess religion incorporates a commitment to social justice as well as ecological balance (Starhawk 1982b:418). Within ecofeminist Wicca the practice of "magic," understood as the "art of changing consciousness at will" (Dion Fortune, cited in Starhawk 1989a:28), and of consciously raising and shaping fields of energy, is seen to assist in focusing the attention of participants on particular issues, as well as empowering them to intervene in overcoming domination and furthering the interests of life on earth.[30] As Starhawk emphasizes, however, magic is not a substitute for political engagement but "a source of healing and energy we can use to heal the wounds of the world" (Starhawk 1982b:418).

Although ecofeminist spirituality draws its inspiration from ancient Goddess imagery and premodern nature religions, this does not mean that it is necessarily antimodern or antiscientific. In most cases it is self-consciously postmodern,[31] aiming not at any kind of wholesale restoration of past cultural forms or social structures but the creation of new myths and rituals out of the residue of history and prehistory to serve the needs of individuals and communities concerned with ecological and feminist transformation in the present. Heide Göttner-Abendroth refers to this conscious and playful redeployment of archaic symbolism as "enlightened mythology" (1989:21–35); in this spirit she also prefigures an alliance of postmechanistic science and feminist spirituality as two dimensions of a new practice of earth-healing (34). Similarly, Starhawk acknowledges the value of an alliance between scientific observation and ecospiritual practice on the grounds that since "the Goddess is manifest in the physical world, . . . the more we understand

its workings, the better we know Her" (Starhawk 1989b:202). Emphasizing the metaphoricity of religious symbolism, she argues for a form
of Goddess spirituality that is informed by the insights of physics, math-
ematics, ecology, and biochemistry, while also acknowledging the prov-
isionality and relativity of the knowledge thereby revealed (203).[32] Here
it is apparent that Goddess spirituality is neither irrationalist nor dogmatic. However, it certainly points toward a wider understanding of
reason than the instrumental and dualistic mode of rationality that has
predominated in modernity—one that sees reason in terms not dissim-
ilar to Plumwood's, namely as in close communication with the evidence of the senses, the promptings of the heart, the flights of the
imagination, and the wisdom of the unconscious—and open at all times
to surprise and wonder.[33]

In summary, I believe, with Karen Warren, that Goddess spirituality,
together with other forms of ecofeminist spirituality, can indeed com-
prise "life-affirming, personally empowering, and collectively constructive challenges to patriarchy," encouraging "ways of thinking and be-
having that challenge patriarchal conceptual frameworks and the
thinking, behaviors, and *isms* of domination they sanction" (Warren
1994:126, 130). In the remainder of this section, I would nonetheless
like to discuss certain aspects of Goddess symbolism that in my view
remain problematic from either a feminist or an ecological perspective.

First, one might ask exactly what kind of female identity and what
kind of connection between women and nature is implied in the figure
of the Goddess. To the extent that the Goddess has been seen as an
Earth Mother figure, it might be feared—as many feminists of equality
certainly have feared—that this form of spirituality identifies women
once more with their reproductive function. In practice, however, the
association of the Goddess with biological fertility tends to be under-
played or radically reconfigured. Thus attention is often drawn to the
association of earlier goddess-figures with agriculture, statecraft, and
the arts and sciences, indicating that a return to the Goddess, while
affirming the female body and the earthbody, does not tie women to
reproduction but rather endorses their movement into culture and society, without denying the wonder of their life-giving capacities. In feminist Wicca, moreover, the Goddess is modeled more closely on the Celtic
triune lunar Goddess than on the prehistoric Earth Mother figure. Here,
the Goddess is said to be mother/lover only in one phase, and even then
it is stressed that as such she represents creativity in general, not only
procreativity, while also conjoining the conventionally opposed attributes of maternal love and sexual desire; in her earlier phase she is virgin
or maiden, not in the patriarchal sense of "sexually pure" but rather

as independent and wild; and finally, she is the crone, the visionary or wise woman. On a more ecocosmic level, one might understand the virgin as a metaphor for the process of individuation, the mother/lover as eros, the power that binds or connects, and the crone as thanatos, the force of death and dissolution that in turn facilitates renewal and rebirth. This is certainly not the "eternal feminine" revisited. As Melissa Raphael has observed:

> although [feminist] thealogies of embodiment might sometimes bear *superficial* resemblance to conservative constructions of female embodiment they draw wholly different conclusions about the meaning, value and relations of almost everything: divinity, nature, history and politics. (Raphael 1996:69)

However, it remains problematic in my view that in symbolizing nature as female the woman–nature link becomes somewhat reified, threatening to obliterate differences among women as well as potentially marginalizing men. For those women who identify themselves with the Goddess, this encourages the view that their connection with nonhuman nature is to some extent pregiven, rather than something that has to be critically reconstructed, and it could also lead to a narcissistic assimilation of all of nature to the self. For men, on the other hand, Goddess symbolism might well perpetuate their construction of nature as other, along with the associated ambivalence of atavistic longing and fear-driven conquest. Arguably, one of the most important tasks of ecosocial transformation is the (re)integration of men into the realm of immanence, allowing them too an appropriate share in the work of care (of self, others, and the earth) and in the celebration of ecocosmic connectedness.[34] From this perspective it is vital that male embodiment also be affirmed and resacralized in ways that simultaneously undermine its traditional association with mastery and transcendence. This reclamation of the male to the sacred earth is also necessary to counter the self-aggrandizement implicit in spiritual ecofemininists' celebration of their own bodily particularity as the privileged metaphor for cosmic creativity. (As far as I know, none of us reproduces parthenogenetically!) The spiritual ecofeminist suppression of the vital male part in the biological generation of new life provides a particularly striking example of feminist bad faith. It should be noted, however, that this tendency is considerably reduced in those forms of feminist Wicca that retain the figure of the Horned God as consort of the Triple Goddess. Whereas nonfeminist Wicca constructs the God and Goddess dualistically along conventionally gendered and heterosexist lines, ecofeminists such as

Starhawk have become highly critical of such sexual stereotypes, emphasizing that different men and women will conceive of and relate to both the God and the Goddess in a variety of different ways and that women cannot claim any intrinsic closeness to nature that men, by nature, cannot share (Starhawk 1989b:214–8).[35]

Whether or not the Goddess appears with a male off-sider, and however many manifestations she assumes, there is however a further problem with this symbolization of nature—namely, as Plumwood has pointed out, its inherent anthropocentrism (1993:127). Imaging the creative energies of nature as human might assist in the process of affirming our continuity with the nonhuman world (especially for those of us raised with an anthropomorphic concept of God as father/son). But the alterity of nonhuman nature—most of whose entities are nongendered—needs to be recognized: learning to honor this tree, or those wetlands, or that crocodile in themselves as others, not just as parts of a whole modeled on an ecocosmic image of woman—and even though in some cases our vital needs might conflict with theirs. (As Plumwood has discovered the hard way—in narrowly surviving a crocodile attack in Kakadu National Park—such recognition of a large beast of prey as earth other does not entail submitting to its appetite for human flesh!)

Plumwood is also critical of what she calls "Goddess pantheism" on the grounds that it overvalues the ecocosmic Whole at the expense of "the great plurality of particular beings," thereby also remaining bound to the hierarchical notion of a central intelligence (1993:127–8). In my assessment, this criticism is less justified, as spiritual ecofeminists do not generally conceive of the Goddess as "out there" or "up there" but, as I have already indicated, as immanent in the glorious diversity of individual entities. However, to the extent that on another level, the image of the Goddess certainly does privilege a holistic concept of nature as ultimately One, it falls prey to the same paradox that Freya Mathews has noted in other forms of deep ecology (1994b: 159–161).[36] For if, as many deep ecologists, including ecofeminist avatars of the Goddess, claim, we are truly part of nature and nature "knows best," then all our creations, from our first tools through to nuclear warheads and the greenhouse effect, would appear to be part of the process of cosmic evolution whereby the drastic depletion of the existing community of the earth merely opens the way to a new stage in the life of the planet. Taken to its logical conclusion, this kind of ecocosmic holism is thus more likely to lead to a quietistic acquiescence in the current course of things than to an ethics and politics of resistance to ecological destruction and social injustice.[37] To ground the latter within the logic of Goddess symbolism, we must either accept that the Goddess is not just tripartite but divided against herself and that our task is to ally ourselves with those aspects of the Goddess that desire the flourishing of earth's existing diversity of human communities, species, and habitats against her "shadow side," which seems hellbent on their destruction; or we must surrender the cosmic image of the Goddess for the more homely one of Earth Mother, embodying the now so gravely threatened capacity of the earth to generate and nourish biological life-systems— a Mother who, in a role reversal, now requires the attentive care of her wayward offspring. Alternatively, we might need to follow Melissa Raphael (1996:47–8) in reconfiguring the distinction between the sacred and the profane, such that the latter is redefined as any attitude or practice that "profanes" by violating, dominating, or needlessly destroying the embodied other or the integrity, diversity, and vitality of the biosphere.

What I am trying to illustrate here is that any attempted revival of ancient life-affirming myths and rituals of the earth that predate the project of the scientific conquest and capitalist expropriation of nature becomes anachronistic if these myths and rituals are not transformed so as to confront the paradox that in modern industrial society nature has seemingly produced its own nemesis. This paradox might be resolved by means of a historical analysis that indicates that although humanity is undoubtedly a part of, and ultimately dependent on, nature, in the course of Western civilization we have sought to suppress this fact by creating a second-order nature that now threatens the first (but that will itself of course be engulfed if the latter collapses). In this situation, a spirituality that teaches accommodation to nature's rhythms is inadequate, since these are themselves presently being altered as a result (unintended and unforeseen) of human intervention. What might it mean to celebrate the cycle of seasonal change, when the seasons themselves are changing under the impact of the greenhouse effect? Or to honor the return of the sun in midwinter, when its rays have become so dangerous in the spring and early summer (and, one might add, when we can readily shield ourselves from the vagaries of climate by air-conditioning and heating, and from the dark of the night by artificial light, and when our livelihood and even diet are largely unaffected by seasonality)?

There is much to be said for a spirituality of immanence that teaches us to delight in our bodies and their interanimation with all the manifold others with whom we share our earthly home. However, for city-dwellers in the affluent West especially, such a spirituality must also confront the extent of our historically constituted disconnection from nature; the ways in which the nature that we inhabit, including our own bodies,[38] has been culturally and technologically reconstituted; and the new ethical and political responsibilities that attend the (by no means unlimited but nonetheless awesome) capacity that our systems of knowledge and economics have acquired to remake the world in their own image, to their own ends.[39] In this regard, I doubt whether the symbolism of the Goddess will ultimately prove adequate to the kind of ecological metaphysics and ethics that are demanded by our current perilous and historically unprecedented situation.

"Let One Hundred Flowers Bloom" (But Don't Neglect the Weeding)

Although I believe that Goddess symbolism is problematic in certain respects, I would like to stress once again that Goddess spirituality has doubtless been inspiring and empowering for many ecofeminists. It may be, however, that the return to the Goddess will turn out to have been less a point of arrival than a stepping stone to other forms of ecocosmic encounter, which might better allow for the recognition of alterity, as well as affinity, in our relations with nonhuman nature and for the historical specificities and ethical complexities of the contexts in which those encounters take place. Although there is a tendency for counter-traditions to generate their own orthodoxies that foreclose a forward movement such as this, there is reason to hope that this will not necessarily be the case with ecofeminist Goddess spirituality, which has always been characterized by a certain playful, makeshift quality, emphasizing openness and spontaneity rather than a dogmatic fixation on particular forms and procedures. Where the divine is perceived to be one with the material universe, symbolism can be recognized as a matter of personal or collective choice; in this sense, ecofeminist spirituality is profoundly antifundamentalist. Living, as we undoubtedly do, at a time of cultural, as well as socioeconomic and geohistorical, transition, there is a need to be open to such experimentation, in the knowledge that what "worked" yesterday might not do so again today and that what feels right today might prove restrictive tomorrow.

Meanwhile, over the past ten years, women in many parts of the world have found other stepping stones toward an ecofeminist spirituality, formed from more conventional frameworks of belief, including the monotheistic "father religions" that have been so strongly criticized on feminist and ecological grounds, as well as Hinduism, Buddhism, and a variety of indigenous traditions.[40] As I have indicated, Goddess symbolism is in itself no guarantee of either feminist or ecological soundness. Conversely, it may well be the case, as Ruether has suggested, that virtually all religious traditions contain elements that might form the basis for a new ecofeminist spirituality. Ruether nonetheless also rightly points out that given the unprecedented nature of our current global situation, no preexisting traditions have ready-made answers to today's problems: all require some degree of reinterpretation and revisioning, preferably by those who "claim community in them," if they are to help us to reorient ourselves in the present (1992:11). In this process, there is a place both for a wider ecumenism, which could allow us to find the common ground underlying our multiple differences, and for an increasing level of regional diversification. For while today's ecospiritualities need to be informed by a global perspective, they are also bound to be shaped by specificities of cultural and, equally important, geographical place. In this regard, the regeneration of an immanental spirituality constitutes a truly postmodern movement away from the universal and toward the particularity of our "storied residence" (Holmes Rolston III, cited in Cheney 1994:174) in the lands we inhabit. For it is in the concrete specificities of our local climatic conditions, land formations, waterways, and biotic communities that we must ultimately seek to ground the bioregional myths and rituals of new ecofeminist spiritualities.

Notes

1. Among the most frequently cited works of this kind are those of Merlin Stone (1976), Marija Gimbutas (1982), Monica Sjöö and Barbara Mor (1987), Riane Eisler (1988) and Elinor Gadon (1989).

2. Christ 1987a, example, draws her inspiration largely from Greek mythology, while Germanic myth has been reappropriated in the main by German feminists such as Ute Schiran, who runs her own school of Shamanic studies); Celtic myth forms the basis for Wicca, that is, contemporary versions of "white witchcraft," example, Starhawk and Z. Budapest (both have active covens and a very wide following); Luisah Teish draws on African spiritual traditions of Voodooism and has a group in Oakland, California, while Paula Gunn Allen (Diamond & Orenstein 1990) draws on Native American traditions. King also reports that other Native American women in the Hopi and Navaho traditions are "attempting to explain their traditions to a wider public while they organize politically to keep their lands from being taken over by developers or poisoned by industry" (King 1990: 112). It should be noted, however, that in Cynthia Eller's assessment, North American Goddess spirituality is still overwhelmingly of white, middle-class origin (Eller 1990:18). It could be argued that this is the case elsewhere in the Western world as well.

3. By 1986, Starhawk's introduction to feminist Wicca, *The Spiral Dance. A Rebirth of the Ancient Religion of the Great Goddess* (1979), had sold around fifty thousand copies, as had Margot Adler's book *Witches, Druids, Goddess-Worshippers and Other Pagans in America Today* (1979), while Starhawk's later

book *Dreaming the Dark: Magic, Sex and Politics* (1982) had sold around thirty thousand copies. Both Adler's book and Starhawk's *Spiral Dance* have since been republished in a revised form, in 1986 and 1989, respectively. On neo-Paganism, including feminist Goddess spirituality in Australia, see Hume 1997.

4. A simple enquiry on "Goddess spirituality" on Altavista brings up 470,000 references, including http.//www.gaia.org/gen/findhorn/press; http://www.missouri.edu/~700100/goddess/links.html; http://www.com/ goddessbk.htm; http://www.agate.net/~scatha /links.html, and http:// www.phenomenalwomen.com/network/religion-spirit.html.

5. Example, Charlene Spretnak, Starhawk, and Margot Adler appear with social ecofeminist Ynestra King and feminist theologian Rosemary Radford Ruether in Plant 1989; Spretnak, Riane Eisler, Carol Christ and Starhawk appear with socialist ecofeminist Carolyn Merchant, Ynestra King, and feminist theologian Catherine Keller in Diamond & Orenstein 1990; and Spretnak also appears with Keller, Ruether, Sally McFague and Jewish feminist theologian Judith Plaskow in Adams, 1993.

6. Commenting on the "indiscriminate hostility" of the academic establishment to the countercultures that emerged from the student and women's movements of the 1970s, Roszak writes in *Person/Planet*: "one must distinguish between the authenticity of the needs people express and the inadequacy of the material that might be offered to meet these needs" (Roszak 1978: xxiv).

7. These include Jewish feminist Judith Plaskow, coeditor with Carol Christ of *Womanspirit Rising*, and Christian feminist theologian Rosemary Radford Ruether, whose work is also included in this book. The field of feminist theology is now vast; among the most prominent contributors are Naomi R. Goldenberg, Judith Plaskow, Tikva Frymer-Kemsky, Elisabeth Schüssler-Fiorenza, Sally McFague, Catherine Keller, Anne Primavesi, Elisabeth Moltmann-Wendel, Dorothee Sölle, and, in Australia, Elaine Wainwright, Maryanne Confoy, and Dorothy Lee.

8. See Caldecott and Leland 1983:6–7; Merchant 1992:184; Mies and Shiva 1993:13–15.

9. It should be noted, however, that the Feminist International Network of Resistance to Genetic and Reproductive Engineering (FINRAGE), founded in Europe in 1984 to oppose the colonization of women's reproductive capacities by patriarchal technologies of the domination of nature (and capitalist economic interests), does have an Australian chapter.

10. Carolyn Merchant provides a good overview of ecofeminism in Australia in the final chapter of her recent book *earthcare* (1995:185–208).

11. One of the best overviews of different approaches within ecofeminist thinking currently available is Carolyn Merchant's in *Radical Ecology* (1992: 183–210). In the following, however, I differ from Merchant, first, in excluding liberal feminist environmentalism from the category of ecofeminism, since liberal feminists seek no more than a strategic alliance with a shallow form of environmentalism, rather than arguing for an intrinsic link between feminist and ecological concerns; and second, in my assessment of cultural ecofeminism, which Merchant views as universally essentialist.

12. Assessments of the extent of this "biocide" vary, but the relatively conservative estimate presently accepted by the World Council of Churches indicates that in the last quarter of this century around 20 percent of the earth's biodiversity will have been lost.

13. Cultural ecofeminism, as a form of radical feminism, identifies the patriarchal domination of women as the primary or "root" form of domination. This contrasts with the relatively greater weight that social(ist) ecofeminists accord socioeconomic domination on the basis of class and race. Social and socialist ecofeminists share a critique of capitalism but differ somewhat in their vision of the society we should work toward, with social feminists favoring the devolution of the state into radically democratized and decentralized communities, as theorized by some anarchist thinkers, while socialist feminists affiliate themselves more closely with the program of democratic ecological socialism. Among the former are Janet Biehl, who draws on the work of anarchist philosopher Murray Bookchin (although in her most recent book, Biehl (1991) has dissociated herself from the term "ecofeminism" altogether, since in her—in my view false—assessment, it has become synonymous with cultural ecofeminism; for a critical response to Biehl, see Buege 1994). Merchant also identifies Ynestra King, Ariel Salleh, and Val Plumwood among those who are currently redefining social ecology (Merchant 1992:195). To this list I would add Vandana Shiva and Maria Mies. Like Mary Mellor in Britain, Merchant defines herself as a socialist ecofeminist. In terms of ecopolitical theory there can be significant differences between socialist and social ecofeminist thought, but with regard to the analysis of the woman–nature connection there is considerable overlap, to the extent that in both frames the social is foregrounded. The currently most prominent poststructuralist ecofeminist is Donna Haraway. However, Jim Cheney (1994) also draws explicitly on poststructuralist and postmodernist thought, as does Melissa Raphael (1996).

14. Among those who do appear to make such a claim are Mary Daly (1978, 1984) and, more recently, Deena Metzger (1989). Interestingly, an early statement by Ynestra King, who has become a prominent social ecofeminist, also includes an essentialist argument: "We have a deep and particular understanding of this [i.e., the link between violence to women and to nature] both through our natures and our experience as women" (King 1984:11). King now avoids according women any such intrinsic "epistemic privilege." Charlene Spretnak sometimes cites biological (neurophysiological) arguments for women's greater sense of empathy and connectedness (e.g., 1989:129) but nonetheless avers elsewhere: "What cannot be said . . . is that women are drawn to ecology and ecofeminism simply because we are female" (1990:4). To some extent, it would appear that the recourse to essentialist arguments in some early ecofeminist statements was a function of the newness of this field of inquiry (and the fact that white Western middle-class feminists were just beginning to have unwarranted generalizations pointed out to them by women of color). Susan Griffin, example, in her recent essay collection (1995), is careful to avoid such essentialisms and stresses the necessity of conjoining the project of feminist and ecological change with endeavors to overcome economic injustice and racism, as do Melissa Raphael (1996) and Chris Cuomo (1998).

15. This is clearly stated in the prologue: "He says that woman speaks with nature. . . . (And when we hear in the Navaho chant of the mountain that a grown man sits and smokes with bears and follows directions given to him by squirrels, we are surprised. We had thought only little girls spoke with animals" (Griffin 1978:1).

16. The critique of dualism is a thread running through all forms of ecofeminist thought and connects it also with the poststructuralist project of the deconstruction of binary oppositions. Plumwood has developed the best ecofeminist analysis of dualism to date. In her account, the web of interlinked dualisms that structure Western thought is ultimately held together by the binary opposition of ("masculine") reason and ("feminine") nature. Within this dualistic framework, nature functions as "a field of multiple exclusion and control, not only of non-humans, but of various groups of humans and aspects of human life which are cast as nature" (Plumwood 1994:4). Thus, workers and colonized peoples, as well as women, have been located historically on the far side of reason, along with parts of the self, such as the body, the emotions, and the unconscious. Unlike distinction or dichotomy, dualism establishes a "relation of separation and domination naturalised in culture and characterised by radical exclusion, distancing and opposition between orders constructed as systematically higher and lower" (47). Dualism is therefore the paradigmatic logic of colonization, whereby the other is defined only in relation to the self as lack or negativity and thereby "incorporated into the self and its systems of desires and needs" (52); objectified and instrumentalized; and stereotyped or homogenized (53).

17. The recuperation of certain patriarchal constructions of femininity is also apparent in the French feminist discourse on "feminine writing" as "writing the body." Some of the best critiques of this tendency are by German feminists such as Sigrid Weigel. See my discussion of this in Beinssen-Hesse and Rigby 1996:83–5.

18. The most significant nineteenth-century theory of matriarchy is J. J. Bachofen's *Mother Right* of 1861 (Bachofen 1967). See Silke Beinssen-Hesse's discussion of Bachofen and his influence in German feminism (Beinssen-Hesse & Rigby, 1996:34–5). Although some German feminists still use the term "matriarchy," the term "prepatriarchal" or "matristic" has become more common in English, as most now agree that this was not so much a period of rule by women as a culture characterized by highly gendered "separate spheres," in which men and women were accorded authority in different areas of cultural and social life and in which women were generally held in higher esteem and had influence in a wider area than was subsequently the case. On the "matriarchy debate" in England, see Ursula King 1989:138–45.

19. This exemplifies the three common pitfalls that Deborah Slicer (1994) has identified in ecofeminist theorizing: (1) the claim that there is a single "root" cause for multiple oppressions; (2) claiming an epistemic privilege for women; (3) claiming that any "adequate environmental ethic must be feminist."

20. See also Bovenschen 1978; Easlea 1980; and Illich 1982:165–9.

21. This transition has also been analyzed along similar lines by a num-

ber of German feminist theorists. See Duden 1977; Hausen 1981; and my discussion of their work in Beinssen-Hesse & Rigby 1996:9–11.

22. In Australia, for example, surveys have indicated that women are significantly more likely to evince environmental concern across a range of issues than men, and more women than men also belong to environmental organisations (Merchant 1996:188–90).

23. This is based on the psychoanalytic theory of Nancy Chodorow (1978), which was in turn drawn on by Carol Gilligan (1982) in explaining perceived differences in the moral outlook of men and women.

24. Because some protofascist ideologues in the 1920s, as well as some contemporary neo-Nazis, are interested in pre-Judeo-Christian myth and ritual, the (eco)feminist reinvention of the Goddess has been viewed with particular suspicion in Germany. In the late 1980s there was also a very virulent debate there concerning anti-Semitic or at least anti-Judaic elements in German feminist spirituality and theology, including the widespread notion that the ancient Hebrews "killed the Goddess" (see Siegele-Wenschkewitz 1988; Heschel 1995). This criticism had also been leveled at American avatars of the Goddess some years earlier, eliciting an explicit disclaimer by Carol (Christ 1987b). For a recent account of anti-Judaism in feminist religious writings in general, see Kellenbach 1994.

25. Similarly, Roger Gottlieb (1996) has recently attempted a reconciliation between deep ecology and the Left.

26. A number of points of contact, as well as divergences, between feminist spirituality and the New Age have nonetheless been identified by Mary Bednarowsky (1992).

27. On the political understandings, affiliations, methods and vision of ecofeminist spirituality, see Spretnak 1982; Eller 1993:185–207; and Raphael 1996:220–61.

28. "Interbeing" is a term coined by the Vietnamese monk Thich Nhat Hanh. Cited in Spretnak 1991:24.

29. The importance of this resacralization of the (female) body in feminist Goddess spirituality is foregrounded by Spretnak (1991:133–55) and explored by Melissa Raphael (1996) with a high degree of theoretical sophistication and philosophical and thealogical depth.

30. Starhawk, example, has led rituals of empowerment such as this in antinuclear protests. On magic and politics, see Starhawk 1982a.

31. Spretnak, example, while highly critical of poststructuralist pantextualism, locates the ecospiritual "recovery of meaning" explicitly in the context of the "postmodern age" (Spretnak 1991).

32. Raphael (1996) also relates the cosmology and politics of ecofeminist Goddess spirituality to the "new science," especially that on nonlinear dynamical systems, popularized as "chaos theory."

33. Spretnak, for example, refers to the "embodied epistemology" that emerges from the practices of ecofeminist Goddess spirituality (1991:149–55).

34. A similar point is made by Ursula King (1989:149–50, 153).

35. Spretnak too sees difficulties with the projection of female identity onto the planet, and suggests the possibility of celebrating the earth in less gender-specific terms (1991:144–5).

36. On the deep ecology–ecofeminism debate, see also Cheney 1987; Fox 1989; Kheel 1990; Salleh 1984, and Zimmermann 1990.

37. Some spiritual ecofeminists have indeed begun to entertain the idea that the Goddess is also manifest in "second nature" but without pursuing the metaphysical and ethical consequences of this notion. See, example, Javors 1990.

38. On the historicity of the body, see the introduction to Duden 1991.

39. As Plumwood observes in the dramatic conclusion of her book, "reason . . . now undertakes the post-Platonic project of remaking the 'chaos' of the biosphere and also the sociosphere in the image of its own abstract perfection"—in accordance with the logic, that is, of economic rationalism (1993:193).

40. Carol Adams's recent collection "Ecofeminism and the Sacred" (1993) contains contributions from Christian, Jewish, Black Womanist, Hindu and Buddhist perspectives. In the United States, African-American and Native American women have been developing ecofeminist spiritualities based on their own indigenous traditions. In Ynestra King's assessment, there is a greater racial—and, I would add, cultural—diversity in spiritual ecofeminism than in any other form of feminism (1990:112). See also Ruether (1996) on feminism, ecology and religion in the Third World.

References

Adams, Carol, ed. 1993. *Ecofeminism and the Sacred.* New York: Continuum.

Adler, Margot. 1986. *Drawing Down the Moon: Witches, Druids, Goddess-Worshippers, and Other Pagans in America Today* [1979]. Rev. and expanded ed. Boston: Beacon Press.

Adorno, Theodor, and Max Horkheimer 1989. *Dialectic of Enlightenment* [Ger. 1944]. Trans. J. Cumming. London: Verso.

Allen, Paula Gunn. 1986. *The Sacred Hoop: Recovering the Feminine in American Indian Traditions.* Boston: Beacon Press.

———. 1990. The Woman I Love Is a Planet; The Planet I Love Is a Tree. In Diamond and Orenstein 1990:52–7.

Bachofen, J. J. 1967. *Myth, Religion, and Mother Right: Selected Writings of J. J. Bachofen.* Trans. R. Mannheim. London: Routledge and Kegan Paul.

Beauvoir, Simone de. 1953. *The Second Sex* [Fr. 1949]. Trans. H. M. Parshley. New York: Knopf.

Bednarowsky, Mary Farrell. 1992. The New Age Movement and Feminist Spirituality: Overlapping Conversations at the End of the Century. In J. L. Lewis and J. G. Melton (eds.), *Perspectives on the New Age.* Albany: SUNY Press: 167–178.

Beinssen-Hesse, Silke, and Kate Rigby. 1996. *Out of the Shadows: Contemporary German Feminism.* Melbourne, Australia: Melbourne University Press.

Biehl, Janet. 1991. *Rethinking Ecofeminist Politics.* Boston: South End Press.

Bovenschen, Silvia. 1978. The Contemporary Witch, the Historcal Witch and the Witch Myth: The Witch, Subject of the Appropriation of Nature and Object of the Domination of Nature [Ger. 1977]. Trans. J. Blackwell et al. *New German Critique* 15:83–119.

Braidotti, Rose, et al. 1994. *Women, the Environment and Sustainable Development: Towards a Theoretical Synthesis*. London: Zed.

―――. 1979. Self-Blessing Ritual. In Christ and Plaskow 1979:269–72.

Budapest, Zsuzsanna. 1986. *The Holy Book of Women's Rituals*. Vol. 1. Oakland, Calif.: Susan B. Anthony Coven 1.

Buege, Douglas B. 1994. Rethinking Again: A Defence of Ecofeminist Philosophy. In Warren 1994:42–63.

Caldecott, Leonie, and Stephanie Leland. 1983. *Reclaim the Earth: Women Speak Out for Life on Earth*. London: Women's Press.

Carlessare, Elizabeth. 1994. Essentialism in Ecofeminist Discourse: In Merchant 1994:220–34.

Carsen, Anne. 1992. *Goddesses and Wise Women: The Literature of Feminist Spirituality 1980–1992. An Annotated Bibliography*. Freedom, Calif.: Crossing Press.

Cheney, Jim. 1987. Eco-Feminism and Deep Ecology. *Environmental Ethics* 9: 115–45.

―――. 1994. Nature/Theory/Difference: Ecofeminism and the Reconstruction of Environmental Ethics. In Warren 1994:158–78.

Chodorow, Nancy. 1978. *The Reproduction of Mothering: Psychoanalysis and the Sociology of Gender*. Berkeley: University of California Press.

Christ, Carol. 1979. Why Women Need the Goddess: Phenomenological, Psychological and Political Reflections. In Christ and Plaskow 1979:271–87.

―――. 1987a. *Laughter of Aphrodite: Reflections of a Journey to the Goddess*. San Francisco: Harper and Row.

―――. 1987b. On Not Blaming the Jews for the Death of the Goddess. In Christ 1987a:83–92.

―――. 1990. Rethinking Theology and Nature [1987]. In Diamond and Orenstein 1990:58–69.

Christ, Carol P., and Judith Plaskow. (eds.). 1979. *Womanspirit Rising: A Feminist Reader in Religion*. San Francisco: Harper and Row.

―――. 1989. *Weaving the Visions: New Patterns in Feminist Spirituality*. San Francisco: Harper and Row.

Confoy, Maryanne, Dorothy A. Lee, and Joan Nowotny. (eds.). 1995. *Freedom and Entrapment: Women Thinking Theology*. North Blackburn, Victoria, Australia: Dove.

Curtin, Deane. 1991. Toward an Ecological Ethic of Care. *Hypatia*. Special issue, Ecological Feminism: 60–74.

Daly, Mary. 1974. *Beyond God the Father: Toward a Philosophy of Women's Liberation*. Boston: Beacon Press.

―――. 1978. *Gyn/Ecology: The Metaethics of Radical Feminism*. Boston: Beacon Press.

―――. 1979. After the Death of God the Father [1971]. In Christ and Plaskow 1979:53–62.

―――. 1984. *Pure Lust: Elemental Feminist Philosophy*. Boston: Beacon Press.

Davion, Victoria. 1994. Is Ecofeminism Feminist? In Warren 1994:8–27.

D'Eaubonne, Francoise. 1994. The Time for Ecofeminism [1971]. Trans. Ruth Hottell. In Merchant 1994:174–97.

Diamond, Irene, and Gloria Feman Orenstein (eds.). 1990. *Reweaving the World: The Emergence of Ecofeminism*. San Francisco: Sierra Club Books.

Duden, Barbara. 1977. Das schöne Eigentum: Zur Herausbildung des bürgerlichen Frauenbildes an der Wende vom 18, zum 19. Jahrhundert. *Kursbuch* 47:125–40.

———. 1991. *The Woman beneath the Skin: A Doctor's Patients in Eighteenth-Century Germany* [Ger. 1987]. Trans. T. Dunlop. Cambridge: Harvard University Press.

Easlea, Brian. 1980. *Witch-hunting, Magic and the New Philosophy: An Introduction to Debates in the Scientific Revolution 1450–1750*. Brighton, Sussex, England: Harvester Press.

Eckersley, Robyn. 1994. Sisters, Subsistence and Survival (Review of Mies and Shiva 1993). *Island* 59:62–5.

Eisler, Riane. 1988. *The Chalice and the Blade*. San Francisco: Harper and Row.

———. 1990. The Gaia Tradition and the Partnership Future: An Ecofeminist Manifesto. In Diamond and Orenstein 1990:23–34.

Eller, Cynthia. 1993. *Living in the Lap of the Goddess: The Feminist Spirituality Movement in America*. New York: Crossroad.

Firestone, Shulamith. 1970. *The Dialectic of Sex: The Case for Feminist Revolution*. New York: Morrow.

Fox, Warwick. 1989. The Deep Ecology–Ecofeminism Debate and Its Parallels. *Environmental Ethics* 11:5–26.

Frymer-Kemsky, Tikva. 1992. *In the Wake of the Goddess: Women, Culture and the Biblical Transformation of Pagan Myth*. New York: Fawcett Columbine.

Gadon, Elinor W. 1989. *The Once and Future Goddess*. San Francisco: Harper and Row.

Gilligan, Carol. 1982. *In a Different Voice: Psychological Theory and Women's Development*. Cambridge: Harvard University Press.

Gimbutas, Marija. 1982. *The Goddesses and Gods of Old Europe, 6500–3500 BC*. Berkeley: University of California Press.

Goldenberg, Naomi. 1979. *Changing of the Gods*. Boston: Beacon Press.

Göttner-Abendroth, Heide. 1989. *Für die Musen: Neun Essays*. Frankfurt: Campus.

———. 1991. *The Dancing Goddess: Principles of a Matriarchal Goddess* [1982]. Trans. M. T. Krause. Boston: Beacon Press.

Gottlieb, Roger S. 1996. Spiritual Deep Ecology and the Left: An Attempt at Reconciliation. In R. S. Gottlieb (ed.), *The Sacred Earth: Religion, Nature, Environment*. New York: Routledge: 516–31.

Gray, Elizabeth Dodson. 1981. *Green Paradise Lost*. Wellesley, Mass.: Roundtable Press.

Green, Karen. 1994. Freud, Wollstonecraft, and Ecofeminism: A Defence of Liberal Feminism. *Environmental Ethics* 16:117–34.

Griffin, Susan. 1978. *Woman and Nature: The Roaring Inside Her*. New York: Harper and Row.

———. 1995. *The Eros of Everyday Life: Essays on Ecology, Gender and Society*. New York: Doubleday.

Gupta, Lina. 1993. Ganga: Purity, Pollution, and Hinduism. In Adams 1993: 99–116.

Hallen, Patsy. 1995. Making Peace with Nature: Why Ecology Needs Feminism [1987]. In A. Drengson and Y. Inoue (eds.), *The Deep Ecology Movement: An Introductory Anthology*. Berkeley, Calif.: North Atlantic Books: 198–218.

Haraway, Donna. 1991. Situated Knowledges: The Science Question in Feminism and the Privilege of Partial Perspective [1988]. In D. Haraway, *Simians, Cyborgs, and Women: The Reinvention of Nature*. New York: Routledge:183–201.

Hausen, Karin. 1981. Family and Role-division: The Polarisation of Sexual Stereotypes in the Nineteenth Century—An Aspect of the Dissociation of Work and Family Life [Ger. 1976]. In L. Evans and W. R. Lee (eds.), *The German Family*. London: Croom Helm:51–83.

Heschel, Susannah. 1995. Configurations of Patriarchy, Judaism, and Nazism in German Feminist Thought. In T. M. Rudavsky (ed.), *Gender and Judaism: The Transformation of Tradition*. New York: New York University Press: 135–54.

Hume, Lynne. 1997. *Witchcraft and Paganism in Australia*. Melbourne, Australia: Melbourne University Press.

Illich, Ivan. 1982. *Gender*. New York: Pantheon.

Javors, Irene. 1990. Goddess in the Metropolis: Reflections on the Sacred in an Urban Setting. In Diamond and Orenstein 1990:211–4.

Kaza, Stephanie. 1993. Acting with Compassion: Buddhism, Feminism, and the Environmental Crisis. In Adams 1993:50–69.

Kellenbach, Katherina von. 1994. *Anti-Judaism in Feminist Religious Writings*. Atlanta: Scholars Press.

Keller, Catherine 1993. Talk about the Weather: The Greening of Eschatology. In Adams ed. 1993:30–49.

Keller, Evelyn Fox. 1983. *A Feeling for the Organism: The Life and Work of Barbara McClintock*. New York: W. H. Freeman.

Kheel, Marti. 1990. Ecofeminism and Deep Ecology. In Diamond and Orenstein 1990:128–37.

King, Ursula. 1989. *Women and Spirituality: Voices of Protest and Promise*. London: MacMillan.

King, Ynestra. 1983. The Eco-feminist Imperative [1981]. In Caldecott and Leland 1983:9–14.

———. 1990. Healing the Wounds: Feminism, Ecology and the Nature/Culture Dualism. In Diamond and Orenstein 1990:106–21.

———. 1994. Feminism and the Revolt of Nature. In Merchant 1994:198–206.

Lloyd, Genevieve. 1984. *The Man of Reason: "Male" and "Female" in Western Philosophy*. Minneapolis: University of Minnesota Press.

Mathews, Freya. 1994a. Ecofeminism and Deep Ecology. In Merchant 1994: 235–45. (Shorter version of 1994b.)

———. 1994b. Relating to Nature: Deep Ecology or Ecofeminism? *Trumpeter* 11(4):159–66.

McFague, Sally. 1993a. *The Body of God: An Ecological Theology*. London: SCM Press.

————. 1993b. An Earthly Theological Agenda. In Adams 1993:84–98.

Mellor, Mary. 1997. *Feminism and Ecology*. Cambridge, England: Polity.

Merchant, Carolyn. 1980. *The Death of Nature*. London: Wildwood House.

————. 1992. *Radical Ecology: The Search for a Livable World*. London: Routledge.

Merchant, Carolyn (ed.). 1994. *Ecology. Key Concepts in Critical Theory*. Atlantic Highlands, N.J.: Humanities Press.

————. 1996. *Earthcare: Women and the Environment*. New York: Routledge.

Metzger, Deena. 1989. Invoking the Grove. In Plant 1989:118–26.

Mies, Maria, and Vandana Shiva. 1993. *Ecofeminism*. Melbourne, Australia: Spinifex.

Moltmann-Wendel, Elisabeth. 1986. *A Land Flowing with Milk and Honey: Perspectives on Feminist Theology* [Ger 1985]. Trans. J. Bowden. London: SCM Press.

————. 1994. *I Am My Body: New Ways of Embodiment* [Ger 1994]. Trans. J. Bowden. London: SCM Press.

Morton, Nelle. 1985. *The Journey Is Home*. Boston: Beacon Press.

Orenstein, Gloria Fenan. 1990. *The Reflowering of the Goddess*. New York: Pergamon.

Plant, Judith. 1990. Searching for Common Ground: Ecofeminism and Bioregionalism. In Diamond and Orenstein 1990:155–61.

Plant, Judith (ed.). 1989. *Healing the Wounds: The Promise of Ecofeminism*. Santa Cruz: New Society.

Plaskow, Judith 1979. The Coming of Lilith: Towards a Feminist Theology. In Christ and Plaskow 1979:198–209.

————. 1990. *Standing Again at Sinai: Judaism from a Feminist Perspective*. New York: Harper and Row.

————. 1993. Feminist Judaism and Repair of the World. In Adams 1993: 70–83.

Plumwood, Val. 1986. Ecofeminism: An Overview and Discussion of Positions and Arguments. *Women and Philosophy*, supplement to *Australasian Journal of Philosophy* 64:120–38.

————. 1988. Women, Humanity and Nature. *Radical Philosophy* 48:16–24.

————. 1991. Nature, Self And Gender: Feminism, Environmentalism and the Critique of Rationalism. *Hypatia* 6(1): 3–27.

————. 1993. *Feminism and the Mastery of Nature*. London: Routledge.

————. 1994a. The Ecopolitics Debate and the Politics of Nature. In Warren 1994:64–87.

————. 1994b. Ecosocial Feminism as a General Theory of Oppression. In Merchant 1994:207–19.

Primavesi, Anne. 1991. *From Apocalypse to Genesis: Ecology, Feminism and Christianity*. Wellwood, Kent, England: Burns and Oats.

Raphael, Melissa. 1996. *Thealogy and Embodiment: The Post-Patriarchal Reconstruction of Female Sacrality*. Sheffield, England: Sheffield University Press.

Ruether, Rosemary Radford. 1979. Motherearth and the Megamachine: A Theology of Liberation in a Feminine, Somatic and Ecological Perspective [1972]. In Christ and Plaskow 1979:43–52.

————. 1984. *New Woman, New Earth*. Minneapolis: Seabury Press.

———. 1989. Toward an Ecological-Feminist Theology of Nature. In Plant 1989:145–54.

———. 1992. *Gaia and God: An Ecofeminist Theology of Earth Healing.* San Francisco: Harper and Collins.

———. 1993. Ecofeminism: Symbolic and Social Connections of the Oppression of Women and the Domination of Nature. In Adams 1993:13–23.

———. 1996. *Women Healing Earth: Third World Women on Ecology, Feminism and Religion.* Hawthorn, Victoria, Australia: John Garratt.

Roszak, Betty 1995. The Spirit of the Goddess. In T. Roszak et al., *Ecopsychology. Restoring the Earth. Healing the Mind.* San Francisco: Sierra Club Books: 288–300.

Roszak, Theodore. 1978. *The Creative Disintegration of Industrial Society.* New York: Anchor Press.

Salleh, Ariel Kay. 1984. Deeper than Deep Ecology: The Eco-Feminist Connection. *Environmental Ethics* 6:339–45.

———. 1997. *Ecofeminism as Politics: Nature, Marx and the Postmodern.* London: Zed Books.

Schiran, Ute. 1988. *Menschenfrauen fliegen wieder: Die Jahreskreisfeste als weiblicher Initiationsweg.* Munich: Droemer Knaur.

Shiva, Vandana. 1989. *Staying Alive: Women, Ecology, and Development.* London: Zed.

———. 1990. Development as a New Project of Western Patriarchy. In Diamond and Orenstein 1990:189–200.

Siegele-Wenschkewitz, L. (ed.). 1988. *Verdrängte Vergangenheit, die uns bedrängt. Feministische Theologie in der Verantwortung für die Geschichte.* Munich: Kaiser.

Sjöö, Monica, and Barbara Mor. 1987. *The Great Cosmic Mother: Rediscovering the Religion of the Earth.* San Francisco: HarperSanFrancisco.

Slicer, Deborah. 1994. Wrongs of Passage. Three Challenges to the Maturing of Ecofeminism. In Warren 1994:29–41.

Sölle, Dorothee. 1984. *To Love and to Work: A Theology of Creation* [with S. A. Cloyes] [Ger 1985]. Philadelphia: Fortress.

———. 1992. *Das Recht auf ein anderes Glück.* Stuttgart: Kreuz.

Spretnak, Charlene. 1986. *The Spiritual Dimension of Green Politics.* Santa Fe: Bear.

———. 1989. Toward an Ecofeminist Spirituality. In Plant 1989:127–32.

———. 1990. Ecofeminism: Our Roots and Flowering. In Diamond and Orenstein 1990:3–14.

———. 1991. *States of Grace. The Recovery of Meaning in the Postmodern Age.* San Francisco: Harper and Row.

———, ed. 1982. *The Politics of Women's Spirituality: Essays on the Rise of Spiritual Power in the Feminist Movement.* New York: Doubleday.

Starhawk. 1982a. *Dreaming the Dark: Magic, Sex and Politics.* Boston: Beacon Press.

———. 1982b. Ethics and Justice in Goddess Religion [1979]. In Spretnak 1982:415–22.

———. 1989a. Feminist, Earth-based Spirituality and Ecofeminism. In Plant 1989:174–85.

————. 1989b. *The Spiral Dance. A Rebirth of the Ancient Religion of the Great Goddess* [1979]. Tenth anniversary ed. San Francisco: Harper.

Stone, Merlin. 1976. *When God Was a Woman.* New York: Dial Press.

Teish, Luisa. 1985. *Jambalaya: The Natural Woman's Book of Personal Charms and Practical Rituals.* San Francisco: Harper and Row.

Wainwright, Elaine. 1998. *Shall We Look for Another? A Feminist Rereading of the Matthean Jesus.* Maryknoll, N.Y.: Orbis.

Warren, Karen. 1987. Feminism and Ecology: Making Connections. *Environmental Ethics* 9:3–20.

————. 1993. A Feminist Philosophical Perspective on Ecofeminist Spiritualities. In Adams 1993:119–32.

Warren, Karen (ed.). 1994. *Ecological Feminism.* London: Routledge.

Williams, Dolores S. 1993. Sin, Nature, and Black Women's Bodies. In Adams 1993:24–9.

Willoughby, L. Teal. 1993. Ecofeminist Consciousness and the Transforming Power of Symbols. In Adams 1993:133–48.

Zimmermann, Michael E. 1990. Deep Ecology and Ecofeminism: The Emerging Dialogue. In Diamond and Orenstein 1990:138–54.

2

Black Truth, White Fiction

The Recognition of Aboriginal Women's Rites

Anne Pattel-Gray

The Omission of Aboriginal Women

As an Aboriginal woman living within contemporary Australian society, being engulfed in the growing trend of gender concerns and awareness, and as a womanist scholar, I cannot overlook the enormous void in academic literature regarding the role of Aboriginal women in the many recordings of history, anthropology, and religious studies. This male-dominated world of scholarship has presented a very unbalanced view of Aboriginal society. Further, when Aboriginal women happen to be given a mention, it is usually in the form of a racist and sexist stereotype, sustaining white ideology of racial supremacy and male domination. Nancy Williams and Lesley Jolly have acknowledged that, unfortunately, many of their

predecessors believed that the white race had a superior culture and religion and was at a far higher stage of evolution than the black race, whom they often viewed as curious living fossils akin to the marsupials (Spencer and Gillen 1927), doomed to extinction in the march of evolutionary progress. Yet for present purposes, it is the gender bias of the recorders that creates the most difficulty. To begin with, most of the writers were men, a fact that reflects not only the greater numbers of white men than white women in contact with Aboriginal society, but also the greater opportunities for European males to publicize their opinions. (1992:10–11)

This racist and gender-biased attitude and thought would undergird the basis of early scholarship, saturating the academic world with such false notions as so-called white supremacy and the objectifying of Aboriginal women as sexual objects for white males to take at their leisure and then discard as you would a piece of garbage.

In 1975, Raymond Evans's essay "Harlots and Helots" challenged the racist and sexist stereotype that white society had constructed about Aboriginal women and their role in Aboriginal society. Jebb and Haebich report thus:

> He recorded a litany of rape, abduction and exploitation justified by racism and greed. Force, not permissiveness, was the order of the frontier, and disease and degradation were the consequences. Evans brought to light the contradictory attitudes and actions of Europeans who indulged in illicit sexual relations with Aboriginal women, yet failed to acknowledge their fully human existence. By 1982, when Evans again focused on the extraordinary brutality shown in Queensland towards Aboriginal women, in an article aptly entitled "Don't you Remember Black Alice, Sam Holt?" academic interest in the conjunction of racism and sexism was beginning to emerge. Buoyed by the increase in anthropological knowledge about women's role in Aboriginal society, but still unconvinced about the efficacy of personal complicity, Evans continued to write of the interplay of racism and sexism and the comparative powerlessness of Aboriginal women:

> > with the onset of white colonization, women's traditional functions were either severely truncated and rendered marginal in a reconstituted social environment or utterly destroyed as their populations were decimated and their society and culture dismembered and fragmented. During this process the position of black women plummeted from being the co-workers of equal importance to men in the balanced use of the environment to that of thoroughly exploited beasts of burden. It fell from being valuable human resources and partners within traditional sexual relationships to that of degraded and diseased sex objects of virtual animal status in the eyes and the belief systems of their exploiters. (Evans 1982:9)

Evans extends the analysis into notions of masculinity and sexual repression which provoked European men's violence towards, and disregard for, Aboriginal women. Thus, he turns the investigation toward European men's perceptions of their own gender which underlay the continuing objectification of aboriginal women. (Jebb & Haebich 1992:28–9)

These racist attitudes, compounded with negative sexist views of Aboriginal women by white males, would have future ramifications on the right of women to access and protect sacred sites. In preparing themselves for future legal and political onslaught, Aboriginal women sought to equip themselves with further education. Several Aboriginal women scholars in various disciplines, when undertaking academic studies, found themselves shocked and angered at the way they had been described and portrayed in much of the research conducted by white Australian males. As an Aboriginal woman, one does not know whether it is best to be made invisible, as opposed to having one's humanity cynically attacked and being subjected to racist and sexist vilification under the guise of academic research. Hazel Carby, a black feminist scholar, writes:

> The black woman's critique of history has not only involved us in coming to terms with "absences"; we have also been outraged by the ways in which it has made us visible, when it has chosen to see us. History has constructed our sexuality and our femininity as deviating from those qualities with which white women, as the prize objects of the western world, have been endowed. We have also been defined in less than human terms. Our continuing struggle with history began with its "discovery" of "us." (Cited by Jebb and Haebich 1992:30)

All scholars must be mindful, when deconstructing historical accounts of the Australian frontier, to bring a critical eye to interpreting the texts, as these often embody the white male narcissism, sexism, racism, and classism of the early frontier:

> Failure to understand gender relationships of the frontier fully is partly explained by the construction of Aboriginal gender relations as necessarily immoral—a sign of savagery and insignificance. Such issues as Aboriginal men's ownership of women, polygamy, child brides, women's profanity, male violence to Aboriginal women and, importantly, Aboriginal women's often mentioned promiscuity, have been taken as pervasive indicators

of black "culture." This is partly a reflection of the state of anthropological knowledge from which historians have borrowed
their cultural information about Aboriginal society. It also indicates historians' unwillingness to develop adequate theoretical
tools for the incorporation of gender relations into Australian history. (Jebb & Haebich 1992:30)

The earlier anthropological writings were considered to be authoritative and unquestionable until the introduction of feminist activism
into academic scholarship. Women scholars brought into academic discourse a critique of gender and race relations in Australia, and "Gender-
biased male colonial attitudes" and interpretation came under fire from
the rising feminist and womanist movements.

> Kaberry's and Berndt's works went almost unheeded by his-
> torians until the 1980s when Annette Hamilton (1981) intro-
> duced Aboriginal women as the key providers in pre-contact so-
> ciety. This trend was re-enforced by Diane Bell's *Daughters Of The
> Dreaming* (1983) in which she berated past masculinist studies of
> Aboriginal social structure for failing to consider women as actors
> or to consult them as informants. Through ethnographic and ar-
> chival research, Bell assessed the changes in women's status and
> in the process challenged many popular misconceptions: women
> are not and were not secondary members of Aboriginal society;
> they can and did control their own sexual liaisons and could or-
> ganize marriages. (Jebb & Haebich 1992:30)

So blinded were the early white male anthropologists and historians
by their own Western patriarchal values and perceived cultural supe-
riority that any endeavor toward obtaining an unbiased interpretation
and objective academic scholarship was nearly impossible to achieve.
The volumes of academic writings denigrating Aboriginal woman's like
are so vast that I can only highlight a few. Diane Bell writes that some

> observers of the twentieth century have been willing to allow the
> economic importance and functional worth of Aboriginal women
> (Stanner 1979:118; Warner 1937), but in discussions of marriage
> arrangements, women are seen as pawns in the games of the
> polygynous gerontocracy (Hart and Pilling 1960; Hiatt 1965); in
> ritual activity they are seen as the excluded, the substance of
> symbols but rarely the creators of their own social reality (Róhiem
> 1933; Hiatt 1971; Cawte 1974). Women, wrote Warner (1937:5–
> 6) on the basis of his work in Arnhem Land, make little social
> progress through life but remain largely profane. "Among the Aus-

tralian Aborigines the condition of women is utterly degraded,"
Briffault (1927:311) stated. In [a] more recent study, Bern (1979:
47), writing of the Roper River area [Northern Territory,] asserts,
"Religion is par excellence, the province of men." (Bell 1984:295)

This in fact was not the case, according to the many traditional
women elder informants with whom I worked for twenty years while
gathering data and researching my doctoral thesis with various language groups throughout Australia. What was referred to at times but
often overlooked or disregarded by the male researchers—and the white
female researchers too—was that not all Aboriginal societies were patriarchal. For example, the notion of Aboriginal women's autonomy and
control comes under challenge by historian professor Ann McGrath,
who argues that:

> despite considerable female autonomy, Aboriginal society was pa-
> triarchal, with the products of the men's labors being more highly
> valued in both hunting and ritual spheres. Men's "business" was
> considered more central to the well-being of the overall social
> group, and in negotiations relating to both sexes men had the
> ultimate power, which they could uphold through the threat of
> violence. (Cited in Saunders & Evans 1992:4)

For McGrath to argue this point of view in 1992 meant that she had
to dismiss numerous academic writings not only by white women scholars but also by Indigenous women scholars, which, in turn, raises questions about her own academic credibility. Nevertheless, the status of
Aboriginal women in their society, and their control over their religious
life continues to be controversial and to invite further debate among
academics.

Sacred or Profane

At one extreme, the issue of the authority and control that Aboriginal
women had over their ritual and life has been considered as having
either little or no significance to the sacred domain of the religious life
of Aboriginal societies. At the other extreme, found in academic writings, is the assumption that white males and females have injected into
their research: that white scholarship has determined Aboriginal people
to be primordial and, therefore, inferior to the people of the so-called
enlightened and civilized West. Historically, anthropology was born out
of an era when science became the basis of all academic understanding.

The perceptions of white Australians have been influenced further by their Western Enlightenment ideas about progress, Darwin's theories on the survival of the fittest, and other European philosophical concepts.

Unfortunately, much of the early work in religious studies and anthropology was—and some of the more recent work is—armchair research. As a result of this form of investigation, a great deal of myth-making took place, leading to inaccurate theories being formulated and regurgitated due to poor research techniques and flawed methodologies. The very detailed work of Phyllis Kaberry (1939)

> challenged several of Róheim's grosser misconceptions about the function of [Aboriginal] women's religious life (ibid.:188–89). She also offered a counter to Warner's (1937:5–6) assertion that [Aboriginal] women make little sacred progress, but remain largely profane. (Bell 1984:298)

In the white male–dominated academic arena, Phyllis Kaberry— along with various other women anthropologists such as Catherine Berndt, Jane Goodale, Diane Bell, Isobel White, and Annette Hamilton— would shatter the androcentric basis and the male dominance in this field. As a result of their extensive field research, these women did a great deal toward the recognition and elevation of Aboriginal women's religious authority and control. Their numerous writings deconstructed and exposed many myths constructed by their male counterparts, and this was considered earth-shattering. Highlighting some of these works produced by these women anthropologists, Diane Bell writes that

> [a]lthough both Kaberry and Berndt show that [the Aboriginal] woman has a sacred side, the Durkheimian prejudice that women represent the profane, and the structural-functionalist equilibrium model wherein women are seen as wives, mothers and sisters, have weighed heavily on female-oriented research in Aboriginal Australia. (Bell cited in Charlesworth 1984:298)

Kaberry writes, regarding the influential power of older women, that

> [t]ogether with the old men, they [Aboriginal women] are the repositories of myth, are responsible for handing on tribal law and custom, and are one of the forces which make possible stability and continuity of tribal life. . . . Also Jane Goodale (1971: 228), in discussing the domestic groups, outlines the extensive powers of the tarramaguti, the first wife. (Karberry cited in Charlesworth 1984:298)

During my time in the Northern Territory, fulfilling some of my cultural and religious obligations with my extended family known as the Gumatj community, my traditional *ngandi* (mother) shared with me during my instruction how the women elders of her community were in fact the keepers of the law and maintained authority and control over all religious practices in their community. This, she said, was acknowledged within the broader community but was not spoken of outside their community. This fact I was to witness on many occasions during my time there. Whenever religious rituals or ceremonies were to take place, the men and male elders would consult the women elders regarding the carrying-out of the ceremony, and they would be instructed as to who would participate, how and when the ceremony would be enacted, and so on.

Mary Magulagi Yarmirr, executive member for West Arnhem of the Northern Land Council, in her essay "Women and Land Rights: Past, Present and Future" in *Our Land Is Our Life*, writes that

> [t]raditionally, Aboriginal People had their own land rights law long before it was put upon us by the *Balanda* (European) land rights legislation. That law was reflected in our names, kinship ties, ceremonies, stories and dance. Both men and women accepted these roles and carried them out in accordance with the law. Today some Aboriginal women's concerns with land are relatively the same as men's, as we have moved into the public and political arenas to protect our rights. We are fighting beside men for recognition and for our country. Women still carry out the roles we have always carried out in relation to the cultural, physical, spiritual, environmental and social maintenance of our land, community and law. (Yarmirr 1997:81)

For anthropologists and religious studies scholars to say that Aboriginal women's business is profane and that only men's business can be considered sacred is to show clearly their ignorance of Aboriginal religious structure and the significance of the egalitarian balance between women's and men's business, and the sacredness found in each. We could even say that, even though the religious spheres of Aboriginal women and men are separate, they still complement each other in the interconnectedness of the spirit world. Through their enactment of the sacred, the Spirit Ancestors—both male and female—are revitalized and the sacred is reborn. There can no longer be any form of marginalization regarding the sacredness of Aboriginal women's religious inheritance, because women possess the same spiritual autonomy, and they too draw on the spiritual power of the Ancestors—all of which are encapsulated in the epistemology of our Dreaming. Thus, Aboriginal women's ritual and ceremonial life "enact[s] a body of knowledge that is both sacred and secret; in other words men had no access to this knowledge nor the right to participate in the religious activities proper to women" (Charlesworth 1984:306).

Sacred Wisdom

In Aboriginal religion, the belief that rites are life-sustaining and life-renewing is the most important aspect of our spirituality and relationship to land, environment, spirits, and humanity. This relationship was strengthened by both genders through the enactment of these sacred rituals. The Berndts highlight our Aboriginal relationship to land, writing that

> [v]arious sacred sites, though not all, have to do with the increase of natural species. The local descent groups whose territories include such sites are (or were) responsible for attending to the rites that ensure increase, or that people believe will ensure it. A site that is spiritually occupied, or possessed by a particular mythic being, can be a center for the increase of the species represented by the being in its shape-changing character. Rites may be performed there. Or particular stones symbolizing the being are anointed. Or, if the site is a cave or rock shelter, the walls are painted with appropriate figures, or existing paintings are restored or renewed (and so on), and songs are sung to release the Spirits of the particular species so that the fertility is ensured. The Spirit essence of the kangaroo, or whatever, is renewed and recharged so that its physical manifestations continue to flourish. This is part of the overall process of trying to keep the whole system going in good working order; not only those living things that were useful to human beings for food or other purposes, but the total systems, involving all living creatures and plants—the whole ecosystem. (Berndt & Berndt 1983:50)

Aboriginal society also recognized that their religious system was not just of a spiritual nature but also included an economic basis, "not merely in terms of immediate aims, such as increase and fertility, but in relation to their organization" (Berndt & Berndt 1983:50). Within the Aboriginal religious system is a web of obligations and responsibilities that have been carried out in all ritual procedures; for example, there are economic obligations, reciprocal duties, payments, and receipts that are incorporated into the religious life and practices of Aboriginal society. Further, these religious systems also laid the bases on which the fundamental principles or the moral behavior and conduct would be guided. In Aboriginal society the sacred authority that is recognized within the religious foundation, coming from the supernatural and sacred source, was and is a powerful and key component in community law and control.

For Aboriginal people, creation is the time long ago, when the mythical Ancestors brought into life their natural environment and also their social environment. These Ancestors vary from one language group to another, and the narratives concerning their actions and interactions in creation is contained in what the anthropologists have made popular as the Dreaming. Because of the multiplicity of languages, however, the terms given to the creation period vary throughout the country:

> [I]n the Great Victoria Desert the term used for the "creative period" is *djuguba* or *djugurba (tjukubi)*; in the Rawlinson Range, *duma*; in the Balgo area, *djumanggani*; in the eastern Kimberleys, *ngarunggani*; *bugari* around La Grange and Broome, and *ungud* among the Ungarinjin (Elkin, 1954:178); *aldjeringa* among the Aranda (Spencer and Gillen, 1938); *mura* for the Dieri; for the Wuradjeri, *maradal* or *galwagi*, but the period before this was *ngerganbu*, "the beginning of all"; among the Jaraldi, *gulal*; and in northern-eastern Arnhem Land, *wongar*. (Berndt & Berndt 1977:229)

Depending on which language group one wishes to draw on, one finds that there were many differing narratives concerning the various Spirit Ancestors. Some of these Spirit Ancestors were considered divine beings, endowed with a special aura of sacredness. The extensive research of Catherine and Ronald Berndt provides a very succinct overview of the varying creation narratives, pertaining to the many names and descriptions of these Spirit Ancestors and their travels throughout Aboriginal Australia.

> In the Western Desert, for instance, among the most famous are the Two men, whose adventures span thousands of kilometres through a number of different dialectal areas. The Red Kangaroo, Malu, left a similar record of his ancestral wanderings. The Dingari group who danced and sang their way across the same wide region are equally important there. The young Kanabuda women, traveling the western expanses of the desert together, tried to keep aloof from men because they were too sacred to mix with men,

so Aboriginal women said. (They used a Western Desert word for this: *darugu* or *daragu*: sacred, holy, set apart.) Dog Man, Possum Woman and hundreds of others roamed across stretches of the desert, through places that now bear names commemorating their . . . Presence. . . .

In Western Arnhem Land, too, characters converged from all points of the compass. Some came from the north-west, through Melville Island and Cape Don from the direction of what is now Indonesia. The great fertility mother Waramurungundji was one; another was her husband for a time—Wuragag, Tor Rock, now a landmark at the edge of the coastal plain near the East Alligator River. . . .

On the eastern side of Arnhem Land there was the same mobile and colorful pageant. The two *Djanggau* (or *Djaanggawul*) sisters, with their brother in some versions, came across the Gulf of Carpentaria in their bark canoe in the light of the rising sun, bringing sacred emblems. They moved westwards, making people and places, including freshwater springs, and finally headed into the sunset. In some accounts they are the sun's daughters. Two other important sisters, the Wawalag (or Wagilag), came north from the direction of the Roper River to a water hole near the central Arnhem Land coast. But the great python who swallowed them there had been established in its waters since time began. . . . In some cases the most important site for a mythical personage is where that personage came to the end of his or her physical earthly story—by going underground there, or into a cave, spring or billabong, or by turning into a hill, or flying away as a bird into the sky: for Moon Man, or for the women who are now the Seven Sisters. Or it may be a "reservoir" for pre-existent Spirits, awaiting rebirth through human women. (Berndt & Berndt 1983: 55–6)

Even in Aboriginal ancestral narratives there is a clear view of the role and gender of our Spirit Ancestors: both male and female Spirits are represented in our creation stories, both are imbued with an aura of the sacredness, and both were Creators. The main factor for Aboriginal men regarding their sacred rituals, however, was in fact their obsession with procreation and female menstruation and fertility.

Women's Rites

One of the most fascinating aspects of the Aboriginal religious system is the ritual focus on the various symbolic elements relating to procreation, menstruation, and fertility. Some rituals can be identified with the male role in procreation, which was symbolized by the use of a large range of phallic symbols. Aboriginal men's emphasis on fertility included an interest in pregnancy and childbirth; they were intrigued by the role of Aboriginal women in the visible creation and nurturing of new life.

> This was the subject of much ritual and symbolic concern. It ramified into other areas as well, such as the division of labor between men and women in directing and controlling sacred ritual and myth. . . . For instance, according to some accounts, in the mythical state of affairs women first owned and controlled everything: all the most sacred objects, rites and songs. In some areas, then, it has been suggested that men act out on a ritual level what women act out naturally, the two complementing each other. The symbolism of blood = life, with red ochre as a secondary symbol for both, was related to this. The implication was that men's blood-letting rites provided a ritual parallel to a process naturally associated with women. (Berndt & Berndt 1983:64)

Female reproduction is considered very sacred within the ritual life and practice of fertility and increase ceremonies. So many of the myths that are encompassed in our Dreaming relate to various female Ancestors, sometimes referred to as Fertility Mothers. Even though many academics, the likes of Émile Durkheim, W. Lloyd Warner, and others, regarded men's religious life as sacred and consequently categorized women's religious life as profane, Aboriginal women themselves give a totally different view. The relationship between men's and women's religious life was never an area of competition or open for debate. Women and men accepted the equivalent status, authority, and ritual responsibilities and obligations to the Law established within the creation period of the Dreaming by both male and female Ancestors. Added to this aspect was the fact stated by many Aboriginal women elders—that in the beginning women owned the most sacred sites and the emblems, which are used today by the men. Following is a short summary of the many references made by other scholars acknowledging the significance of Aboriginal women's role, authority and ownership:

> Writing in reference to the eastern Kimberleys, Kaberry (1939: 277) says: "The sacred inheritance of the tribe includes the system of totemism, a number of myths of the totemic Ancestors . . . [and] the mourning and increase ceremonies, in which both

men and women are associated and have their part . . . [T] here can be no question of identifying the sacred inheritance of the tribe only with men's ceremonies. . . ." Among the Aranda, according to Spencer and Gillen (1938:195–6), many mythical traditions tell how women played an equal part with men, and possessed the sacred emblems. Strehlow writes (1947:94) ". . . The Female Ancestors which are celebrated in Aranda myths are usually dignified and sometimes awe-inspiring figures, who enjoyed unlimited freedom of decision and action. Frequently they were much more powerful beings than their male associates. . . ." The same is the case over most of the Great Victoria Desert. It is not stated specifically there that women originally possessed all sacred rites and emblems, but this is inferred in the myth telling how women first circumcised such beings as Njirana. Another myth tells how men performed circumcision with a firestick, and as a result many novices died. *Galaia* (Emu) women came up, however, and pushing aside the firestick showed the men how to use a stone flake. In the Western Desert south of Balgo, women in the mythical era are said to have possessed all sacred ritual, which was later taken from them by men. In western Arnhem Land, the *ubar* ritual belonged first only to women. In the myth the headwoman, *Mingau* (a Kangaroo Women of the fire Dreaming), was holding a ceremony with other women when *Gandagi* (a Kangaroo Man) appeared among them. He stood watching their dancing. At last he drove the women back to the main camp, taking over their sacred emblems. He got together all the men and they began their own ritual: but it was the same as the women's. (Berndt & Berndt 1977:257)

Aboriginal women do testify and insist that Gandagi would not have learnt the right steps if the women had not taught him. The fact that Aboriginal women were the owners of sacred rituals and emblems never seems to count in the equation formulated by the earlier white male writers. Aboriginal women today are just fed up with the Eurocentric, patriarchal, and racist views that continue to be regurgitated in the writings of many male historians and anthropologists and also in the area of religious studies. Such fallacies have portrayed Aboriginal women as religious paupers and, therefore, as profane, restricted to the margins and devoid of possessing any spiritual divinity, and lacking within their own humanity any resemblance of the sacred.

I now look further into some of the ancestral narratives to which Aboriginal women refer regarding their ownership and the theft of sacred rituals and emblems.

The Djanggawul *Sisters*

The *Djanggawul myth* in northeastern Arnhem Land tells how the two Sisters came to *Marabai*, where they built a shelter and hung inside it their sacred dilly bags, or long baskets, full of emblems. Then they went out to collect mangrove shells. While they were away their Brother and his companions, men whom the Sisters had made, sneaked up and stole the baskets. The Sisters heard the whistle of the *djunmal* mangrove bird, warning them that something was wrong. They hurried back to their shelter to find their belongings gone, and saw on the ground the tracks of the men who had stolen them. They followed these, but had not gone far when the Brother began to beat his singing sticks rhythmically. As soon as they heard the beat of the sticks and the sound of the men singing they stopped, fell to the ground and began to crawl. They were too frightened to go near that place, fearful not of the men but of the power of the sacred songs. The men had taken from them not only these songs, and the emblems, but also the power to perform sacred ritual, a power which had formerly belonged only to the Sisters. Before that, men had nothing. The myth continues: The elder Sister said . . . "Men can do it now, they can look after it . . . We know everything. We have really lost nothing, because we remember it all, and we can let them have that small part. Aren't we still sacred, even if we have lost the baskets?" (Berndt & Berndt 1977:257–8)

Catherine Berndt's comments regarding this ancestral narrative and other such material are revealing:

Such myths reveal something about the relationship between men and women in these societies. In one sense this many be interpreted as a fall from grace on the part of the women, or as a symbolic statement of their subordinate position. But it can also be interpreted as a statement about the dependence of men on women, the insecurity underlying their control of the sacred rites, emblems and myths, and the authority they exercise over women on the basis of control. In a complementary fashion the converse situation is emphasized in rituals which are still the prerogative of women. (See Kaberry, 1939; Elkin, 1954:180–184; C.Berndt, 1950a). (Berndt & Berndt 1977:258)

The first interpretation she describes would certainly have been the interpretation that conservative evangelical Christian white men would have given—anything to justify the subjugation of women.

A second myth comes from the Canning Stock Route region of the Western Desert.

The Ganabuda Women

The Ganabuda were a party of women (in some versions, one woman identified with the Gadjeri or Galwadi) in the *dingari* "mob." As they traveled from one place to another they danced the *bandimi*. (This is now one the preliminary rites leading up to circumcision, as in the eastern Kimberleys, where a row of women dances with a shuffling step making parallel grooves in the soft earth.) But Lizard Man, Gadadjilga ("spiny-head"), saw them, and sang *djarada* love magic for them. By this means he was able to catch one of the young Mangamanga girls from among them, and had sexual relations with her. This was *wadji*, wrong. The Ganabuda resented him: and they killed him by breaking off his penis with a *gana* (digging stick). Then they went on, still dancing the *bandimi*, and swinging bullroarers. They owned the sacred objects and the rites connected with them. The older Ganabuda women used to send the girls out to hunt and collect food for them, and in return they showed the rituals: that is, the girls "paid" them by supplying them with meat. (This is what men do today: the older ones expert "pay" from the young men in return for revealing the sacred rituals.) The Ganabuda women had all the *daragu* (sacred things), men had nothing. But one man, Djalaburu, creeping close and watching them secretly one night, discovered that they kept their power (*maia*) under their armbands. He succeeded in stealing this. Next morning the women tried to swing their bullroarers, but they could hardly manage to do so: they had lost their power. After that, Djalaburu led them down to where the men were; the men went up to where the women had been, and took over their responsibility for attending to sacred matters. They changed places. (Berndt & Berndt 1977: 266)

Even though the men had stolen the sacred objects, Aboriginal women have insisted that this held no threat to them as they still had all the secret/sacred knowledge. They also have felt that this said more about their men—highlighting the men's insecurities and need for power and control. The women felt that the men could have it, as this did not disempower them, for they knew that through the collective wisdom the real power and knowledge still remained with them, regardless of what appearances may indicate to the contrary.

Black Truth, White Fiction

For far too long white fiction has distorted the recognition of **Aboriginal** women's rites, yet black truth remains. Our lived experience speaks volumes about the women of Aboriginal societies and our silent wisdom that remains forever the basis of out spiritual knowledge and strength. We know we are still the keepers of the Law.

References

Bell, Diane. 1983. *Daughters of the Dreaming.* Melbourne, Australia: Mcphee Gribble.

———. 1984. Introduction to Women and Aboriginal Religion. In Charlesworth 1984:295–303.

Berndt, Catherine H., and Ronald M. Berndt. 1983. *The Aboriginal Australians: The First Pioneers.* Melbourne, Australia: Pitman.

Berndt, Ronald M., and Catherine Berndt. [1964] 1977. *The World of the First Australians.* Sydney: Lansdowne Press.

Charlesworth, Max (ed.) et al. 1984. *Religion in Aboriginal Australia: An Anthology.* Brisbane: University of Queensland Press.

Cuomo, Chris J. 1998. *Feminism and Ecological Communities: An Ethic of Flourishing.* London: Routledge.

Evans, Raymond. 1975. Harlots and Helots. In Raymond Evans et al. (eds.), *Exclusion, Exploitation and Extermination; Race Relations in Colonial Queensland.* Sydney: Australia and New Zealand Book Company: 102–17.

———. 1982. Don't You Remember Black Alice, Sam Holt? Aboriginal Women in Queensland History. *Hecate* 8 (2): 7–21.

Jebb, Mary Anne, and Anna Haebich. 1992. Across the Great Divide: Gender Relations on Australian Frontiers. In Saunders and Evans: 20–41.

Kaberry, Phyllis M. 1939. *Aboriginal Woman, Sacred and Profane.* London: Routledge.

Saunders, Kay, and Raymond Evans, eds. 1992. *Gender Relations on Australian Frontiers.* Sydney: Harcourt Brace Jovanovich.

Williams, Nancy, and Lesley Jolly. 1992. From Time Immemorial? Gender Relations in Aboriginal Societies before "White Contact." In Kay Saunders and Raymond Evans (eds.), *Gender Relations in Australia: Domination and Negotiation.* Sydney: Harcourt Brace Jovanovich: 9–19.

Yarmirr, Mary Magulagi. 1997. Women and Land Rights: Past, Present and Future. In Galarrwuy Yunupingu (ed.), *Our Land Is Our Life: Land Rights—Past, Present and Future.* St. Lucia: University of Queensland Press: 80–83.

Between Worlds

Approaching the Indigenous Sacred in Australia

Lyn McCredden

In one form or another, Australian cultural commentators of the 1980s and 1990s have espoused largely materialist views of culture, often opposing or repressing the category of the sacred or metaphysical. Cultural critic John Docker, writing in his 1984 book *In a Critical Condition*, argues that the context for this repression is a strong resistance to the earlier hegemony of the "metaphysical ascendancy" in Australian literary criticism. In fact many literary commentators of the postwar era, both Australian and international, formed their approaches in contradistinction to the often hegemonically disseminated literary critical methodologies of New Criticism and Leavisism. Such methodologies, according to Docker, saw

> the social and political (as) "surface" realms, local and temporary, and therefore "non-literary." The metaphysical realm of existence (they said) . . . because its problems are more abiding and permanent than social and political problems are presumed to be, is somehow, by magical fiat, "strictly literary." (Docker 1984:91)

Influential Australian literary critics of the 1960s and 1970s—Vincent Buckley, Harry Heseltine, Gerry Wilkes, Leonie Kramer—are accused by Docker of promulgating dichotomous thinking, including a

70

pitting of the social and political against the aesthetic, literary, and metaphysical; *and* the social, national, and communal against individualist, internalized humanism. However, Docker's critical net catches an unexpected fish in its attack on metaphysics: himself. His diatribe against such dichotomies merely ends up placing him, by implication, on the side that was supposedly crushed by the metaphysical ascendancy—that is, political and ideological criticism—and therefore does nothing to deconstruct the dichotomizing habit of thought he is condemning.

In the past decade—after Leavis and the New Criticism—postcolonial theory, with its social and political concerns, has developed in Australia and internationally as a critical methodology in the humanities and has become mainstream in tertiary curricula. It can be argued that it too has often become mired in dichotomous thinking, with a number of practitioners writing versions of postaesthetic, ideological criticism, often with a secular, materialist, and sometimes actively antimetaphysical basis. Such an approach often remains fixed in what American ethnographer Arnold Krupat calls, after Donald Bahr, "victimist history" (Krupat 1992:20), a simplistic delineating of the central postcolonial dichotomy: victim and perpetrator.

This essay will analyze procedures within postcolonial criticisms that focus on Aboriginal claims to sacred sites and beliefs. The poetic and political work, as well as the critical reception, of aboriginal poet and activist Oodgeroo Noonuccal forms the illustrative final section of this essay. I will argue that the most productive approaches to questions of the Aboriginal sacred, in its many forms, and to the work of a writer such as Oodgeroo, continue to struggle with this question of dichotomous thinking, to imagine beyond the Enlightenment binaries—civilized/primeval, sophisticated/childlike, secular/sacred, perpetrator/victim—that demonstrably permeate and plague much white, Western thinking.

In the many discourses of academia and the media that surround questions of indigenous spirituality and sacred sites, a very large full stop appears as soon as the concept of "the sacred" is raised. For some it is the full stop of suspicion, skepticism, and even hatred of such a category. For others this full stop is an indication of eager compliance with Aboriginal claims, a compliance that does not always do justice or give credence to the complex claims of the sacred it is purportedly embracing. By "justice" here is meant an allowing of the category of "the sacred" to send its own questions back to the supposedly objective white observer, interested in so-called discourses of the sacred but perhaps not in the value-challenging and more disturbing claims of the sacred.[1] To be alert to the discursive and rhetorical questions of aboriginal sacredness is one (powerful, usually academic) approach; to allow the values and claims of such an embracing category to challenge and change social and personal practices is another.

. *Historical Encounters with the Sacred*

In 1995, the state of South Australia became the focus of national attention when claims by Aboriginal women to a specifically women's sacred site and counterclaims for development by an Adelaide construction company collided. The site, on what is presently called Hindmarsh Island, south of Adelaide off Encounter Bay, was claimed by women of the Ngarrindjeri tribe to be a historical sacred women's place. Further complicating this issue was the claim that a large portion of the women's sources about this place and their practices were traditionally not to be seen by men's eyes. National debate staggered, hardly able to cope under the weight of this "preposterous" claim: that only women—and *select* women from among the Ngarrindjeri at that—should view the proofs and signs of the traditional links to this part of the land. As anthropologist Diane Bell writes: "[t]he existence of gendered knowledge presents a real problem for a legal system which claims to be gender- and race-neutral" (Bell 1998:15).

But the Hindmarsh bridge affair, as it has come to be known, was also highly instructive in its potential to loosen up the full stop around the question of *sacredness* in Australian society into a comma at least, as commentators swirled around the proposition that Hindmarsh Island was not just a sacred site, but a *women's sacred site;* not necessarily for all aboriginal women of the Ngarrindjeri tribe either, but known to be so only by *some,* a select eldership; and not even this is agreed on by all female Ngarrindjeri.

The then federal minister for the environment, Ian McLachlan, a member of Australia's conservative coalition, in a near-gleeful ABC (Australian Broadcasting Corporation) radio interview, was pleased to keep the conversation going when news of the disagreement *within* the Ngarrindjeri became known. McLachlan transparently whipped up the *ambiguity and indecipherability* of the situation, as the reporter asked: "Well don't you believe the women then?" "Which ones?" McLachlan replied triumphantly, his political opportunism almost palpable down the airwaves as he attempted to deliver the question involving declarations of sacred belief safely back into the party political basket. Political assumption number one about the category of the sacred: all believers are of one mind and can have no disagreements or political differences among themselves. That is, the sacred and the political should never converge. Politics, Lachlan's attitude implies, is where you debate; issues of sacredness are either true or false.

The June 1995 edition of *Time Australia* carried the tendentious headline "Disputed Secrets" and added in its byline: "The Hindmarsh Bridge affair takes an ugly turn, igniting fresh anger and finger pointing on all sides" (*Time* 1995:38–9). This report goes on to quote Wendy Chapman, bankrupt entrepreneur and would-be developer of the proposed Hindmarsh marina:

> Everything we've worked for all our lives has been taken from us . . . These Aboriginal claims came out of nowhere, they can't be tested in court or even seen by anybody other than a chosen few We tried hiring our own female anthropologist to look at the evidence but we were denied access. What kind of society is this?[2]

In response to this, *Time* quotes University of Adelaide anthropologist Deane Fergie, on behalf of the Aboriginal Legal Rights Movement, who says in support of the women's claims to Hindmarsh: "This is not some remote claim to a patch of desert nobody will ever see; this is in our backyards. And we're going to be seeing a lot more of it" (*Time* 1995: 39). Fergie, perhaps a little ineptly, manages here to point to one of the central dilemmas for discussions of Aboriginal beliefs and sacred sites: that Aboriginal traditions and sites *are* secret, private, belonging not to the global media, not to Western anthropology, male or female, nor to Western developers, even if they've worked for it all their lives, but to traditions of belief and practice, the sacred as living, sustaining, and educating a community and individuals in that community over many lifetimes. Yet ironically the only way such sites, and the beliefs and practices they sustain, can be fought for in Western societies is through the media and through demands for explicit proofs of sacredness, through "seeing a lot more of it."

Post Colonial Scrutiny

How can Aboriginal concepts of the sacred be scrutinized by white settler Australia, particularly if it is granted that such concepts are at the very least problematic to a "modern," largely secular, capitalist society? Who has the right to scrutinize such concepts and the closely attendant social and political rights of indigenous Australians, and by what processes? More specifically, how does materialist-oriented *academic* criticism cope with and examine claims to the sacred and traditional? For many white *and* black critics, discourses about the aboriginal sacred are problematically *romantic and aboriginalist,*[3] constructed by invocations of presence, authenticity, freedom, wholeness, and reclamation of an originary past. Whether the individual Aborigine is imaged alone, discovering his or her "own poetic voice," or deeply entrenched within a community, a tradition, or a past, what is often too easily called for in such liberal humanist discourse is "authentic" Aboriginal humanity, a humanity not yet constructed by white education or desecrated by colonizing impurities. This Manichean approach—black innocent/white polluter—is understandable, perhaps, within the larger political context with its demands for strategic, polemical representation. Yet it also leaves the further, vital questions of how a diverse citizenry can live together in the future, and valuably interact, hard to ask. If the Aboriginal claims to the sacred, based on relationship to the land, on traditional practices and stories, and on beliefs and modes of life enacted from generation to generation, are to be seen as anything more than discourses for white scrutiny—discourses that are then able to be used for whatever ends, be they policy making, or spiritual, or touristic—then questions of the power of the category of the Aboriginal sacred to influence and change broader social values and practices need to be broached.

In his stinging review of the much-publicized book on cultural theory, *Uncanny Australia: Sacredness and Identity in a Postcolonial Nation* (Gelder & Jacobs 1998), Barry Hill attacks the white academic authors[4] who deal merely in *discourses of representation* rather than lived beliefs that are personally, politically, and legally defensible. He sees such academic work as "founded on bookish conceits written without getting out of the car":

> [H]ow does one's own sense of the sacred bear upon the cultural predicament of indigenous people? As if our secularizing culture has done the thinking and feeling for them (the white critics), they have danced about the sacred without their feet touching the ground—least of all the ground of their own religious beliefs or lack of them. It's a class act, writing so much about a troubled condition in such an untroubled way.[5]

The justness of Hill's claims needs to be tested by each individual reader of the text involved in the debate, but what needs to be examined here are the terms of Hill's attack. A white critic himself, having produced some very valuable discussions of aboriginality and the sacred,[6] Hill points in his review to an "untroubled" academic approach to Aboriginal sacredness that applies a new form of supposed objectivity—discursive analysis—and that is in danger of merely perpetuating dichotomies such as sacred and primitive, secular and modern. Such academic work is in danger because it does not or cannot take the sacred seriously—personally, experientially, and with any sense of the lived, continuing importance of such beliefs and practices. The sacred in such academic work can never be anything more than *discourses about the sacred.*

If Hill's argument is worth contemplating, it sets up a range of questions about whether there are real differences between such postcolonial and postmodern critical approaches to the Aboriginal sacred and earlier anthropologies. Don't both objectify sacred objects, and Aboriginal subjects, clearing a space for them as museum pieces, or exotic primitives, with no real impact on the intellectual and spiritual beliefs and ideas of the modern? Hill's approach here and elsewhere does contemplate real meetings between peoples and imaginative interchange between the monoliths of Sacred and Secular, without fixing and objectifying such categories simply as discourses.

Another, less dichotomized form of debate around the sacred can be found in political activism that engages white academic and political expertise in the cause of Aboriginal claims. In her essay "Earth Honoring: Western Desires and Indigenous Knowledges" feminist geographer Jane Jacobs discusses in detail what she suggests might be *appropriational* activities of ecocentric and ecofeminist groups around questions of Aboriginal sacred sites. Her particular case study concerns the attempts to dam the Todd River outside Alice Springs, a point of fierce contestation since the 1960s between the Arrernte Aborigines and the Northern Territory government. Jacobs details the debate, with its ensuing support for Aboriginal women, who became the true spokespersons for the endangered sites. The main site, Welatye Therre, or "two-breasts," was designated by the women of the Arrernte tribe as sacred and secret, a secrecy that was strategically broken by the tribal women themselves, to a certain extent, in order to protect the site. Support came from such groups as Greenpeace, Friends of the Earth, feminist antinuclear groups, feminist bookshops and refuges. Jacobs writes powerfully about such alliances between the aboriginal women and white groups:

> The alliances . . . may well be an example of a colonizing, self-aggrandizing feminism. But Welatye Therre is also a site that . . .

operates to provide guidance: it is a pedagogical site that teaches
Aboriginal women and men about appropriate behaviors . . . how
to avoid the violence of patriarchy and how to care for the land.
(Jacobs 1994:187)

Jacobs here begins to deflate a number of Western-bred dichotomies
regarding the sacred. As she carefully reads it, the sacred is gendered,
it can be violent as well as utopic, it is politically strategic *and* visionary.
But what can be said of these white, Western alliances with the sacred?
Are they merely examples of "a colonizing, self-aggrandizing feminism"?
Jacobs answers affirmatively and negatively:

> [T]he issue of secrecy and nondisclosure provides a key to an
> important complexity in the way "appropriation" needs to be un-
> derstood. Under the conditions of secrecy the desires of non-
> aboriginal sympathizers to support Aboriginal rights did not di-
> minish, but intensified. Secrecy may enhance desires of
> sympathizers, providing an unknowable space into which their
> imaginative desires about Aboriginality are projected. (Jacobs
> 1994:191)

Jacobs sees this intensified desire as problematic in two ways: in its
essentializing of Aboriginality as "primitive sacredness," the premodern;
but also as instrumental, as one of the strategies by which the sacred
site was indeed saved.

The Sacred: Gendered, Racial, and Embodied

My debate with Jacobs takes up at this point. Yes, there is a burden,
and perhaps it is a colonialist burden, placed by these white sympathizers upon aboriginality to provide "an imaginative space" outside of
Western development-driven capitalism. Yes, the alliance of ecocentric
and ecofeminist Westerners to overlay their desires on Aboriginal beliefs
and traditions is inevitably part of what is going on. But at the same
time, Jacobs herself, as white academic, has been free to narrate her
tale of the struggles around this Aboriginal site. She has been able,
meticulously, to describe Aboriginal sacredness as a dynamic series of
desires and actions that sustain both traditional, centuries-old rituals
and teachings as well as a lived reality that must be strategically protected. She too is implicated in the meeting of white academic and black
social and sacred beliefs and claims.

Jacobs's work here does begin to problematize, if not open up, the category of the sacred as a variously situated reality, lived by some men and women, some Aboriginal and some white Australians, and rejected, sometimes on political grounds, sometimes ontologically, by others. It is perhaps those who grasp the social and political justice of Aboriginal claims but who do not or cannot accept the actual challenges to values and modes of living of the sacred who are in the most intellectually contradictory position.

Surely then, while certain white political alliances can be read as hypostasizing aboriginality and the sacred, they can also be read as desiring an encounter with the sacred, albeit this desire is clumsily affixed to or envisioned through Aboriginality. If the Aboriginal sacred, narrated by Jacobs, can be read as dynamic, gendered, violent, both political and visionary, and highly prized, then surely white desires toward "the sacred," expressed politically in practical sympathy for something beyond consumerism and materiality, must imaginatively be granted a space. Is the white post-colonial subject only ever able to speak from some "modern" state, one fixedly removed from "the sacred"?

Of course "predatory appropriation" of aboriginality cannot be eliminated, both in intellectual and in consumer activities, but the intentions and practical outcomes of this white desiring should not all be monolithically assigned to "appropriation." To do so would be to interpret Western motives as *purely* colonialist, *purely and statically* political—surely a dichotomous, Western-oriented way of thinking. If we are willing to read *beyond* a model of essentialist Aboriginality and static, fetishized, and dehistoricized concepts of sacredness, in solidarity with Aboriginal peoples and their contemporary claims to sacred sites, then one must ask whether, surely, the same deconstructing of the logocentric dichotomies sacred/political, Aboriginal/Western, pure/impure can be brought into operation when scrutinizing those "white sympathizers," as it should when thinking about "Aboriginality."

A Difficult Position, between Worlds

Oodgeroo Noonuccal, a pivotal figure in Australian literary and political culture, did not feel the need, in either her poetry or her political speeches and essays, to monolithically homogenize "white Australia," even as she exposed the effects of colonialist violence on indigenous Australians. Her poetry and her activism continually negotiated both the grief and horror of colonialism right up to the present day, as well as the possibilities for amelioration. In 1988, the bicentennial year of white settlement of Australia, the then Kath Walker changed her name to Oodgeroo of the Noonuccal tribe, her people centered on North Stradbroke Island (Minjerriba), off the southern coast of Queensland. This act disturbed some observers, who failed to understand the symbolic power of such an act. And symbolic, prophetic power—of words, of storytelling, of relationship with the land, of myth, of tradition—was what Oodgeroo drew on in her negotiations with white Australia.

Oodgeroo published four books of poetry, *We Are Going* (1964), *The Dawn Is at Hand* (1966), *My People* (1970a), and *Kath Walker in China* (1988), as well as many stories of the Dreamtime, stories and picture books for children, and political and historical essays and speeches. As with many indigenous writers, there have been accusations—mainly from white, aesthetic critics—that her writing tends to be "didactic and propagandistic," but Oodgeroo was capable in a number of ways of short-circuiting such criticism: "I agreed with them because it *was* propaganda. I deliberately did it" (Noonuccal cited in Shoemaker 1994:19). Consistently, Oodgeroo found ways of refusing the dichotomies white aestheticians imposed on her work: aesthetic/political, crafted/naïve, individual artist/spokesperson. For example, she spoke often about "poetic voice" in communal terms. In a 1977 interview she said: "I'm putting their voices on paper, writing their things. I listen to the Aboriginal people, to their cry for help—it was more or less a cry for help in that book *We are Going*. I didn't consider it my book, it was the people" (Noonuccal 1977:429).

Although Oodgeroo Noonuccal does not apply the term to herself, these words, and so much of the power of her interventions, are what might be called prophetic. With unrancorous determination, she spoke of the genesis of her first book of poetry, *We Are Going:*

[T]he only book that the Aboriginals were allowed to be literate about was the Bible. And whenever they tried to express themselves—right up to the sixties—was to say, like Samuel, or, like Noah, in order to compare, to put their message over, to be understood. And whenever the old men would come into the meetings they would always have the Bible under their wing, you see. And I thought, My God it's time we recorded the cries of the people and gave them a book they could call their own. So I wrote *We are Going* . . . [I]t's their voices, their hopes, their inspirations, their frustrations, their aspirations. (Turcotte cited in Rutherford 1988:18–19)

If we analyze such a motivation, it may at first seem oppositional—European bible/a book they could call their own, their words/our voices—yet Oodgeroo here is demonstrating a prophetic line of action, if by prophetic is meant a lifting of spirit out of matter, or better, an enabling of spirit through delineating the real matter. For the old men, "the Bible under their wing," the reality was one of oppression, a ventriloquist condition in which quoting Samuel or Noah was necessary "in order to compare, to get their message over." The new possibility envisaged by Oodgeroo was to use the tools of the oppressor to write for her people "their voices, their hopes, their inspirations, their frustrations, their aspirations."

For postcolonial critic Bob Hodge it is the *multiplicity* of voices Oodgeroo lets into her verse that is valuable: "A major part of her poetic work went into the construction of this complex 'we,' this emerging, contradictory and shifting Aboriginal subjectivity which incorporates suffering and hope, anger and goodwill" (Hodge & Mishra 1991:73). Eva Rask Knudsen connects such multiplicity to an ancient Aboriginal practice of storytelling: "[w]ithin this tradition—in which literature and politics in the broadest sense are not at all seen as antagonistic—individuality is subjected to the concerns of the community" (Knudsen cited in Shoemaker 1994:110).

Knudsen goes on to place the voices of Oodgeroo's poetry as emerging from such traditions but heading toward another place. It was a difficult position: between worlds, writing in the language of the colonizer, judged by predominantly white critics, writing for a passing world and the perpetrators, "the peculiar fringe world, a third cultural reality midway between the traditional Aboriginal world and white society" (Knudsen cited in Shoemaker 1994:111).

In her poetry Oodgeroo uses a range of rhetorical and ideological weaponry as she constructs and inhabits this third cultural reality, seeking the ear of her people and the ear of the colonizer: dialogue, irony, sarcasm, lament, diatribe, protest, and rallying cry are all employed. She takes up no one, monolithic position but attempts to represent the real voices—the lived expressions—of her people. Sometimes this leads to a poetry of seeming defeat and racial disappearance, in such laments as "We Are Going" or "No More Boomerang" (1970:30–):

> No more boomerang
> No more spear;
> Now all civilized—
> Color bar and beer.

No more corroboree,
Gay dance and din.
Now we got movies,
And pay to go in.

No more sharing
What the hunter brings.
Now we work for money,
Then pay it back for things.

Now we track bosses
To catch a few bob,
Now we go walkabout
On bus to the job.

In these first four stanzas of "No More Boomerang," first published
in 1964, a number of Oodgeroo's characteristic strategies, both rhetorical and ideological, are evident. The short, blunt lines pick up the in-
tonations of Aboriginal speech, a direct, no-nonsense series of statements, and a grim humor mixed with the lament. The Aboriginal here
is the victim of colonialism, in its modern, capitalist form, but the victor
too is seen as a victim, inscribed by a system that is threatening both
black and white. Under this regime, work is alienating and unreward-
ing. The inheritance of this system is competitiveness and prejudice,
lack of sharing and community, shame, mortgages, long hours of work,
all "mod-cons" that aren't necessarily an improvement, high art élitism,
television with ads, and the atom bomb. The final stanza (1964:37):

Lay down the woomera,
Lay down the waddy.
Now we got atom-bomb,
End *every*body.

The strange mixture of down-to-earth, anarchic humor, together
with a plea for mercy from, *and* a criticism of, white society, is haunting.
The victim is not simply self-pitying but abrasive, cynical, and dismissive
about what has been gained under civilized colonial rule. What disturbs
here are the restless, mixed tones of what is both lament and protest,
coming out of the mouth of a victim who won't quite lie down and
who won't settle for the dichotomies "them and us," "colonizer and
colonized." Civilization is attacked as a system—white, capitalist, and
consumerist—that swallows up all its adherents.

The same refusal to merely promulgate oppositions can be found in
the 1962 poem "Aboriginal Charter of Rights," written for the fifth an-

nual General Meeting of the Federal Council for the Advancement of Aborigines and Torres Strait Islanders (FCAATSI). In its driving octosyllabic rhyming couplets it belts out a range of demands in a powerfully repetitive formulation (1970:36–7):

> Give incentive, not restriction,
> Give us Christ, not crucifixion.
> Though baptized and blessed and Bibled
> We are still tabooed and libelled.
> You devout Salvation-sellers,
> Make us neighbors, not fringe-dwellers;
> Make us mates, not poor relations,
> Citizens, not serfs on stations.
> Must we native Old Australians
> In our land rank as aliens?
> Banish bans and conquer caste,
> Then we'll win our own at last.

While the whole poem is patterned around the real, experienced oppositions of racism, the utopic drive of the poem envisages a state for Aboriginal people that surpasses the current moment of bigotry and serfdom. What is envisaged beyond the present is again grasped in prophetic terms, the sacred—earthed and embodied in the form of neighborliness, mateship, citizenship, a freedom from fringe-dweller existence. Oppositional states are powerfully represented but are simultaneously dissolved within the ambit of the highly utopic rhetoric.

The same drive toward possibilities of change can be seen in other poems written in the 1960s, in for instance "The Dawn is at Hand," which envisages "Dark and white upon common ground/In club and office and social round. . . . For ban and bias will soon be gone,/The future beckons you bravely on/To art and letters and nation lore,; shFringe-dwellers no more." This is very early for such reconciliatory gestures, as it wasn't until 1967 that white Australians voted to grant the vote to all Aboriginal Australians, not just landowners. And with that vote, considered a watershed in Australian history, came a growing realization for many Australians that a different future beckoned. Oodgeroo's combative, politicized but never simply oppositional rhetoric was among the earliest of rallying cries. Some may read the lines of a poem such as "The Dawn is at Hand" as reflective of the assimilationist government policies of earlier decades. However, this would be to read them denuded of the context of Oodgeroo's fuller work as poet, relentless activist, and spokesperson, a context that sees her consistently prompt-

ing white and black Australians to move into a future, equipped to fully
acknowledge a past that stretched back to well before white invasion.

The utopic, prophetic impulse has not been highly regarded in postcolonial discourses, and for good reasons. The drive to establish the real,
horrific, and continued effects of colonial invasion on Australian Abor-
igins—what prime minister John Howard simplistically dubbed "the
black arm-band version of history"[7]—should not be lost. But the need
for poetic and political acts of reconciliation that envisage the future
with real change possible, and occurring, has been there from the beginning too. Postcolonial critic Leela Gandhi has recently written, in
regard to the kinds of directions postcolonial writing could fruitfully
take in India, as follows:

> Without seeking to determine the shape of an alternative ortho-
> doxy, we might still observe that perhaps what postcolonial liter-
> ature needs is a properly romantic modality; a willingness to cri-
> tique, ameliorate and build upon the compositions of the colonial
> aftermath. It is possible, in other words, to envision a transformed
> and improved future for the postcolonial nation. (Gandhi 1998:
> 166)

In Oodgeroo's poem "Oration,"[8] written for FCAATSI (the Federal
Council for the Advancement of Aborigine and Torres Strait Islanders)
to read in the Federal Parliament on March 27, 1970, there is a carefully
measured tension between lament and utopic optimism and a fine balance among critique, amelioration, and a vision of the future. The poem
begins:

> Here, at the invaders talk-talk place,
> We, who are the strangers now,
> Come with sorrow in our hearts.
> The Bora Ring, the Corroborrees,
> The sacred ceremonies,
> Have gone. All gone.

There is both dignity and grief in this poetic lamenting of a past
irretrievably desecrated. While the victims measure the dimensions of
their loss, displaying their sorrow in this public place of the victorious
invaders, they are also, miraculously, speaking, invoking presence and
a will to perpetuate a future. The poem swerves surprisingly at line 9,
after the opening lament, as we realize that the speaker is not in fact
addressing the worthy white politicians but "spirits from the unhappy

past." These spirits are the victims of colonial genocide, and the speaker seeks "strength and wisdom in your memory." In the Australian Parliament House, the speaker effectively ignores the presence of the white politicians and seeks future direction and strength from those who have been made invisible, voiceless. The poem is simultaneously a moving lament, a politically canny rallying cry for Aboriginal people, and a plea for justice and acknowledgment from white Australia. In its carefully balanced tension between oppositions, it gathers power to forge a future utopically, if tentatively, envisioned in its final lines: "And let it be so. Oh spirits—let it be so."

White Australian poet and activist Judith Wright worked closely with Oodgeroo on a number of poetic and environmental projects. Her moving and prophetically pessimistic 1970 poetic tribute to Oodgeroo, "Two Dreamtimes (For Kath Walker)" (in Noonuccal 1970:109–12), admirably echoes the spirit of Oodgeroo's third reality, between worlds. Both women, from different perspectives, faced the horrors of degradation registered by indigenous Australians and perpetrated on the body of the land. Further, Wright, the daughter of a pastoralist—by implication one of the conquerors—responsible for such degradation, uses "Two Dreamtimes" to confess her role as conqueror and to seek a stern forgiveness:

> I am born of the conquerors,
> you of the persecuted.
> Raped by rum and an alien law,
> progress and economics,
> are you and I and a once-loved land
> peopled by tribes and trees;
> doomed by traders and stock exchanges,
> bought by faceless strangers.
>
> And you and I are bought and sold,
> our songs and stories too
> though quoted low in a falling market
> (publishers shake their heads at poets).
>
> Time that we shared for a little while,
> telling sad tales of women
> (black and white at a different price)
> meant much and little to us.
>
> My shadow-sister, I sing to you
> from my place with my righteous kin,
> to where you stand with the Koori dead,
> "Trust none—not even poets."

The knife's between us. I turn it round,
the handle to your side,
the weapon made from your country's bones.
I have no right to take it.

But both of us die as our dreamtime dies.
I don't know what to give you
for your gay stories, your sad eyes,
but that, and a poem, sister.

Wright's representation of two women from different tribes and different dreamtimes is measured and moving, fully aware of the violence
of colonialism—the persecution, rape, continuing economic pillage, the
knife, the country's bones—to both human lives and to the land. But
the poem is also powerfully struggling for a way beyond such violence.
In the ritualized gesture of turning the knife-handle toward her
"Shadow-sister" and in the balanced but properly differentiated image
of the two women sitting facing each other in a time that simultaneously "meant much and little to us," Wright pays tribute to a woman
whose strong, prophetic contribution has been one of storytelling *and*
anger, lament *and* activism.

The "romantic modality" of Oodgeroo's work, what I have been calling her prophetic and utopic impulse, both exposes the atrocity and
violence of colonialism and envisions a future, just condition. This double impetus is powerfully telescoped in the 1970 poem "Time Is Running
Out," a jeremiad against the miner who "rapes / the heart of earth /
With his violent spade." With its instilling of both gentleness and
strength into Aboriginal resistance and its rhetorical transformation of
violent harm into violent love, the poem dissolves simple oppositions,
oriented as it is toward change and invoking its listeners to enact the
conditions of a future justly informed by history. Such an invocation is
a major part of the legacy left by Oodgeroo, whose approaches to the
sacred were always earthed and powerfully ameliorative rather than
merely divisive (1970:87):

Come gentle black man
Show your strength;
Time to take a stand.
Make the violent miner feel
Your violent
Love of land.

For Australian cultural commentators working at the end of the
twentieth century, such ameliorative and utopic directions cannot be

ignored. This does not mean that there is no room for anger and rage. But it does mean that "the sacred" as a multifarious category needs to be addressed by white and black Australians, not merely as one discourse among others, not merely as primitive, and not in opposition to the material, but as a reality that must and will speak powerfully into the party-political, the consumerist, the gendered, and the racial realities of Australian lives.

For white and black Australians to be satisfied with a "merely" discursive approach to questions of the sacred would be to lose the whole point of Oodgeroo's and others' prophetic interventions. Oodgeroo's contribution has been one that moves beyond a victimist history, beyond the dichotomous thinking of civilized/primitive and material/sacred. It seeks justice, because it seeks out an audience that needs to respond, and that is called on to take up the challenge of "the sacred," not merely to discourse about it and to express guilt or confusion regarding to whom the sacred belongs.

Such a challenge demands that sacredness be contemplated and experienced in all its earthed and political aspects, as much as its transcendent and transhistorical claims. It is, in the work of Oodgeroo and many other Aboriginal and white Australians, a reality that refuses to be fixed or made monolithic but seeks the constant activity of remembrance, lament, anger, honoring of tradition, a regard for the past, *and* political activism, an awareness of the physical, earthed, material, and historical in sustained relationship with the transcendental. It is at this intersection that prophets have so often stood, never *merely speaking* about justice but reordering the discourse so that new possibilities might emerge. Such hard-won changes will of necessity be freighted with what is precious, valued, and communally and individually experienced from the past. Today in Australia, the prophetic voices of Aboriginal Australians—Oodgeroo, Jack Davis, Roberta Sykes, Gatjil Djikura, Mandawuy Yunupingu, Lionel Fogarty, Kevin Gilbert, Mudrooroo, Ruby Langford Ginibi, Maureen Watson, Sally Morgan, Patricia O'Shane, Paddy Roe, Sam Watson, Archie Weller, and many others[9]—are being heard and acted on. They in no way speak monolithically, but neither are they mere victims or ventriloquists of an imposed system of beliefs and laws. They speak both to remember and to transform, their voices and actions challenging black and white Australia to think into the sacred.

Notes

1. For two very different perspectives on the challenge of the sacred to Australian culture, see literary critic David Tacey, *Edge of the Sacred* (1995), a highly influential, Jungian, and some have argued "Aboriginalist" ap-

proach to Aboriginal spiritualities; and ethnographer Diane Bell, *Ngarrindjeri Wurruwarrin: A World That Is, Was, and Will Be* (1998), an anthropological and passionately detailed account of the Ngarrindjeri people of South Australia, and in particular of the Hindmarsh bridge affair.

2. *Time Magazine* (Australia), June 5, 1995, 39.

3. For a discussion of "Aboriginalism" see Hodge & Mishra 1991 or Knudsen 1994:107–8.

4. For further discussion of legal, political, and postcolonial discourses of the Aboriginal sacred, see Gelder & Jacobs 1998. See also the highly polemical and disparaging review of *Uncanny Australia* by Hill (1998b: 15–16).

5. See Hill 1998a: 4–5.

6. See for example, Hill 1994.

7. The phrase "black arm-band version of history" was first used by Professor Geoffrey Blainey in "Drawing up a Balance-Sheet of our History" in *Quadrant* 37 (7–8) 1993:11.

8. *Origin*, April 1970:2. For a precise technical discussion of "Oration," see Brewster 1994.

9. The work of Djikura and Yunupingu has been in national politics around issues of land rights; Davis, Oodgeroo, Sykes, Fogarty, Langford Gunibi, Watson, Morgan and Gilbert are preeminently writers; Weller is a writer and singer; Paddy Roe's oral storytelling has been extensively transcribed; Watson and O'Shane have legal backgrounds, and Watson is also a novelist. All have a national profile among both Aboriginal and white Australians.

References

Bell, Diane. 1998. *Ngarrindjeri Wurruwarrin: A World That Is, Was, and Will Be*. Melbourne, Australia: Spinifex.

Brewster, Anne. 1994. Oodgeroo: Orator, Poet, Storyteller. In Shoemaker 1994:95.

Cataldi, Lee. 1994. *Yimikirli-Warlpiri Dreamings and Histories*. San Francisco: HarperCollins.

Docker, John. 1984. *In a Critical Condition: Reading Australian Literature*. Ringwood, Victoria, Australia: Penguin.

Gandhi, Leela. 1998. *Postcolonial Theory: A Critical Introduction*. St Leonards, Australia: Allen and Unwin.

Gelder, Ken, and Jane M. Jacobs. 1998. *Uncanny Australia: Sacredness and Identity in a Postcolonial Nation*. Carlton: University of Melbourne Press.

Hill, Barry. 1994. *The Rock: Travelling to Uluru*. Sydney: Allen and Unwin.

———. 1998a. Letter to the editor. *Australian Book Review* 205:4–5.

———. 1998b. Review of *Uncanny Australia*, by Ken Gelder and Jane M. Jacobs. *Australian Book Review* 203:15–6.

Hodge, Bob, and Vijay Mishra. 1991. *Dark Side of the Dream: Australian Literature and the Postcolonial Mind*. North Sydney: Allen and Unwin.

Jacobs, Jane. 1994. Earth Honouring: Western Desires and Indigenous Knowledges. In Alison Blunt and Gillian Rose (eds.), *Writing Women and Space: Colonial and Postcolonial Geographies*. New York: Guilford Press: 169–96.

Krupat, Arnold. 1992. *Ethnocriticism: Ethnography, History, Literature.* Berkeley: University of California Press.

Noonuccal, Oodgeroo. 1964. *We Are Going.* Brisbane, Queensland: Jacaranda Press.

———. 1970a. *My People.* 3rd ed. Milton, Queensland: Jacaranda Press.

———. 1970b. Oration. *Origin* (April): 2.

———. 1977. Interview. *Meanjin* 36(4): 428–41.

Rutherford, Anna (ed.). 1988. *Aboriginal Culture Today.* Sydney: Dangeroo Press–Kunapipi.

Shoemaker, Adam (ed.). 1994. *Oodgeroo: A Tribute.* Australian Literary Studies. St. Lucia: University of Queensland Press.

Stockton, E. 1995. *The Aboriginal Gift: Spirituality for a Nation.* Alexandria NSW: Millenium Books.

Tacey, David. 1995. *Edge of the Sacred: Transformation in Australia.* Ringwood: HarperCollins.

Turcotte, Gerry. 1988. Recording the Cries of the People Interview with Oodgeroo. In Rutherford 1988:17–30.

Part Two

Interrogating "Matriarchy"

4

"Inanna and the Huluppu Tree"

An Ancient Mesopotamian Narrative of Goddess Demotion

Johanna H. Stuckey

A lluring and assertive, Inanna was one of the "great gods" of the male-dominated Sumerian pantheon and the most prominent of all the goddesses (Kramer 1967:153). Her symbols occur on some of the earliest Mesopotamian seals (Adams 1966:12), and she is among the first female deities about whom written material is extant (Hallo & Van Dijk 1968).[1] In the second half of the fourth millennium B.C.E., most Sumerian cities had deities, usually goddesses, as "their titulary divine owners," Inanna being originally the deity who "owned" the developing city-state of Uruk. As such, her primary realm was earthly fecundity, especially that of human beings and other animals (Steinkeller 1999: 113 forthcoming). Because of her power over fertility and her central role in the fertility ritual known as the "sacred-marriage" rite, Inanna retained her importance in the pantheon even as Sumerian culture became increasingly male-dominated (Wakeman 1985:8). However, some of the poems about Inanna suggest that she once ruled over not only the earth's fertility but also the heavens and the underworld.

One such text, "Inanna and the *Huluppu* Tree,"[2] recounts a major alteration in Inanna's role in human affairs, indeed among the first of the limitations and demotions that she underwent. Part of an episode of the Gilgamesh epic, the poem contains an exemplary and explanatory myth that supports and validates the status quo of the time when the poem in its extant form was composed or, more likely, written down. Further, it speaks eloquently to some of the ways male-dominated society influenced, and even used, ritual and myth to further its aims.

The *huluppu*-tree poem starts with a description of the beginning of time, when "everything needed was brought into being" (Kramer 1967: 199; Wolkstein & Kramer 1983:4). It was then that ovens first began to function and bread was baked; it was then that earth and sky were first separated. When the great god Enki sailed to the underworld, a destructive storm uprooted a tiny *huluppu* tree. A young female was roaming about in the vicinity, and she, a "woman, respectful of [the sky god] An's word," rescued the *huluppu* from the river (Shaffer 1963:100, 1. 32).[3]

Though early interpretations of the poem demonstrated some uncertainty about the identity of the woman who rescued the *huluppu* tree, there is now general agreement that she was the goddess Inanna (Kramer 1938:45). Normally, in cuneiform texts, the phrase "*the* or *a* woman" refers to Inanna. Even when Inanna was describing herself as a warrior, she still used the designation "the woman": " 'I, the woman, am a noble warrior' " (Shaffer 1963:29 n. 3).

Although Inanna took the roles of sister, daughter, sweetheart, bride, and widow, she never filled those of wife and mother, "the two [roles] which call for maturity and a sense of responsibility" (Jacobsen 1976: 141). Feminist scholar Tikva Frymer-Kensky interprets this aspect of Inanna quite differently: she understands her as a divine role model that society did not expect women to emulate. Since Inanna represented "the non-domesticated woman," she was "an essentially marginal figure" (1992:25, 27). Frymer-Kensky is not entirely correct in this interpretation, for Inanna was too important to Sumerian religion to be "essentially marginal." Indeed, almost in contradiction to her own interpretation, Frymer-Kensky points out Inanna's enormous diversity in "powers and roles" and her exercise of some sort of control over heavens, earth, and sovereignty, in addition to being in charge of warfare (1992:27).

In the texts, Inanna is certainly a changeable, impulsive, and sexually aware young goddess of "Infinite Variety," almost as if she were many goddesses in one (Jacobsen 1976:35). However, all the evidence suggests that the Sumerians understood her as a single goddess—and also as central—so that her various aspects may have had some kind of unified meaning. Some scholars have argued that her "changeableness" was the result of her association with the Venus star, the epitome of mutability. However, Inanna stood for "both love (life) and war (death)"

(Wakeman 1985:19). Something in her nature encompassed this and the other oppositions that were her domain.

Inanna's areas of power and influence were certainly diverse. They seem to have included storehouse, storm and rains, war, morning and evening stars, and sexuality/prostitution (Jacobsen 1976:135–9). Though scholars have queried elements of his interpretation, Jacobsen was probably right that the Sumerians understood Inanna as "the power in the storehouse": the famous Uruk or Warka vase depicts Inanna's receiving the bounty of the land into her storehouse-shrine (Wakeman 1985:12; Wolkstein & Kramer 1983:104; Oates & Oates 1976:115).

Some evidence suggests that the Mesopotamians may have seen Inanna as "the power in the rains." It may be she who, in iconography, rides the liquid-spewing beast that draws the Storm God's chariot (Wolkstein & Kramer 1983:94). At least one hymn addresses her as "Loud Thundering Storm," who pours out rain over the land (Wolkstein & Kramer 1983:95; Jacobsen 1976:136).

Further, images often closely associate her with a bird usually interpreted as the *Anzu*, the "lion-headed thunder-bird" (Williams-Forte 1983:177; Wolkstein & Kramer 1983:102). Usually, Inanna stands on a lion, "typically an image or emblem of thunder gods" (Wolkstein & Kramer 1983:36, 93, 98, 100, 102; Jacobsen 1976:136).

Although the lion may also have been the emblem of Inanna as a storm goddess (Jacobsen 1976:136), the beast probably indicated her ferocity as spirit of both storm and war. Certainly, the Mesopotamians understood her as the war goddess, who was present on battlefields and in warfare generally (Jacobsen 1976:137). A Sumerian epithet, *nin-me*, designates her as "mistress of battle" (Frymer-Kensky 1992:66–7).

Another of Inanna's symbols, the eight-pointed star or rosette, signals her identity with the planet Venus, the morning and evening stars (Wakeman 1985:19; Williams-Forte 1983:182; Wolkstein & Kramer 1983:27, 92; Jacobsen 1976:138). As such, she is "Lady of Heaven," one of the possible meanings of her name. Her identity with the Venus star perhaps partially explains the fact that Inanna is a very peripatetic goddess, for Venus seems seasonally to change position in the heavens (Frymer-Kensky 1992:28).

The many figurines and other images of nude and voluptuous females found all over Mesopotamia may represent Inanna and indicate her function as spirit of sexuality and love (Jacobsen 1976:139). Her epithets include *kar-kid* (Sumerian for "harlot") and *harimtu* ("prostitute" in Akkadian). In textual descriptions, she often behaves like a prostitute, roaming the streets and frequenting taverns. She was the patron of prostitutes: "the beautiful girl standing in the street, the young prostitute, is the daughter of Inanna' " (Frymer-Kensky 1992: 29, 282 n. 53). Above all, Inanna represents "raw sexual experience and power" (Frymer-Kensky 1992:47).

Inanna's usual roles—little sister and daughter, sweetheart, bride, and young widow—all present her as in late adolescence, as a permanent teenager, who is permanently poised on the edge of womanhood (Jacobsen 1976:141). Not surprisingly, then, Inanna was a female who behaved like a male and who lived "essentially the same existence as young men," exulting in battle and seeking sexual experience. Transvestism was also part of her worship (Frymer-Kensky 1992:29; Wolkstein & Kramer 1983:99).

It seems likely that Inanna stood for potentiality and transformation, the essence of life. That is why she was central and unified and why, at the same time, she seemed infinitely variable. What is "the power in the storehouse" but the potential of dried food and seed, seemingly dead, but in reality harboring the ability to support and generate life? Rains, especially in Mesopotamia, can make the difference between fertility and sterility, life and death. In war, humans can change their fortunes and even lose their lives, the ultimate transformation. Morning and evening stars herald change: they appear at the boundaries of light and dark. Sexuality and love provide two of the most effective ways for humans to change. Transvestism also is societal boundary crossing. All of Inanna's powers, attributes, and aspects involve transformation and stretching or crossing of boundaries and limits (Friedrich 1978).

The Sumerian sign for Inanna—a pair of specially shaped standards, usually interpreted as gateposts—is a clue that the Sumerians viewed her essence as transformation (Wolkstein & Kramer 1983:27, 47, 85; Jacobsen 1976:7). On the top register of the Uruk vase, Inanna stands in front of the standards greeting worshippers who bring the land's produce to her shrine (Wolkstein & Kramer 1983:104; Oates & Oates 1976:115). The pair of standards frame her shrine's threshold. Thresholds and doors lead from one place to another, from one reality to another. Changeable Inanna was, then, goddess of the doorway and, thus, of the eternal threshold. Consequently, she had always to be adolescent, not being but becoming, permanently "the maiden" poised at the threshold of change. Essentially she was life—the great, continually changing cycle of being and becoming.

It is not surprising that the Sumerians understood Inanna to be essential to the making of a monarch, the transforming of a man into a king (Frymer-Kensky 1992:237 n. 40). In the "sacred-marriage" ritual, Inanna and the man to be validated as king had sexual intercourse (whether this was actual and/or symbolic is debated) on a specially constructed and appointed bed in her temple (Steinkeller 1999:132 forthcoming; Frayne 1985:18). Afterward, she installed him on a throne and bestowed on him the symbols of power (Jacobsen 1976:38). Thus, a mortal man became identified, at least temporarily, with Inanna's bridegroom Dumuzi, and something further of immortality rubbed off on him because of his relationship with the goddess. So long as she regularly reconfirmed him through the ritual, he was able to maintain both his power and the fertility and prosperity of the land. Originally, this ritual and its necessity must have given Inanna and her temple enormous influence (Steinkeller 1999:116, 135–136, forthcoming; Cooper 1993; Frymer-Kensky 1992:237, n. 40; Frayne 1985; Wakeman 1985:12–3; Teubal 1984:77 and chapter 8; Kramer 1969). It is therefore quite a shock to find Inanna as the weeping protagonist of the huluppu-tree poem.

Inanna's rescue of the *huluppu* tree took place at the time of beginnings; appropriately, the sapling too was just starting its life. Since the incident occurred when everything necessary for sustaining life was coming into existence, it follows that the *huluppu* tree was also necessary for the maintenance of life.

That the *huluppu* tree was the Sumerian version of the World Tree, the Tree of Life, seems highly likely. In a variety of mythologies, the World Tree usually houses a serpent in its roots and often has a bird living in its branches (Campbell 1964:41). As the *huluppu* tree matured, it acquired a snake in its roots and a bird in its crown.

What was a *huluppu*? Scholarly consensus is that no one knows; it was "perhaps a willow" (Williams-Forte 1983:178; Kramer 1967:198). It seems certain, however, that the *huluppu* was a sacred tree. *Huluppu* may have been another word for date palm, for there is considerable evidence that the date palm was sacred to the peoples of the ancient eastern Mediterranean (Danthine 1937:6). Visual material often associates Inanna with the date palm. In one image she holds a date frond in her hand (Wolkstein & Kramer 1983:ii). In another she sits enthroned, her feet on her lion and the *anzu* by her head. Between her and her worshipers a stylized date palm grows in a vase, "the focus of ritual libations before the goddess in other scenes" (Williams-Forte 1983: 102; Wolkstein & Kramer 1983:102). It was often a stylized date palm of this kind that later Mesopotamian kings watered to demonstrate their sole ability to maintain the fertility and prosperity of the land (Gray

1982:29, 45, 5963; Widegren 1951:chapter I). Since the *huluppu* tree was, as I shall argue, sacred to, or identical with, Inanna, it is possible that it was a date palm.

Inanna took the little tree to her sacred garden, where she may or may not have tended the tree with her hand—translations contradict one another here. However, after tamping it into place with her foot, she left it to grow in the fecundity of her garden, probably the cultic garden, "pure Inanna's fruitful garden," in her huge temple complex in her favorite city, Uruk (Kramer 1967:200; Shaffer 1963:30 n. I). Each ancient Mesopotamian temple seems to have had a sacred grove complete with a sacred tree, of which the ruler of the temple's city functioned, both in myth and in cult, as caretaker. He usually included among his honorifics the title "Gardener" (Widegren 1951:9, 11, 15).

In ancient Mesopotamian literature, tending a garden, cultivating land, could be a metaphor for the male role in sexual intercourse. This metaphor was especially applicable to the central rite in the "sacred-marriage" ritual. One of the "sacred-marriage" hymns has "maiden" Inanna sing of her vulva that it is her "untilled plot . . . [her] hillock land . . . [her] (well) watered lowlands," and she asks "who will be their ploughman?" The king incorporating Dumuzi answers that he will plough them for her, whereupon she responds that he is the "man of [her] heart!" (Jacobsen 1976:46). At the metaphorical level, the fertile garden is the goddess, and particularly her womb, her vulva. In the *huluppu* poem, the sacred garden was "fruitful" in and of itself, a fecund matrix. Inanna did not need to do more than put the little tree into the ground. Clearly, in the *huluppu*-tree poem, Inanna's sacred garden did not yet have a gardener, no male stimulator of fertility. Thus, in this poem with its focus on the interests of a male-dominated society, the *huluppu* tree could not grow as other trees do. The Garden, with no Gardener, was not capable of producing "normal," healthy growth. Instead, it became infested with unwanted creatures.[4]

That a snake took up residence in the roots of Inanna's tree is not at all surprising if, in fact, the *huluppu* is the World Tree. Further, in ancient Mesopotamia as elsewhere, snakes were usually connected with fertility and fertility goddesses (Henshaw 1994:173; Wolkstein & Kramer 1983:3). In many ancient cultures, indeed, serpents, creatures of goddesses of earth and underworld, lived under their shrines. Snakes can also move around in water and often live in or near springs, which, in many ancient cultures, were entrances to the underworld.[5]

The "serpent who could not be charmed" would not move from the roots of the *huluppu* tree. Roots constitute a threshold, joining the surface of the earth and the area below the earth. In the *huluppu*-tree

poem, the snake's abode made possible its moving easily between the
earth's surface and the underworld (Wolkstein & Kramer 1983:180). In
addition, if the *huluppu* tree were the World Tree, the serpent's presence
in the roots was normal. Could the snake as a threshold creature also
have been an aspect of Inanna, her underworld self? Maybe its identity
with Inanna was another reason why it remained in her sacred *huluppu*
tree and why it was reluctant to leave the sacred garden.

The bird in the tree's branches, the Anzu, seems to have had a relationship to thunder and thus to storms, to which Inanna also had a
close connection (Williams-Forte 1983:180, 194; Wolkstein & Kramer
1983:95–6, 102; Jacobsen 1976:136–7). Thus the *anzu*'s presence in Inanna's tree was appropriate. Keeping itself to the branches in the crown
of Inanna's tree, the bird was also a boundary creature, living between
earth and sky. It too was able to move across thresholds. It is therefore
possible that the *anzu* was another aspect of Inanna.

The female "demon," the "dark maid," who took up residence in the
trunk of the *huluppu* tree is attested in Mesopotamian literature as far
back as the third millennium B.C.E. (Hutter 1995:973).[6] She was "a female demon," a kind of *lilu* (feminine *lilitu*), the name of a family of
demons (*Chicago Assyrian Dictionary* 1956). The term comes from the
Sumerian *lil*, "air, wind, spirit" (Douglas Frayne, personal communication, December 10, 1996). The *lilu* demons controlled "stormy winds,"
and the *lilitu* could fly like a bird (Hutter 1995:973).

The *lilu* class of demons also had decidedly negative sexual characteristics, which were especially marked in the females. They were not
married, they wandered about seeking to entrap men, and they were
apt to steal into a man's house through the window. More important,
the Mesopotamians considered their sexuality not to be "normal," for a
man does not have intercourse with them "in the same way as with
his wife" (Hutter 1995:973).

These female demons sound very much like Inanna and Ishtar, Inanna's Semitic counterpart: she "stands at the window looking for a
man in order to seduce him, love him and kill him" (Hutter 1995:973–
4). Not only did Inanna stand seductively in doors and windows (Jacobsen 1976:140), but, like Ishtar, she also was "*sahiratu*, 'the one who
roams about' " (Frymer-Kensky 1992:28). Hymns describe her as going
"from house to house and street to street," a phrase that later texts
apply to demons (Frymer-Kensky 1992:28).

This connecting of free, unattached woman and demon suggests that
male-dominated society had slowly separated Inanna's independent, societally uncontrollable self from her other attributes and divided that
difficult self in two, prostitute and demon. The former was societally

useful, if stigmatized and marginalized; the latter was feared and rejected. The fact that many translators render the word *lilitu* as "Lilith"
could indicate indirect support for such a hypothesis (Kramer 1967:200;
Wolkstein & Kramer 1983:6). They understand that the Mesopotamian
demon was the ancestor of Lilith, in much later Jewish myth the vilified
first wife of Adam (Ausubel 1979:393–4; Graves & Patai 1964:68).

In a discussion of Lilith, Raphael Patai argues that a famous image
on Babylonian baked clay plaque, which he dates as "roughly contemporary with the [*huluppu*-tree] poem," depicts a *lilitu* like the one who
lived in the trunk of the *huluppu* tree (Patai 1990:222 and plate 31;
Wolkstein & Kramer 1983:6). Naked and voluptuous, she stands on two
lions and is flanked by two owls. Wearing the multihorned headdress
of a great deity, she holds two ring-and-rod symbols that denote royal
power (Henshaw 1994:240; Williams-Forte 1983:181; Jacobsen 1976:
38). Because of the owls, Patai sees her as a goddess of the night and
because of the lions as a tamer of wild beasts.

If Patai is correct that this clay plaque depicts a *lilitu*, he is also right
that she is no ordinary demon. Almost certainly, the plaque depicts the
goddess Inanna. This Inanna can fly and has the feet of a nocturnal
bird of prey; the image demonstrates that Inanna had a death and
underworld aspect, entirely appropriate for the goddess of the transformation (Williams-Forte 1983:189). Another piece of visual evidence
supports the argument that the figure on the plaque is a female deity.
A cylinder seal, dated 2000–1600 B.C.E., shows an oversized, winged
goddess, standing with multihorn crowned head in the top register of
the seal and taloned feet in the bottom one. The top register displays
deities and human worshipers, the bottom "demonic creatures." Some
scholars have identified this winged figure with Lilith and thus with the
lilitu, although it seems clear that the figure is that of Inanna (Williams-
Forte 1983:189; Wolkstein & Kramer 1983:51). Over time, Mesopotamian society probably separated Inanna's underworld aspects, originally
integral to her being as goddess of life, from her other traits and turned
them into the demon, the *lilitu*.

The seal also adds another piece to the puzzle of Inanna's nature.
Not only does its two-register arrangement attest to the goddess's duality, her head in the realm of deities and her feet in the underworld,
but it also argues that it is she who makes the connection among the
realms. Like the *huluppu* tree, she stands with feet, roots, in the underworld and head, branches, in the heavens, her body, the trunk with its
lilitu, serving to join them.

In the *huluppu*-tree poem, Inanna did not see the three interlopers
as other selves, for the poem presents her as already co-opted by male-

dominated society. She wanted the unwelcome monsters gone so that she could use the wood of the sacred tree for a throne and a bed. She no longer understood that, as the poem implies, the sacred tree and herself were originally one, that she herself had connected heavens, earth, and underworld, "a goddess . . . symbolized . . . by a cosmic tree of life" and death (Campbell 1965:64). No wonder male-dominated society needed to tame and control her!

Eventually the *huluppu* tree attained the girth necessary to provide wood for Inanna's wished-for throne and bed, but its unwelcome residents refused to leave, despite Inanna's distress. Her feminine weeping is quite out of character for the demanding, assertive goddess, but Inanna had now to operate in a male-dominated world. Her plea for help to her brother, the sun god Utu, "guardian of justice," was unsuccessful (Jacobsen 1976:134). Perhaps because he was the god of one of the most important necessities of life, the sun, he would not cooperate in the destruction of any other.

On the other hand, Inanna's request to the hero Gilgamesh, renowned builder of the walls of Uruk, received a favorable response (Kovacs 1989:3). Gilgamesh was *lugal*, "king," of Inanna's Uruk. He also held the priestly title *en*, though in the *Epic of Gilgamesh*, he showed scant respect for his city's goddess. An androcentric, individualistic monarch, he delighted in spurning the goddess Ishtar, Inanna's counterpart and successor, thus announcing that he did not need her to validate his kingship and maintain the fertility and prosperity of the land. On the contrary, not only did he reject the goddess's proposal that he become her mate, presumably by taking part in the "sacred-marriage" ritual, but he also insulted her grievously and with impunity (Kovacs 1989:51–3).[7] This episode represents a later stage of goddess demotion than the relatively tame version in the *huluppu*-tree poem.

Without hesitation, Gilgamesh entered the sacred garden, heavily armed to face what clearly were ferocious enemies. He wasted no time trying to persuade the creatures to leave. Unerringly, he chose first to attack the snake, the most dangerous and deadly of the creatures, and dispatched it. The snake was the only one of the *huluppu*'s residents that Gilgamesh had to dispose of directly. The poem implies that he killed it. In so doing, he cut off forever one of the links between earth and underworld.

The other creatures left of their own accord. The survival of the bird and its brood argues that the connection to the heavens, though damaged, was not yet irretrievably severed. Society still needed Inanna to retain her association with the heavens. The bird took its stormy self and its brood off to the mountains, where it had less potential to do

damage than in the middle of Uruk; its absence was an advantage for
the city. Inanna's anger could still, of course, unleash it (Wolkstein &
Kramer 1983:95). As the demonization of Inanna as both unattached,
independent, and societally uncontrollable female and underworld goddess, the *lilitu* fled to "wild, uninhabited places," whence she returned
to plague men (Wolkstein & Kramer 1983:9). Again it was to the advantage of the city that she should keep to the wastelands but be available to take the blame for a myriad miseries.

When Gilgamesh had disposed of the *huluppu* tree's inhabitants, he
uprooted it, thus eliminating finally any natural connection between
earth and underworld. He then gave the wood to Inanna to make into
a bed and a throne, the furniture used in the "sacred-marriage" rite.
Both she and the furniture would henceforth serve male monarchy in
a male-dominated society. In this way, society was able to circumscribe
her and direct her undoubted power into channels that would be useful
to the male-dominated city.

Inanna made the roots of the tree into an object and branches into
another object and gave them to Gilgamesh (Heidel 1963:94).[8] In the
verses following the *huluppu*-tree poem, the objects fell into the underworld, and the attempt to retrieve them not only failed but resulted in
the death of Gilgamesh's beloved friend. Obviously Gilgamesh had no
right to appropriate either extremity of the tree. He could not yet serve
his people as a conduit between earth and heaven; Gilgamesh still
needed the relationship with Inanna to mediate that connection. The
focus on the construction of the throne and the bed make that patently
clear. Moreover, neither he nor other kings would try to effect any rap-
prochement with the dreaded underworld.

It is ironic that Gilgamesh was the destroyer of the *huluppu* tree, for,
in the *Epic of Gilgamesh*, he is so horrified by death and the prospect of
the underworld that he sets out to learn the secret of immortality (Kovacs 1989). However, it was he who was instrumental in producing a
world in which, without the *huluppu* tree and its snake, human beings
could no longer have natural and easy access to the underworld, now
a "place of no return." Inanna's threshold snake was dead, and the
sacred tree no longer put its roots down into the nether regions. Inanna
was now a goddess only of the heavens and the earth, and the cycle of
life had suffered irreparable damage.

Inanna did finally get her throne and her bed, both of which were
crucial to the "sacred-marriage" rite and its validation of kingship in
Mesopotamia. Initially the "sacred-marriage" rite undoubtedly would
have given Inanna and her temple great power. However, the cost to
Inanna and for society was high. In return for the influence afforded

her by the throne and the bed, Inanna actually had to instigate the murder of one aspect of herself and the banishment from her city of two others. Perhaps a more important point, she had to sanction, indeed beg for, the destruction of the *huluppu* tree, that is, her united self. In return, she got two items of furniture and a central role in a king-making ritual. However, the furniture, which was essentially constructed from her body, was no longer entirely hers. The institution of kingship had appropriated it to its use and, with the furniture, Inanna herself. What is more, the poem presents her as willingly cooperating in her own demotion.

The way the poem treats the *huluppu* tree gives every indication that it was the World Tree, like the ash tree Yggdrasil in Norse myth, the World Axis, that which joins heavens, earth, and underworld (Campbell 1965:486–89). As identical with the *huluppu* tree and as goddess of boundaries, Inanna too connected heavens, earth, and underworld. As a result of the action the poem describes, both Inanna and the tree became confined to earth as the furniture, the literal underpinning, of kingship. At the end of the *huluppu*-tree narrative, Inanna was not only clearly separate from the three aspects of herself in the *huluppu* tree but also so distant that she could see them as her enemies. She also was completely alienated from the sacred tree that was herself, so much so that she could not only allow but actually arrange for, her body and her transformative power to be at the disposal of the male-dominated city-state. In the "new world" that was coming into being, it was the king who was to function, at first through his relationship with Inanna, as the connector of heavens and earth. The instruments of that relationship, the throne and the bed, were once, in their natural form, the living trunk, itself a direct conduit between heavens and earth, and, through the tree's roots, the trunk also joined heavens and earth with the underworld. The result of the destruction of the *huluppu* tree was that humanity could no longer maintain a cyclical view of death and the underworld, through Inanna's underworld aspects and the World Tree. Instead, humans were to inhabit a frightening world. Gone was the old cyclical world view of death as merely one stage in the eternal round of birth, death, and renewal. In their new, male-dominated society, men feared death and dreaded the underworld (Kovacs 1989:59–75; Wolkstein & Kramer 1983:51–89).

The charming and seemingly innocuous little poem "Inanna and the *Huluppu* Tree" provides a male-centered mythic explanation for Inanna's participation in the "sacred-marriage" ritual. Her necessary involvement as goddess of transformation, without whose approval no change could take place, became her presence as both pieces of furniture and cooperative goddess who bedded and enthroned the prospective king. Powerful goddess subject, the sacred Tree of Life, had, over the centuries, turned into limited goddess objects—pieces of furniture, bed and throne.

In her insightful essay "Why Women Need the Goddess . . . ," Carol Christ discusses the meanings or functions of the goddess symbol for feminists and other women today. The most important—"the acknowledgment of the legitimacy of female power as a beneficent and independent power"—does not immediately seem to be the lesson of the *huluppu*-tree story. At first glance, indeed, it is clear that it comes from one of the goddess traditions in which goddesses "are subordinate to gods" and which, Christ says, feminists ignore (1982:74). However, subjected to careful feminist analysis, the story yields up riches that are very empowering for women.

For example, a feminist analysis of the poem demonstrates the consolidating of a stage of male dominance, and thus it adds confirmation to the feminist assertion that male dominance is not natural but constructed (Lerner 1986). That a strong, assertive goddess like Inanna could in the *huluppu*-tree poem be rewritten as a feminine woman, dependent on males to help her out of trouble, shows how effectively myth can be transformed in the service of ideology. It is indeed probable that, slowly, over time, priests reworked and subtly altered a story from another period, a story in which Inanna and her sacred tree played very different roles. It is frustrating to think that we will probably never know what they were. We are lucky to have the glimpses we do have.

Notes

1. The survival of written and visual material about ancient deities and their worship is very much a matter of chance. The fact, therefore, that the goddess Inanna seems to have been the most prominent and powerful female deity of ancient Sumer may be no more than archaeological accident.

Since I cannot read ancient Mesopotamian texts in the original languages, I work with translations. However, my training in ancient Greek, Latin, and Biblical Hebrew has taught me that comparison of different translations produces a good understanding of an original text. In analyzing Mesopotamian texts, I also check my understanding with colleagues who can read the originals. Nonetheless, I am responsible for any errors in interpretation.

2. The huluppu-tree episode is part of the Sumerian tale known as "Gilgamesh, Enkidu, and the Netherworld" (Kramer 1967:197). It is preserved among the great collection of Sumerian texts unearthed at Nippur (Kramer 1972:9).

The writing of most of these tablets dates to approximately 1750 B.C.E but at least some of the texts were composed earlier, between 2150 and

2050 B.C.E. by which time Mesopotamian society was fully male dominated (Kramer 1972:19; Kovacs 1989: xxiii). However, the huluppu-tree poem shows every indication of having had its origin in oral material that probably went back into Sumerian prehistory (Wolkstein & Kramer 1983:4–9; Kramer 1972:19; Kramer 1967:199–205; Shaffer 1963:99–105).

3. In Kramer's translation, she is a "woman, roving about in fear of the word of An," a significant difference in interpretation (Kramer 1967:200; Wolkstein & Kramer 1983:5).

4. Elsewhere in Mesopotamian myth, a goddess who created alone without the assistance of a male partner gave birth only to aberrations: Tiamat, who, with her male consort Apsu, produced all the other gods, gave birth to only monsters after her consort's demise (Heidel 1967:23–4,ll.132–45). This pattern also occurs in mythologies of other cultures, for example, that of ancient Greece: when Hera, queen of heaven, bore a child not fathered by her husband Zeus and perhaps even unfathered, she gave birth to the physically deformed Hephaistos.

5. For example, the snake who stole the plant of youth from Gilgamesh lived in or near a spring (Kovacs 1989:106–107).

6. The Sumerians called her *ki-sikil-lil-la*, in Semitic Akkadian, *(w)ardat-lilla or ardat-lili*; both phrases mean "Young Woman (Air) Spirit" (Douglas Frayne, personal communication, December 10, 1996).

7. When Ishtar retaliated by arranging to loose the voracious Bull of Heaven on Uruk, Gilgamesh and his friend Enkidu killed the Bull, and Enkidu contemptuously threw its "hindquarter" in the goddess's face (Kovacs 1989:53–6). Confronted with such arrogance and lack of respect, Ishtar could do nothing except retreat to the wall of her city and mourn the Bull (Kovacs 1989:56).

8. A *pukku* and a *mikku*—it is unclear what these were.

References

Adams, Robert McC. 1966. *The Evolution of Urban Society: Early Mesopotamia and Prehispanic Mexico*. Chicago: Aldine.

Ausubel, Nathan (ed.). 1979. *A Treasury of Jewish Folklore*. New York: Crown.

Campbell, Joseph. 1964. *The Hero with a Thousand Faces*. New York: Meridian.

———. 1965. *The Masks of God: Occidental Mythology*. New York: Viking.

Chicago Assyrian Dictionary. 1956. Chicago: University of Chicago Press.

Christ, Carol P. 1982. Why Women Need the Goddess: Phenomenological, Psychological, and Political Reflections. In Charlene Spretnak (ed.), *The Politics of Women's Spirituality: Essays on the Rise of Spiritual Power within the Feminist Movement*. Garden City, N.Y.: Doubleday Anchor: 71–86.

———. 1997. *Rebirth of the Goddess:Finding Meaning in Feminist Spirituality*. Reading, Mass.: Addison-Wesley.

Cooper, Jerrold S. 1993. Sacred Marriage and Popular Cult in Early Mesopotamia. In E. Matushima (ed.), *Official Cult and Popular Religion in the Ancient Near East: Papers of the First Colloquium on the Ancient Near East— The City and Its Life*, held at the Middle Eastern Culture Center in Japan (Mitaka, Tokyo), March 20–22, 1992. Heidelberg: C. Winter: 81–96.

Crawford, Harriet 1992. *Sumer and the Sumerians*. Cambridge, England: University of Cambridge Press.

Danthine, Hélène. 1937. *Le palmier-dattier et les arbres sacrés dans l'iconographie de l'Asie occidentale ancienne.* 2 vols. Paris: Librairie Orientaliste Paul Guethner.

Frankfort, Henri. 1978. *Kingship and the Gods.* Chicago: University of Chicago Press.

Frayne, Douglas. 1985. Notes on the Sacred Marriage Rite. *Bibliotheca Orientalis* 42:5–22.

Friedrich, Paul. 1978. *The Meaning of Aphrodite.* Chicago: University of Chicago Press.

Frymer-Kensky, Tikva. 1992. *In the Wake of the Goddesses: Women, Culture, and the Biblical Transformation of Pagan Myth.* New York: Free Press.

Graves, Robert, and Raphael Patai. 1964. *Hebrew Myths: The Book of Genesis.* London: Cassell.

Gray, John. 1982. *Near Eastern Mythology.* London: Hamlyn.

Hallo, William W., and William K. Simpson. 1971. *The Ancient Near East: A History.* New York: Harcourt Brace Jovanovich.

Hallo, William W., and J. Van Dijk. 1968. *The Exaltation of Inanna.* New Haven: Yale University Press.

Heidel, Alexander (trans.). 1963. *The Epic of Gilgamesh and Old Testament Parallels.* Chicago: University of Chicago Press.

———. 1967. *The Babylonian Genesis.* Chicago: University of Chicago Press.

Henshaw, Richard A. 1994. *Female and Male, The Cultic Personnel: The Bible and the Rest of the Ancient Near East.* Allison Park, Penn.: Pickwick.

Hutter, M. 1995. Lilith. In Karel van der Toorn et al. (eds.), *Dictionary of Deities and Demons in the Bible.* Leiden: E. J. Brill: 973–976.

Jacobsen, Thorkild. 1976. *The Treasures of Darkness: A History of Mesopotamian Religion.* New Haven: Yale University.

Kovacs, Maureen Gallery (trans.). 1989. *The Epic of Gilgamesh.* Stanford: Stanford University Press.

Kramer, Samuel Noah. 1938. *Gilgamesh and the Huluppu Tree.* Chicago: University of Chicago Press.

———. 1967 [1963]. *The Sumerians: Their History, Culture, and Character.* Chicago: *University of Chicago Press.*

———. 1969. *The Sacred Marriage Rite: Aspects of Faith, Myth, and Ritual in Ancient Sumer.* Bloomington: University of Indiana Press.

———. 1972. *Sumerian Mythology.* Philadelphia: University of Pennsylvania Press.

———. 1983. Sumerian History, Culture and Literature. In Wolkstein and Kramer 1983:115–126.

Lerner, Gerda. 1986. *The Creation of Patriarchy.* New York: Oxford University Press.

Oates, David, and Joan Oates. 1976. *The Rise of Civilization.* [New York]: Elsevier Phaidon.

Patai, Raphael. 1990. *The Hebrew Goddess.* 3rd enl. ed. Detroit: Wayne State University.

Schüssler Fiorenza, Elisabeth. 1992 [1983]. *In Memory of Her: A Feminist Theological Reconstruction of Christian Origins.* New York: Crossroad.

Shaffer, Aaron. 1963. Sumerian Sources of Tablet 12 of the Epic of Gilgamesh. Ph.D. diss., University of Pennsylvania (University Microfilms 1974).

Steinkeller, Piotr. Forth coming 1999. On Rulers, Priests and Sacred Marriage: Tracing the Evidence of Early Sumerian Kingship. In Watanabe, K. ed., *Priests and Officials in the Ancient Near East: Papers of the Second Colloquium on the Ancient Near East* The City and its Life held at the Middle Eastern Cultural Center in Japan (Mitaka, Tokyo) March 22–4, 1996. Heidelberg: C. Winter: 103–137.

Teubal, Savina. 1984. *Sarah the Priestess: The First Matriarch.* Athens, Ohio: University of Ohio: Swallow Press.

Wakeman, Mary K. 1985. Ancient Sumer and the Women's Movement: The Process of Reaching Behind, Encompassing and Going Beyond. *Journal of Feminist Studies in Religion* 1 (2):7–27.

Widegren, George. 1951. *The King and the Tree of Life in Ancient Near Eastern Religion.* Uppsala: Lundquist.

Williams-Forte, Elizabeth. 1983. Annotations of the Art. In Wolkstein and Kramer 1983:174–199.

Wolkstein, Diane, and Samuel Noah Kramer. 1983. *Inanna, Queen of Heaven and Earth: Her Stories and Hymns from Sumer.* New York: Harper Colophon.

The Sovereignty as Co-Lordship

A Contemporary Feminist Rereading of the Female Sacred in the Ulster Cycle

Frances Devlin-Glass

In a postbiblical age, pre-Christian narratives are finding new audi-
tors/readers, among them those interested in a post-Christian theology and spirituality.[1] It is necessary at the outset to distance my approach from others that search for an empowering past and for
compensatory woman-centered myths as antidotes for patriarchal ones.
Such searches have often taken a separatist, romantic, and nostalgic
form and have been marked by serious ahistoricity (Hutton 1991), especially in the hands of New Age reconstructionists of spirituality. My
intention is this paper is to offer a gynocritical recuperation of archaic
Irish narratives and to read a small selection of this material through
the deconstructing lens of feminism, with a view to exposing the androcentric process at work reshaping and resignifying a body of material
in which, I argue, traces of a different ideological focus may be dis-
cerned. Archaic Irish narratives have a translation and reception history
that has seen them serve a variety of ideological agendas, possibly even
at the point of their earliest transmission in written form (Aitchison
1987). Modern translations (notably Kinsella 1969) reveal a body of
narratives that are surprisingly rich for feminist deconstructive purposes
and indeed have gender-political implications not just for women but
for men's and women's understandings of how the sexual contract
might be refigured.[2] The notion of an interdependency of power be-

tween women and men, which assumes a particular view of the body of woman, and its sacredness,[3] is at the center of what I shall be arguing that these myths offer. My project takes the view that to be aware that patriarchal understandings are not natural, universal, and trans-historical is emancipatory.

One of the problems of dealing with such narratives is that an adequate (deconstructed and deconstructing) nomenclature has not been established. The problem is centrally that of the gender polarities built deeply into language and cultural formations of all kinds and the need to continue to deconstruct them. Many scholars, with good reason (Lerner 1986; Sanday 1981; Coward 1983), object to a nomenclature that has patriarchy preceded by *matriarchy*, with the implication that power might have been vested in the women in a style of social organization that is the inverse of patriarchy. Historical, anthropological, and ethnological evidence for such societies does not exist; matriarchy exists only in myth and legend, such as legends of the Amazons (Lerner 1986: 31), and has usually served either evolutionist and social Darwinist agendas or patriarchal ones—agendas that tend to overlap.[4] Nor do the terms that are usually substituted, *matrifocality* and *matricentrism*, serve, though one often needs to use such terms in order to signal the difference in discursive styles. What is most striking about the body of narratives I shall be examining is the notion of power exchange, of sexual contracts, rather than domination by one group over another, of cultures in which women had separate and different, and privileged, religious functions, but ones that are exercised contractually and not at men's expense. Not being aware of a single word that might be used to characterize these complex processes, I shall have to be content with describing and interpreting them carefully.

The suppression and repression of narratives in which women have spiritual and political significance has a long history in Western culture and is increasingly well documented. Theories about the rise of patriarchy proliferated in the second half of the nineteenth century[5] and fueled such productions as Freud's phylogenetic accounts in *Totem and Taboo* (1912–13) and *Moses and Monotheism* (1939). Feminists were later in weighing into the debate (Condren 1989; Lerner 1986; Gimbutas 1991), often doing so in polemical ways, and many academic disciplines (biology, psychology, anthropology, archaeology) continue to contribute hypotheses to it. Undoubtedly (as Lerner argues, 1986:36–53) the process whereby patriarchal assumptions became the norm in the West was multifactorial, occurring differently in different groups and cultures and at different times. But of central significance to this process is the imbrication of two processes: the rise of patriarchy is predicated on the almost complete exclusion of women from writing and religious practices. The role of literacy in this process, and the shift from oracy to literacy, are crucial. Women were systematically excluded from symbol- and meaning-making, from knowledge-formation (especially theology), and from history (Lerner 1986:231). Once stories were committed to writing rather than being handed down orally, the transition from narratives concerned with heterosexual exchange to ones in which men have exclusive power was almost always achieved. It is, of course, the qualification ("almost") in the preceding sentence with which this essay concerns itself.

A series of factors serve to explain why matrifocal narratives survived much longer in Ireland than in the Middle East and in Greco-Roman culture:

- Ireland's geographical isolation and Agricola's failure to invade Ireland;
- The late (and peaceable) arrival in Ireland of patriarchal Christianity in 432 A.D.;
- The "anthropological" methodology of monks who committed the Irish narratives to vellum and who appear to have been reasonably open to the culture they sought to displace;
- The monks' susceptibility to the culture they displaced and nonetheless transmitted: Christianity in Ireland acquired a Celtic character (until it was extinguished by the English-dominated Synod of Whitby in 664 A.D.) (Lehane 1994); the assumption that the monks transcribed these oral narratives has been challenged by Aitchison (1987:101–3), who speculates that the scribes might have been former *filidh* (bards) who had converted to Christianity and literacy and found themselves working in antiquarian ways in church-run scriptoria.[6] The implications of this suggestion are enormous;
- The maintenance of the local system of brehon laws (until the seventeenth century and the collapse of the Gaelic order after the decisive Williamite victory at the Boyne) in the face of considerable church pressure to Christianize them) (Power 1976; O'Corráin 1984, 1985; Devlin-Glass 1997).

For these reasons and undoubtedly others, narratives that bear traces of a prepatriarchal ideology survived in Ireland, admittedly in a compromised form. Gimbutas speculates that insular Celticism underwent the patriarchal Indo-European revolution less thoroughly than its continental counterparts (1991:348). Nonetheless, enough survives of these ancient texts, and texts (often in archaeological and legal discourses:

Glob 1969; Mac Cana 1956; Power 1976; O'Corráin 1984, 1985) cognate with them, and they have been translated (on this point there is much to say later in this essay) in recent decades in ways that disclose more fully their different value systems and make possible new interrogations of what they have to say about embodiment, sexuality, and heterosexuality. The codes they seem to enact are, I contend, significantly different from those to be found contemporaneously in mainstream patriarchal culture. A further point that needs to be made is that the study of these myths using methods drawn from feminist, specifically gynocritical, and poststructuralist practices and from the cognitive symbolic anthropology of Geertz (1973) yields insights that have gender-political uses well beyond an enclosed and separatist feminist enclave.

Outside Ireland, *The Táin* is not well known other than to Irish scholars. This epic-scale narrative poem, comprising more than eighty heroic tales, comes to us in fragments in a variety of manuscripts, the oldest of these being a twelfth-century manuscript compiled in the monastery at Clonmacnoise. But the matter of this song cycle is much older and predates literacy in Ireland. As transmitted by monks, it is a "boys' own" tale of Celtic warmongering, with much of the narrative devoted to bloodthirsty trials of strength. However, the action is almost always propelled by the agency of women who are arguably the deities of a recently eclipsed religion. The fore-tales that help to clarify the main action are dominated by women who are feisty, outspoken, intelligent, and able to "shape their worlds through the judicious use of speech acts," as Findon (1997) claims of Emer.[7] Furthermore, they are sexually proactive as lovers, and perhaps give evidence of an ideological nexus between the female body and notions of sacredness.

Narrative as Manipulable

What feminist historians, archaeologists, palaeoanthropologists, and those who study large changes in agricultural practices and urbanization have to offer on the subject of the entrenchment of patriarchy is usefully augmented by the study of narratives and their evolution over time. By their very nature, narratives are both conservative and also susceptible to ideological massaging: a slight shift of emphasis here, a highlighting of a particular potent symbol at the expense of another, a shift in point of view, a changed ending are the cruder ways of effecting an ideological shift. More usually, though, when one analyzes incremental changes to a particular narrative over time, one is struck by the

subtlety and minuteness of the changes in signification. What seems
an insignificant change of focus at one point in history may, by several
changes in a congruent pattern of signification, effect a radical shift in
significance. Page duBois (1988:130–1, 165–6) offers a cogent example
of how in Greek literature one may chart a shift in signification from
the female body (conceived of as analogous with the earth) as auton-
omous source of life, flowering and burgeoning without human labor,
to that of a furrow that must be ploughed by the husband, with the
focus shifting to the act of ploughing. She argues that as Athens abandoned its dependence on agriculture, the earth metaphor gave way to
the metaphor of the stone tablet, which is passive, to be labored over
and inscribed, and in this metaphoric shift the active work of the in-
scriber becomes the focus of the metaphor. In this symbolic evolution
what is lost is the notion of interchange between earth (and its human
referent) and the human agent of the plough.

Ancient Irish texts reveal similar shifts in signification. Mary Condren's account of the ways that Christian and patriarchal discourses,
by means of subtle incremental shifts in narrative ·significance, implement patriarchal ideologies is instructive, as is a close reading of the
key text of ancient Ireland, *Táin Bó Cúailnge*. Looking at a number of
different narratives, she details a story of increasing control over women
in the religious, social, physiological, and political aspects of their existence (1989). Most significantly, it is women's bodies, their sexuality,
that must be controlled in order that male paternity be secure. The
most efficient way to establish paternity is by restricting women's sexuality through monogamy. The narrative of Cúchulainn's birth in Kinsella's ordering of the events (which is significantly different from Lady
Gregory's [1902] 1970:21–4)[8] is a curious one, as he is born not once
but three times. Condren reads this excess as (male) anxiety about
women's freedom and as an exploration in narrative form of increasing
male consciousness of the role of semen in reproduction (Condren
1989:38–43). This is a reading that is difficult to credit since the Celts
were pastoralists of some sophistication who certainly knew a great deal
about breeding cattle in the period the tale is set.[9] A sounder reading,
I think, is to see the three incarnations as a locus of ideological anxiety
about paternity rather than as an evolutionary dawning of understanding. Certainly, the Deichtine[10] who fosters the first incarnation of the
hero and who successfully brings to term the third is the king's sister
and is one who is located symbolically as journeying to the Boann;[11]
she finds welcome in a house that men had wrongly designated as
inhospitable and gives birth simultaneously with a horse that delivers
twin foals (a story that resonates with Macha's story), which are pre-

sented as a gift to the child. In this account of the birth, the paternity of the child is not an issue. In Rolleston's (1990:182) and Lady Gregory's (nineteenth-century) recountings of the myth, a further suggestive detail is added: Deichtine is represented as wandering with her retinue of fifty maidens for three years, unencumbered by men. In Rolleston, she lures the king and his followers, whom they had previously shunned, to the Boyne tumuli, referred to in Rolleston as "the Fairy Mound" (182). Although the tale reads like a traditional hero's extraordinary birth (the father is the sun god), there are many motifs to interest a reader whose focus is on prepatriarchal and pretranscendental spirituality. Because of the place of birth, perhaps Newgrange, and the links with the story of Macha, it is possible that Deichtine is a vestigial sovereignty goddess, cast here in a maternal aspect.

The Sovereignty of Ireland, "one of the oldest and most pervasive patterns of Irish myth" (Tymoczko 1994:96), enacts the "notion of a mystical or symbolic union between the king and his kingdom" (Mac Cana 1968:92). The Irish conceived the kingdoms anthropomorphically as goddesses/queens who exercise physical power as the land itself (its fertility, its productiveness and also its devouring qualities), legal power (as legitimators of the king's sacral rule, which was negotiated socially and according to portents), and both sexual and spiritual power (in giving and taking life, conferring fertility and prosperity).

In Kinsella's brilliant 1969 translation, there is an ironic twist to the tale in that, despite the environment of plenty, the child proves feeble and dies. The second conception is the most magical and, to the storytellers, unaccountable, involving as it does conception by means of a drink in which there is a "tiny creature." This phenomenon is acknowledged to be puzzling and to need explanation.[12] This is offered in two forms: a dream proclaims the father to be the sun god, Lug mac Ethnenn; the social anxiety that the brother might be the father necessitates his giving Deichtine in marriage to Sualdam mac Roich (who is deemed subsequently to be the father of Setanta, Cúchulainn's given name). It is significant that at this point in Kinsella's narrative, Deichtine is represented as experiencing shame: "She was ashamed to go pregnant to bed with her husband, and got sick when she reached the bedstead. The living thing spilled away in the sickness, and so she was made virgin and whole and went to her husband" (Kinsella, 1969: 23).

Fertility, which has no conditions on it in the first story, metamorphoses into shame that causes her to miscarry. Psychic health and fertility in the final version is dependent on allegiance to a husband. This single episode with its multiple versions of a hero birth constitutes, then, I suggest, a dramatic illustration of a culture in transition from one set of social practices and understandings of what conception means to a radically different one in which certainty about paternity is critical. A further change that should be noted is the way child-bearing moves from being the concern of a group of independent women to being a matter controlled by men. The three attempts to explain birth also point up the highly dynamic way in which the narrative process is exploited to effect ideological change, perhaps those changes required by Christian monks.

Translation and Reception History of The Táin

The processes by which Irish narratives have been relegated to the margins, if not suppressed, in the modern period (nineteenth and twentieth centuries, for my purposes), and the ideologies that were served by such maneuvers, can be exposed for scrutiny, and the archaeology of their reception can be understood.

The chart dramatizes the different cultural uses to which Irish mythology, in particular *The Táin*, was put in the course of its long history. The divisions between strata should be thought of as permeable, with significations leaving "traces" that are read and understood by cultures in which the job of appropriation and transformation might seem complete and hegemonic. Medb, for instance, might in the Celtic stratum be given a history and a location and a politics designed to explain the primacy of Ulster, but many of her attributes/deeds are superfluous to this (for example, her monumental menses) and understandable in terms of earlier significations—her Sovereignty. In the nineteenth century, new nationalist imperatives and the accelerating loss of the Irish language meant that the myths came to serve different ideological agendas, those driven by the need to contradistinguish Irish culture from an increasingly dominant Anglo-Saxon culture and the Irish one that had to some extent become hybridized. Furthermore, the comparison with mainstream myths (in particular Greek, Roman, and Judeo-Christian) gave rise to translations heavily influenced by the morality and literary conventions attaching to those bodies of narrative. Feminist and gender-conscious scholarship in our own times in many disciplines (from language studies to archaeology) makes new readings of these myths imperative.

The Táin was originally an oral text, or rather, and this is crucial to understanding the editorial problems it constitutes, a collection of interrelated and interlaced tales. These existed long before they first took

Phases (in cross-section)	The Formation of Political and Cultural Ideologies
Feminist Rereadings 1970–	Features: • Reading for "traces" • Reading deconstructively • Resistant readings • Focus on marginalized women characters • Epistemologically and hermeneutically reflexive readings
Modern Ireland **c. 1800–2000** **Celtic Revival** • Irish literary renaissance, 1890–1922 • Language revival, 1880 • Young Ireland movement, 1842–46	Features: • Political and cultural nationalism • Philology-led recovery and translation of Irish traditions • Sanitization, bowdlerization of myth • Construction of Celticism and sentimentalism (after Arnold) • Quest for a shaped narrative • Assimilation to Christian, Greek, and Roman models of "epic"
Defeat of the Gaelic Order • Williamite victory, 1690 • Tudor Plantation—late 1600s	Features: • Proscription of Irish under the Penal Laws • The *Aisling* tradition (coded political poetry using the tropes of Sovereignty)
Christianization 432 A.D.: **Patrick and Palladius**	Features: • Euhemerization of myths • Oral poetry written in Irish • Laws written in Irish • Influence of Greek and Roman myth and law
Celtic Stratum (Dates uncertain: a series of migrations beginning from perhaps 1000 B.C.E.)	Features: • Warrior myths—pastoral in focus • Sun gods • Sovereignty given a political face
Pre-Celtic Stratum (Hypotheses based on what is not replicated in Continental Celticism)	Features: • Sovereignty • Land- and water-based female deities • Matricentered • Contractual heterosexuality

Archaeology of a Myth-System

literary form and were committed to writing, probably around the eighth century. In its most ancient written form, it exists as fragments in fifteen manuscripts ranging in date from the eleventh to nineteenth centuries (Smyth 1988:142–5). The two main medieval manuscripts used by Kinsella (the most recent and authoritative edition) are *Lebor na hUidre*, often referred to as *The Book of the Dun Cow*, compiled in a textually flawed manuscript by the monks at Clonmacnoise in the twelfth century, and a later, fourteenth-century manuscript, *The Yellow Book of Lecan*. Modern reconstructions tend to have to be more than translations; they are more like creative reworkings, and this has permitted a degree of both conscious and unconscious distortion and ideological massaging.[13] Just how many cognate texts were necessarily imported into his translation of *The Táin* to make the text more coherent, motivated, and comprehensible is made clear in the textual notes supplied with Kinsella's translation (1969:255–83).

The problem with the translations that are available as a result of philological recovery and rediscovery in the late nineteenth and early twentieth centuries is that such translations accorded with current notions of epic literature drawn from the epics of Greece and Rome and with current moral standards (Tymoczko 1982, 1987; Marcus 1970). These versions of the nature of the epic genre performed the function of straitjackets. As a result, the comedy of the Ulster cycle and its very different version of human sexuality were deliberately obscured, sanitized, and made serious (Tymoczko 1987:90; Clark 1991). Standish O'Grady deliberately rewrote episodes in *The Táin* to accord with contemporary sentimental, moral, and nationalist taste (Marcus 1970:22–6, 35). Furthermore, some nineteenth-century philologists and ethnographers, tainted by programmatic nationalism, found it necessary to privilege what is noble and tragic (Tymoczko 1987:92) in the myths at the expense of what to an Anglo-Irish Victorian ear might seem comic, crude, sexually uninhibited, or less than civilized. It comes, then, as no surprise to find Lady Gregory sanitizing the departures from Victorian decorum of King Conchobar's mother, Ness, in these terms: "Now Ness, that was at one time the quietest and kindest of the women of Ireland, had got to be unkind and treacherous because of an unkindness that had been done to her, and she planned to get the kingdom away from Fergus for her own son" (Gregory [1902] 1970:21).

Such prose works to preclude a reading that sees such (female) interference in the political process as legitimate and to encode versions of feminine conduct congruent with Victorian codes. These interests, then, Victorian morality and moral seriousness on the one hand and nationalism on the other, contributed to the difficulties of Irish epic being assimilated into the canon of Western literature, especially in the nineteenth century. Its comedy grotesquerie and explicit sexuality offended Victorian sensibilities and notions of the "aesthetic." The wider European context of production of nineteenth- and early-twentieth-century translations of this material is also relevant. Outside Catholic Ireland (and an Ireland for which Catholicism was one among several convenient markers of difference from the colonial oppressor), the work of deprivileging the master-myth status of Christianity and reading it as one among many fertility myths was occurring (Frazer's *Golden Bough* began its monumental publication history in 1890 and was finally completed in 1915), and interest in matriarchy had existed in ethnological and anthropological circles for half a century before that in the work of such writers as J. J. Bachofen (*Das Mutterrecht*, 1861), Lewis Henry Morgan (*Ancient Society*, 1871), and Friedrich Engels (*The Origin of the Family, Private Property and the State*, 1884). Androcentric versions of fertility myths were common in the early part of the century, and in particular Frazer's decentering of goddesses in favor of a focus on dying god figures in ancient fertility myths is a symptom of this. The sea-change from the point of view of feminism did not occur until the 1970s. Then we find an awareness that hero tales are often associated with colonial expansion and legitimating conquered territories and that the symbology of such narratives typically underwent a significant and gendered change. The shift in focus of these feminists was welcome, but their reliance on military theories of the demotion of goddesses was probably overly dramatic and overstated. In the case of the Irish myths, the "takeover" was probably more gradual and the process more syncretic than is often suggested.

Reading for Traces/Reading Slant

To read the myths of ancient Ireland for what they reveal of the pre-Christian attitudes to women and the body is to read for traces and to read against the grain, and to penetrate to a stratum of the tale that underlies its heroic, dying-god surface. *The Táin*, as Condren points out (1989:226 n. 73), both explicitly and implicitly functions as a satiric denigration of goddesses, an ironic antifeminist poem (Kinsella, 1969: xii) and as an exaltation of male bonding and warfare. Sanday (1981: 135–60) argues that historically, colonialist discourses (among others) radically disrupted matrifocal ones, and certainly this set of stories has as its focus the hero's success in battle and a reading and naming of the land in terms of these military exploits. But the text contains within

it certain tensions that make clear its reliance on, and incomplete transformation of, older narratives. What is remarkable about the text, and
it is more obvious in Kinsella's translation than in many others, is that
despite the focus on male heroic action, the text "continually turns" on
the "strong and diverse personalities" (Kinsella 1969:xv) of a cast of
women characters, who undoubtedly (Kinsella expresses a modicum of
reserve on this point) take their power from their roles in this and other
cognate texts as goddess figures,[14] and specifically as Sovereignty goddesses.

These myths, I think, may be read as implicitly contesting hierar-
chically organized binarisms, especially that which posits that women
are universally assigned to the low ground of nature and men to the
high ground of culture (Ortner 1974) or that male dominance is
achieved through woman's symbolic association with nature (Herbert
1991:20). As with Australian Aboriginal culture (and many other matrifocal cultures; see Sanday 1981), nature, the earth, is the religious
focus, and much of this poem functions as *dindshenchas* (the lore of
place-names), designed to demonstrate how particular landforms came
about and why they are sacred. It is partly the sacralization of the earth
that ensures what Sanday refers to as "a reciprocal flow between the
power of nature and the power inherent in women" (1981:5). The
scripts offered women and men in the discourses of Irish culture (actual
contemporary scripts are very different—unhappily) go much further
than Sanday suggests, however, and enact a contractual heterosexual
exchange, based not on "the triumph of authority, but on mutual respect and cooperation" (Herbert 1991:20) and are based on the analogy
of the cultivator and the soil and the impossibility in that relationship
of anything other than a mutuality of gift-giving. Furthermore, the
metaphor of sexual congress freely and mutually engaged in appears to
have been a highly important symbolic vehicle for expressing this contract. It should be noted, however, that the utopic character of this
metaphor in both literature and in what we know of ancient Irish history is a model rather than a realizable modus vivendi.

Disruption of a free contractual exchange, which usually takes the
form of Cúchulainn turning his back on offers of assistance or sexuality
from female deities or seizing his sexual pleasures by force (as with Aife),
is what the narrative invariably codes as etiological.[15] This is well illustrated by the Derdriu story. Maria Tymoczko's reading (1985–86) of
various redactions of the tale points specifically to the animal and pastoral metaphors in the earliest version of the tale and to the complex
interweaving of desire and death symbolism (signaled by complex use
of red/black/white signifiers). Reared in an enclosure constructed by

King Conchobar, supposedly for her own protection, Derdriu longs for escape from bondage. Her desire is initially awakened (ironically, given the outcome of the tale) by a vision of a dead calf (the Irish word *lóeg* is also used in Old Irish to mean "beloved") whose blood is being drunk by a raven on the snow. The courtship between the young lovers is conducted in terms that both highlight the pastoral context of the poem and place the focus on embodiment. The natural world and the desirable body are typically metaphors for one another in these discourses:

> The chanting of the sons of Uisliu was very sweet. Every cow or beast that heard it gave two thirds more milk. Any person hearing it was filled with peace and music. Their deeds in war were great also. . . . Besides this they were swift as hounds in the chase, killing the wild beasts in flight.
>
> While Noisiu was out there alone, therefore, she slipped out quickly to him and made as though to pass him and not recognize him.
>
> "That is a fine heifer going by," he said.
>
> "As well it might," she said. "The heifers grow big where there are no bulls."
>
> "You have the bull of this province all to yourself," he said, "the king of Ulster."
>
> "Of the two," she said, "I'd pick a game young bull like you."
>
> "You couldn't," he said. "There is Cathbad's prophecy [that because of her beauty she will bring evil on the province]."
>
> "Are you rejecting me?"
>
> "I am," he said.
>
> Then she rushed at him and caught the two ears of his head.
> (Kinsella 1969:12)

Derdriu shares with other female divinities in *The Táin* (Macha and Nes among them) a directness of approach in matters sensual and erotic, and what should be noted in this interchange is the way in which language fails to binarize and hierarchize the distinction so important in Judeo-Christian discourses between human and animal. What the archaic Irish discourse invites is deconstructive interrogation and theoretical contestation of the notion of continuity/difference between the sexual behavior of animals and humans.

What is pivotal in the outcome of the Derdriu narrative, however, is a different hierarchy, symbolized, as Tymoczko wittily argues, by her psychic reduction of status in her unwanted marriage to King Conchobar from the status of heifer to that of ram. Although the narrative has often been read and reconstructed in terms of the conventions of the courtly love tradition (especially in nineteenth- and early-twentieth-century versions of it, especially Synge's and Yeats's plays), to do this is to impose a very different paradigmatic grid on the tale. Tymoczko speculates that the significance is quite different:

> [T]he status of the conflict has dropped from bulls to sheep [sheep being less valuable "currency" than bulls] with the concomitant economic correlates regarding the importance of large stock versus small stock and their respective symbolic significance as status indicators. Having once lived with a fine "bullock" one can scarcely imagine Deirdriu settling for a [mere] "ram."
>
> The meaning of this episode is that here Deirdriu rejects the status of an animal; she chooses death rather than continue life in a sheep's role. Her last act is [she suicides by breaking her own skull] is an assertion of her human self in the only way remaining to her—the destruction of her animal body. . . . She both refuses to be dehumanized by others at the end and she refuses to be party to the human and societal destruction that could ensue from her dehumanization. (Tymoczko 1985–86:153)

While agreeing with her hierarchy, I would contest Tymoczko's coding of the animal body as negative. Body, here, is made to signify in an interconnecting web of symbols of many things: beauty (it is significant that Derdriu destroys her own most desired features—her face and body), desire (which is active and potent), psychic health, the health of the kingdom, and the frustration of the due process of real-politik that provided for contested rather than lineal kingship. It is also noteworthy that the death of her lover is not in itself a cause for her suicide, as is conventional in some courtly love tales.

The Embodied Female and Sexuality

The Táin furnishes many examples of how bodies, both male and female but especially female, are to be valued for their sexuality. In these discourses, sexuality is nonproblematic morally. Medb offers her "friendly thighs"[16] as proper and the ultimate good in a set of proposed exchanges for the Donn Cuailnge (the brown bull of Cuailnge) because of the prosperity such a loan can bring to Cruachan (modern Connaught), without jeopardizing the prosperity of Ulster. In Kinsella's translation, it is the disruption of this system of exchanges, effected by a male and based on loose talk between messengers about Medb's intentions to take by force what she cannot have through exchange, that sets the bloody events of the epic in train.[17] Medb's rebuff by Dáire (the owner of the bull) and the importance of cattle as signifiers of wealth and fertility necessitate the descent into violence. As Neumann points out ([1955] 1991:12), the more archaic the story, the less likely it is that contradictory attributes are functionally separate: she who is responsible for the fertility of the province is also responsible for carnage. At the point that her armies, resplendent and drawn from the four provinces of Ireland, are ready to march into battle against Ulster, Medb ruefully notes: "Everyone leaving a lover or a friend today will curse me. . . . This army is gathered for me" (Kinsella 1969:60).

To reduce Medb merely to the status of cattle- or fame-hungry queen is to overlook her symbolic function as a Sovereignty: fertility comes at a price. Medb, like the Morrígan/Badb,[18] both gives and destroys. In the pre-Indo-European iconography of Old Europe, Gimbutas speculates that such goddesses represents both tomb and womb (1991:305), and there is much evidence in the poem to support this.

Although Medb's offer of "friendly thighs" is not constrained by moral prohibitions as it would be in a Christian framework, such liberality should be seen as occurring in a context in which the exchange of bodies signifies not only sovereignty but also a number of ethical requirements and a certain understanding of gendered power. When Medb chooses her partner, she is represented as making demands of "equal lordship" (O'Corráin, 1984:2) in the relationship:

> I asked a harder wedding gift than any woman ever asked before from a man in Ireland—the absence of meanness and jealousy and fear.
>
> If I married a mean man our union would be wrong, because I'm so full of grace and giving. It would be an insult if I were more generous than my husband, but not if the two of us were equal in this. If my husband was a timid man our union would be just as wrong because I thrive myself, on all kinds of trouble. It is an insult for a wife to be more spirited than her husband, but not if the two are equally spirited. If I married a jealous man that would be wrong, too: I never had one man without another waiting in his shadow. (Kinsella 1969:53)

What is valued here is precisely what is valued and considered normative and ideal in the customary laws of ancient Ireland: equal lordship (Ó'Corráin 1978:2), a marriage in which not only dowries and status are equivalent, but virtue and largeness of soul are matched.[19]

The Comic, the Grotesque, and Embodiment

There are many episodes in *The Táin* that accord neither with the notion of epic as celebrating deeds of high heroism nor with the tone of high seriousness that is epic's usual mark. And often the comedy pivots on the fact of embodiment. One such episode concerns Cúchulainn's advance on Emain Macha (modern Armagh) at the age of seven, having successfully massacred the three sons of Nechta Scéne, as well as some other Ultonian warriors, and having done what few grown men could do, take alive a wild stag and some swans. Conchobar issues the order: "Naked women to him!" and Kinsella renders Cúchulainn's response thus:

> He hid his countenance. Immediately the warriors of Emain seized him and plunged him in a vat of cold water. The vat burst asunder about him. Then he was thrust in another vat and it boiled with bubbles the size of fists. He was placed at last in a third vat and warmed it till its heat and cold were equal. Then he got out and Mugain the queen gave him a blue cloak to go round him with a silver brooch in it, and a hooded tunic. And he sat on Conchubor's [sic] knee, and that was his seat ever after. (Kinsella 1969:92)

The narrative goes to extraordinary lengths to signify the hero's special supranatural powers. However, it is worth noting that in this episode, women's bodies are instrumental in quelling the reckless young war-machine, suggesting that a still powerful but earlier set of ideologies underlie those of the martial hero. In the same set of stories, and elsewhere in *The Táin*, it is made quite clear that the boy (and later the man) is capable of disposing of large numbers of opponents single-handed, so it is not in any physical sense that the women represent a threat, nor does Cúchulainn's body language have to be read as shame, as Lady Gregory does.[20] The women control the hero's "warp spasm," the frenzy that enables the heroic feats, and a phalanx of (one hundred and fifty, in Lady Gregory's account, [1902] 1970:33) "red-naked" women strip "their breasts at him" (Kinsella 1969:92). They represent a counterbalance to Cúchulainn's destructive powers. This is not to essentialize, to construe as male the act of making war and as female nurturance of life, since women/goddesses are frequently represented as violent, ruthless, and war-mongering in these tales (though historically such warrior women among the Celts seem to have been the exception rather than the rule). The women of *The Táin* are vicious, blood-thirsty, and scheming in defense of the *tuath* (tribe),[21] and, above all, proactive. Gender performances are by modern standards very fluid. What should be stressed is the situated nature of the ethics at work in the tale.

The Christian heroic reading of the tale stresses the hero's independence of the goddess. However, an alternative reading is possible, I think, one that focuses on the interdependence of mortal king (for I take Cúchulainn to be a potential ruler) and goddess. Cúchulainn is twice offered the sacred marriage, once (indirectly) by Medb (Kinsella 1969:116–7) and on another occasion by the Morrígan (Kinsella 1969: 132–3), and on each occasion he spurns it. The Morrígan appears initially to the hero as King Buan's daughter, offering herself and her assistance, and is rudely rebuffed: "It wasn't for a woman's backside I took on this ordeal" (Kinsella 1969:133). The Morrígan's identification with the animal life of the kingdom, its territorial sovereignty, is made very clear in her threat to take the form of an eel, a gray she-wolf, and a hornless red heifer in order to impede his progress. It is a threat she effects. At the climax she presides over his death in the form of a raven. The damage done to her (Cúchulainn puts out one of her eyes) and his own battle fatigue, are, however, rectified by his unwitting taking suck of her:

A great weariness fell on Cúchulainn. The Morrígan appeared to him in the shape of a squint-eyed old woman milking a cow with three teats. He asked her for a drink and she gave him milk from the first teat.

"Good health to the giver!" Cúchulainn said. "The blessing of God and man on you."

And her head was healed and made whole. She gave him milk from the second teat and her eye was made whole. She gave him milk from the third teat and her legs were made whole.

"You said you would never heal me," the Morrígan said.

"If I had known it was you I wouldn't have done it," Cúchulainn said. (Kinsella 1969:136–7)

What seems to be at issue here is the notion that Cúchulainn's warrior status cannot be maintained independently of women, and the image, the maternal/child symbiosis, of the hag giving suck to the young and temporarily defeated boy, is powerfully symbolic. Clark (1991:21–52) argues that, even more than Medb, Macha, and Derdriu, the Morrígan was the Sovereignty goddess least susceptible to being Christian-ized and patriarchalized. Clark's case (1991:1–52) is that intertexts that detail the Morrígan's instigation of the cattle raid (notably *Táin Bó Regamna* and *Echtra Nerai*) have been overlooked in modern editions because editors have tended to euhemerize the narrative and present it as a hero tale rather than as one that deals in a spirituality that is immanent in the land and expressed via metaphors of sexuality, maternity, and embodiment. The tale ends with an episode in the *dindshenchas* genre, in which the land itself is scarred by the bulls' final frenzy. The narrative parallels two dire outcomes of Cúchulainn's failure to acknowledge that he must share power with the goddess: the mortal[22] heroes leave a trail of battle landmarks, and the supranatural bulls as they battle to the death leave a series of landforms that memorialize the heroic contests. It is perhaps not accidental that, contrary to what happens in the *Dindshenchas*, where female place-names are much more common than male ones, *The Táin*, with only two exceptions, memorializes men and their battles. The more important of these exceptions concerns Medb.

Cúchulainn's ultimate showdown with Medb is averted, for a reason that is, I think, unique in epic literature: the arrival of her menses.

> Then Medb got her gush of blood.
> "Fergus," she said, "take over the shelter of shields at the rear of the men of Ireland until I relieve myself."
> "By god," Fergus said, "you have picked a bad time for this."
> "I can't help it," Medb said. "I'll die if I can't do it."
> So Fergus took over the shelter of shields at the rear of the men of Ireland and Medb relieved herself. It dug three great channels, each big enough to take a household. The place is called Fual Medba, Medb's Foul Place, ever since. Cúchulainn found her like this, but he held his hand. He wouldn't strike her from behind.
> "Spare me," Medb said.
> "If I killed you dead," Cúchulainn said, "it would only be right."
> But he spared her, not being a killer of women. He watched them all the way westward until they passed Ath, and there he stopped. He struck three blows of his sword at the stone hills nearby. The Bald-topped Hills is their name now, at Ath Luain, in answer to the three Bald-topped Hills in Meath.
> The battle was over.
> Medb said to Fergus:
> "We have had shame and shambles here today, Fergus."
> "We followed the rump of a misguiding woman," Fergus said. "It is the usual thing for a herd led by a mare to be strayed and destroyed." (Kinsella 1969:250–1)

It is important to remember that the epic functions to legitimate the rule of Ulster and to denigrate the Connaught leadership of Medb and to be aware of the probable misogynist contamination by Christian scribes. With these caveats in mind, it is nonetheless possible to engage in a resistant reading of the passage, which might involve focusing on the hyperbole of the details of Medb's menstruation and its symbolic registration not necessarily of her foulness but of her fertility. This is to reconstrue radically what the Christian misogynist scribe deems scatological and to point to the fact that menstruation is normally negatively coded in Western discourses, in much the same way as excreta, rather than as a signifier of fertility. Furthermore, I would suggest that this particular example of the dindshenchas genre is particularly significant both structurally (at the point of a frustrated climax!) and because of the rarity in *The Táin* of dindshenchas that mark sacred female places.

Macha as Sovereignty

In my reading of it, this Irish myth gives a central place to the contract at the base of heterosexual bonds, and many stories function to illustrate this, often exposing the ideal by representing its breaking-down and the disastrous consequences that follow from that. Macha, the eponymous goddess of Emain Macha (in modern times, Armagh, the preeminent seat of Catholicism in Ireland), has many incarnations in myth, legend, and pseudohistory. As in many archaic myths, the sign of antiquity of the myth is the nonspecialization of functions that are normally separated in later, allegedly "more civilized" cultures: Macha is associated with Badb and the Morrígan in the trio of goddesses that make up the Morrígan (Smyth 1988:93–4) and represents both death and rebirth/fertility. The story of Macha and her curse on the Ultonians is an instructive one: despite its transmission via the monks, and its clear misogyny, the story deals with a broken sexual contract, and the power of the goddess prevails in the story, an illustration incidentally of the way in which this particular narrative was resistant to patriarchal reformulation. As one of the *remscéla* (or fore-tales, tales leading up to the main events of *The Táin*), this story both reinforces the notion of equal lordship, which is so important to Medb in her dispute with her husband Ailil, and functions to explain why the Ulstermen are not free for some time to fight in the epic battle *The Táin* describes. Further, it is congruent with a significant intertext to be found in the *Prose Tales in the Rennes Dindshenchas* (the narrative is outlined in some detail in

Condren 1989:30–1), which details the establishment of Emain Macha as the royal court and the legitimate line of succession. The last-mentioned narrative is a graphic demonstration of what happens when a woman's right to succession of the kingship is not honored by men, and it tracks the shift in Ulster from a culture in which the contract based on trust and understanding gave place to a culture in which the right of conquest by arms is deemed to be legitimate. In this story, the rule of trust is established in Ulster by three brothers who ruled under the supervision of druids, poets, and captains and according to a series of conditions agreed between them. The contract was clearly one de-signed to ensure continuing fertility and prosperity for the group and indicate the centrality of women in the contract. The signs of the suc-cess of the rule of the king are the goddess's provision of crops, success in dyestuff (women's art), and that no woman should die in childbirth. The contract remained successfully in place until the early death of Aed Ruad. Macha, his daughter, demanded she take her father's place, which was resisted by the brothers, whereupon she fought and defeated them and ruled for her seven years. Because she deemed the contract to have been invalidated by the brothers, she made a further claim to retain the kingship. One by one, in the shape of a lepress she lay with the claim-ants and captured them, but rather than kill them (which was in her power), she forced them to build her ring fort, Emain Macha (Navan Fort). The story, then, argues a code based on contractual understand-ings, honor, and nonviolence (Condren 1989:30–1), though she was subsequently slain by an enemy of the father. The motif of the leprous, disfigured, or haglike woman who must be embraced for the kingship to be ratified is a common one in Irish narratives and one that trans-gresses what in our culture would constitute age, class, and beauty norms. While it is easy to relegate this pattern of signification to the realms of romance and fantasy, it might perhaps be read in terms of other paradigms, paradigms in which power depends on a mutuality of contracts.

Like the tale of Macha in the *Dindshenchas*, the story concerning Macha that Kinsella uses as one of the remscéla for *The Táin* gives similar prominence to the contract between a woman and a man and the consequences of breaching the contract. In this case, an argument between Macha and her husband Crunniuc[23] demonstrates the way her body ought be properly honored and contests the male "right" to the appropriation of women's bodies. Like many of the fertility figures of Irish epic, Macha offers her body (and her domestic arts) to Crunniuc to assuage the loss of his wife, and his affairs predictably flourish. It is hinted (according to Condren 1989:31) that she may have the attributes of a sun goddess:

> There was a very rich landlord in Ulster, Crunniuc mac Agnomain. He lived in a lonely place in the mountains with all his sons. His wife was dead. Once, as he was alone in the house, he saw a woman coming toward him there, and she was a fine woman in his eyes. She settled down and began working at once, as though she were well used to the house. When night came, she put everything in order without being asked. Then she slept with Crunniuc.
>
> She stayed with him for a long while afterward, and there was never a lack of food or clothes or anything else under her care. (Kinsella 1969:6)

What might be noted here is the offering by the woman of her person, her skills, and her body (in that order), the lack of courtship rituals, the uncomplicated place of sex in the transaction; it should be noted that the narrative locates the point of view in the male participant. However, just as casually noted is the *geis* (or prohibition) she puts on him: "It would be as well not to grow boastful or careless in anything you say" (Kinsella 1969:7).

The taboo calls to mind the contractual nature of their relationship: there are conditions that must be honored for her free act and his enjoyment of it to continue. Crunniuc does not abide by the conditions of their contract; he boasts that his wife can run faster than the king's horse-drawn chariot, and he is imprisoned pending proof of his boast. Macha protests that she should not run because she is pregnant:

> "It would be a heavy burden for me to go and free him now. I am full with child."
>
> "Burden?" the messenger said. "He will die unless you come."
>
> She went to the fair, and her pangs gripped her. She called out to the crowd:
>
> "A mother bore each one of you! Help me! Wait till my child is born."
>
> But she couldn't move them.
>
> "Very well," she said. "A long-lasting evil will come out of this on the whole of Ulster." (Kinsella 1969:7)

Then she raced the chariot. As the chariot reached the end of the field, she gave birth alongside it. She bore twins, a son and a daughter.

The name Emain Macha, the Twins of Macha, comes from this. As she gave birth she screamed out that all who heard that scream would suffer from the same pangs for five days and four nights in their times of greatest difficulty. This affliction, ever afterward, seized all the men of Ulster who were there that day, and nine generations after them. Five days and four nights, or five nights and four days, the pangs lasted. For nine generations any Ulsterman in those pangs had no more strength than a woman on the bed of labor. Only three classes of people were free from the pangs of Ulster: the young boys of Ulster, the women, and Cúchulainn. (Kinsella 1969:7–8).

What might be noted here, I think, is the construction of the female pregnant body as both frail and its opposite at different moments: in her prime and most strikingly, she is the robust pregnant chariot-racer, the opposite of "frail, imperfect, unruly, and unreliable" (Grosz 1994: 23). In her time of birthing, though, the text underscores her weakness. Condren offers several interpretations of this episode (1989:33–5) and traces Macha's evolution from mother goddess to consort, to daughter, and from fertility goddess to war goddess, and sees in this process a subtle shifting of meaning in line with patriarchalization of the figure of Macha.

Cúchulainn as Lover/Hero

If there is a single continuous feature of Irish literature, and a feature that draws readers to it as a body, it is probably what Vivian Mercier identified in *The Irish Comic Tradition*—the tradition of comedy that stretches back from contemporary literature to the earliest narratives we have. This is not to say that what is perceived as comedic does not change from age to age. It clearly does: there is a difference between the comedy of *The Táin* (one cannot be sure what Iron Age men found amusing)[24] and that of Brian Merriman or James Joyce (who are much closer to our own culture). However, what these writers have in common, according to Mercier, is their grotesquerie, their tendency to hyperbole and irony. I perceive another common element specific to the treatment of gender issues in these writers, that of a refusal to take relations between men and women, and the body itself, too seriously. Until the advent of Kinsella's translation in 1969, the nature of the comedy of *The Táin* had been obscured by too-solemn renderings; its reliance on hyperbole, exaggeration, and grotesquerie adds much to our understanding of gender relations. Cúchulainn's hero-body is frequently described both at rest and in battle frenzy (in his "warp spasm"), and although it could be concluded that Cúchulainn's posturings are those of a narcissist, what is striking is his consciousness of giving pleasure to the women (and men) and the generous interchange of awe and delight between the admirers and the admired body:

> Cúchulainn came out the next morning to view the armies and display his noble fine figure to the matrons and virgins and young girls and poets and bards. He came out to display himself by day because he felt the unearthly shape he had shown them the night before had not done him justice. And certainly the youth Cúchulainn mac Sualdaim was handsome as he came to show his form to the armies. You would think he had three distinct heads of hair. . . . He had four dimples in each cheek—yellow, green, crimson and blue—and seven bright pupils, eye-jewels, in each kingly eye. Each foot had seven toes and each hand seven fingers, the nails with the grip of a hawk's claw or a gryphon's clench. He wore his festive raiment that day. . . .
>
> The Connacht women climbed on the soldiers, and the Munster women climbed on their own men, to see Cúchulainn. (Kinsella 1969:157–8)

I have quoted at length to make the point that there is much here that is excessive for a hero tale. More is being established than the hero's prowess and status as a warrior. His body has become in the narrative a signifier that renders public and communicable his sacred standing, and that it does so in terms so extravagantly nonnaturalistic is, I suggest, a sign of the narrative's conscious departure from more familiar and established signifying systems. The framing audience of women stresses both their existence as warriors in their own right and the sexual pleasure to be derived from the male beauty that Cúchulainn's raiment and body constitute. On another occasion, much is explicitly made of Cúchulainn's ability to arouse desire in Scáthach's daughter Uathach, and it is considered natural by the mother that her daughter should sleep with such a one. This relationship continues while he is trained by Scáthach as a warrior. The powers of the hero and the lover are certainly not mutually exclusive as is normative in mainstream Western hero tales. Indeed, victory seems to be signified by, and to be ensured by, honoring the sexual bond. Cúchulainn, in his hubris, chooses to stand alone. A feminist reading cannot but appreciate the significant place of women in this sexual economy, even if the hero in his naiveté does not. And such a reader is aware that s/he reads the myth in this way very much against the grain of its transmission and reception over twelve centuries, and probably much longer than that.

Conclusion

The differing politics of patriarchy, of nationalism, of class, and of gender have for over a millennium resulted in repressing, and almost effectively erasing, an intriguing body of mythic narratives. Irish myth represents the body, heterosexuality, and even homosexual relations in
ways that do not conform to the mind/body, spirit/body dualisms and
asymmetrical binaries so central to mainstream Western thinking.[25] In
these discourses, the body is not coded as superior to the animal realm,
or as a source of moral defilement, or as a distraction from the enterprise of war (especially war in defense of a territory). Rather, it is seen
as sacred, as analogous with the earth and water, both figures of fertility. Maleness and femaleness, if coded as antagonistic, are never unproblematically so, and when they are, one becomes aware of paradigmatic tensions and interference by monks in what seems to be an older
story, and one that is difficult to disentangle from its heroic and Christian reworkings. A resistant reading, one that attempts to discard the
distorting lens of Christian ideology and is alert to gender, especially if
one's focus is the most misogynist passages, exposes a variety of tensions in the narrative. To read such discourses resistantly, critically,
and in deconstructive ways is to begin to understand that the versions
of gendered power that seem natural and universal in our culture may
not always have been so and to understand perhaps how and why
such myths came to occupy a marginal place in Western culture.
Myths like these, which challenge cultural and religious hegemonies,
need to reenter the cultural conversations of our times. Such myths
raise questions about the heterosexual exchange, and more radically
about sexual difference and performance, sexual specificity, and gender
roles as they may have existed in one of the earliest documented fringe
Western cultures. *The Táin* can be seen to constitute a set of narratives
in which spirituality and sexuality, and male and female, are conceived
of not as polarities and binaries but as complementary and interdepen-
dent.

Notes

1. The Ulster Cycle, also known as *Táin Bó Cúailnge*, is referred to
throughout as *The Táin*.
2. This project has been to a large extent inspired by Julia Kristeva's
semiotic deconstruction of images of maternity and her call for a new post-
Christian and post-virginal discourse of maternity in her article "Stabat
Mater" (1986).

3. For a postmodern feminist rereading of the sacrality of the female body, see Raphael 1996.

4. Rosalind Coward (1983:9) argues that modern definitions of sex, developed in the second half of the nineteenth century, and especially in the social sciences (which provided the foundation of Marxism and psychoanalysis), were crucially predicated on essentializing gender concepts and the assumption of the existence of matriarchy and patriarchy.

5. A fine critical account of the debates is to be found in Coward 1983, especially chapters 1–3.

6. Aitchison (1987) specifically mentions a Monaghan monastery of the early seventh century and points to the particular richness of vernacular literature in the Ulster province.

7. For an intriguing feminist account of Emer, the first wife of Cuchulainn, that focuses on her verbal prowess, her enmeshment in patriarchal constraints, and her resistance to them, see Findon 1997.

8. By way of contrast, it should be noted that Lady Gregory's account of Cuchulainn's birth takes the marriage to Sualtim son of Roig for granted, and it begins the tale.

9. There is much debate on this matter. Clark argues that it is set earlier than the fifth century, basing her view on the date at which Emain Macha functioned as a capital (1991:190). Aitchison (1987:106) cites archaeological evidence contesting the historical reality of Emain Macha as a royal residence or even as a fortified settlement, and says that it did not function beyond about 100 B.C.E.

10. I have adopted Kinsella's orthography.

11. The River Boyne is a particularly sacred place in Irish prehistory because of its association with the cow goddess, Boand, and as the site of ancient fertility rituals at Samain, and of large prehistoric tumuli; it is also significant in the historical period as the location of the decisive Williamite defeat of Gaelic culture in 1690. It is also worth noting that cattle were not only the major item of exchange and currency but signified the acme in wealth and fertility in Irish prehistoric tales.

12. The gift of an intoxicating drink (wine, mead, or ale) is highly significant in Irish myths of sovereignty where the recipient is usually the king. The gift is offered by the goddess disguised as an ugly hag. The acceptance and drinking of the potion, and often lying with the woman (who is usually transformed into a ravishing bride) are the tests and rituals of kingship, which is conceived of in terms of a sacred marriage between the human political king and the tutelary goddess of the kingdom. Bowen (1975) notes the etymological connection between the words *flaith* ("sovereign" or "sovereignty") and *laith* ("beer"). It might be speculated that in this detail in *The Táin* something survives from a earlier stage of human knowledge when the male role in reproduction was not understood.

13. It is possible too that if the scribes were monks, as Hutton suggests, the inscriptions of the tales were influenced (even unconsciously) by familiar Greco-Roman genres.

14. Charles Bowen (1975) makes a strong case for reading Medb as a goddess and divinity rather than as merely a human queen and for seeing Irish epic as incorporating the discourses of epic, history, and myth in in-

terdisplinary ways (the categories are those of much later epistemologies). He argues that it was the eighth- and nineth-century redactors of the Ulster Cycle, the monks, who effected her euhemerization and diminution: she is diminished by being reduced from the status of goddess to that of masterful woman and historical figure. Bowen further argues that the monks' "robust antifeminism" (p 30) is responsible for the bad press she is given in the action.

15. The rape of Aife, the forced union of Finnabair, and the rejection of the Morrigan are other examples.

16. On another occasion, Medb offers her both her own and her daughter's bodies as part of a bargain with Ferdia (Kinsella 1969:169).

17. Rosalind Clark (1991), who otherwise admires Kinsella's edition immensely, argues that Kinsella is unconsciously influenced by Standish O'Grady's (and subsequent translators') tendency to euhemerize and secularize a spiritual narrative. In particular, she believes that Kinsella underplays the role of the Morrigan in being the indirect cause of the events of the cattle raid. In *Táin Bó Regamna*, she mates a cow with the Brown Bull; subsequently the calf of this union is worsted by the White Bull and calls on its father, whereupon Medb swears to see the two bulls fight.

18. Clark 1991.

19. Findon (1997:40), in her reading of courtship tales and especially the courtship of Emer and Cuchulainn, argues that the arcane riddling games that constitute a prelude to commitment are an index of the lovers' "equality in mental and verbal dexterity."

20. Lady Gregory's accounting for Cúchulainn's gesture as 'shame' (Gregory [1902]1970:33) is a good example of a narrowly Christian/Victorian reading.

21. Medb is prevented by Fergus from murdering 3,000 Galeóin whom she sees as a potential threat to her province (Kinsella 1969:66).

22. Cuchulainn, though part god, is mortal.

23. Sometimes transcribed as Crunnhuc or Cruind. I have used Kinsella's orthography, unless specifically dealing with another writer's version of the spelling.

24. Tymoczko (1987) gives an account of the difficulties of translating archaic humour.

25. A most striking attempt to read bodies in terms other than the binaries of the mainstream philosophical and Judaeo-Christian traditions is that by Liz Grosz (1994).

References

Aitchison, N. B. 1987. The Ulster Cycle: Heroic Image and Historical Reality. *Journal of Medieval History* 13 (2): 87–116.

Bowen, Charles. 1975. Great-Bladdered Medb: Mythology and Invention in the *Táin bó Cualinge. Eire–Ireland* 10 (4): 14–34.

Clark, Rosalind. 1991. *The Great Queens: Irish Goddesses from the Morrígan to Cathleen Ní Houlihan.* Gerrards Cross, England: Colin Smythe.

Condren, Mary. 1989. *The Serpent and the Goddess: Women, Religion and Power in Celtic Ireland.* San Francisco: Harper and Row.

Coughlan, Patricia. 1991. "Bog Queens": The Representation of Women in the Poetry of John Montague and Seamus Heaney. In Johnson and Cairns 1991:88–111.

Coward, Rosalind. 1983. *Patriarchal Precedents: Sexuality and Social Relations.* London: Routledge and Kegan Paul.

Devlin-Glass, Frances. 1997. The Fathers as Gatekeepers: Ancient Irish Laws and the Divorce Referendum of 1995. *Canadian Woman Studies/Les Cahiers de la Femme* 17 (3): 11–5.

Dillon, Myles. 1946. *The Cycles of the Kings.* London: Oxford University Press.

du Bois, Page. 1988. *Sowing the Body: Psychoanalysis and Ancient Representations of Women.* Chicago: University of Chicago Press.

Findon, Joanne. 1997. *A Woman's Words: Emer and Female Speech in the Ulster Cycle.* Toronto: University of Toronto Press.

Freud, Sigmund 1966–74. *Totem and Taboo.* Vol. 13. *Moses and Monotheism.* Vol. 23. In *The Standard Edition of the Complete Psychological Works of Sigmund Freud,* trans. J. Strachey in collaboration with Anna Freud. London: Hogarth Press.

Geertz, Clifford. 1973. *The Interpretation of Cultures, Selected Essays.* London: Hutchinson.

Gimbutas, Marija. 1991. *The Civilization of the Goddess: The World of Old Europe.* San Francisco: Harper.

Glob, P. V. 1969. *The Bog People: Iron-Age Man Preserved.* Trans. Rupert Bruce-Mitford. London: Faber and Faber.

Gregory Augusta. 1970 [1902]. Cuchulainn of Muirthemne: The Story of the Men of the Red Branch of Ulster, 5th ed. Gerrards Cross, England: Smythe.

Grosz, Liz. 1994. Volatile Bodies: Toward a Corporeal Feminism, St. Leonards, New South Wales, Australia: Allen & Unwin.

Herbert, Máire 1991. Celtic Heroine? The Archaeology of the Deirdre Story. In Johnson and Cairns 1991:13–22.

Hutton, Ronald. 1991. *The Pagan Religions of the Ancient British Isles: Their Nature and Legacy.* Oxford: Blackwell.

Johnson, Toni O'Brien, and David Cairns (eds.). 1991. *Gender in Irish Writing.* Milton Keynes: Open University Press.

Kinsella, Thomas (ed). 1969. *The Táin: Translated from the Irish Epic Táin Bó Cúailnge.* Dublin: Oxford University Press.

Kristeva, Julia 1986. Stabat Mater. In *The Kristeva Reader.* Ed. Toril Moi. Oxford: Blackwell: 160–86.

Lehane, Brendan. 1994. *Early Celtic Christianity.* London: Constable.

Lerner, Gerda. 1986. *The Creation of Patriarchy.* New York: Oxford University Press.

Mac Cana, Proinsias. 1956. Aspects of the Theme of King and Goddess in Irish Literature. *Etudes Celtiques* 7:357–413 and 8:59–65.

Marcus, Phillip L. 1970. *Standish O'Grady.* Lewisburg, Pa.: Bucknell University Press.

Mercier, Vivian. 1962. *The Irish Comic Tradition.* Oxford: Clarendon Press.

Neumann, Erich. [1955] 1991. *The Great Mother: An Analysis of the Archetype* Trans. Ralph Mannheim. Princeton: Princeton University Press.

O Cathasaigh, Donal. 1982. The Cult of Brigid: A Study of Pagan-Christian

Syncretism in Ireland. In J. J.Preston (ed.), *Mother Worship*. Chapel Hill: University of North Carolina Press: 75–94.

Ó'Corráin, Donncha. 1984. Women in Early Irish Society. In Margaret MacCurtain and Donncha Ó'Corráin (eds.), *Women in Irish Society: The Historical Dimension*. Arlen House: 1–13.

Ó'Corráin, Donnchadh. 1985. Marriage in Early Ireland. In Art Cosgrove, (ed.), *Marriage in Ireland*. Dublin: College Press: 5–22.

Ortner, Sherry B. 1974. Is Female to Male as Nature Is to Culture? In M. Z. Rosaldo and L. Lamphere (eds.), *Women, Culture and Society*. Stanford: Stanford University Press: 67–88.

Power, Patrick. 1976. *Sex and Marriage in Ancient Ireland*. Cork, Ireland: Mercier Press.

Raphael, Melissa. 1996. *Thealogy and Embodiment: The Post-Patriarchal Reconstruction of Female Sacrality*. Sheffield, England: Sheffield Academic Press.

Rolleston, T. W. 1990. *Myths and Legends Series: Celtic*. London:Studio Editions. (Facsimile edition (n.d.–1934?).

Sanday, Peggy Reeves. 1981. *Female Power and Male Dominance: On the Origins of Sexual Inequality*. Cambridge, England: Cambridge University Press.

Smyth, Daragh. 1988. *A Guide to Irish Mythology*, Dublin: Irish Academic Press.

Synge, John Millington. [1910] 1964. *Deirdre of the Sorrows*. In *J. M. Synge's Plays, Poems and Prose*. London: J. M. Dent.

Tymoczko, Maria. 1982. Strategies for Integrating Irish Epic into European Literature. *Dispositio* 7:123–40.

———. 1983. Translating the Old Irish Epic *Táin bó Cúailnge*: Political Aspects. *Pacific Quarterly Moana* 8 (2):6–21.

———. 1985. Unity and Duality: A Theoretical Perspective on the Ambivalence of Celtic Goddesses. In Paul Jefferiss and William J. Mahon (eds.), *Proceedings of the Harvard Celtic Colloquium* 5:22–37.

———. 1985–86. Animal Imagery in *Loinges MacnUislenn*. *Studia Celtica* 20–21:145–66.

———. 1987. Translating the Humour in Early Irish Hero Tales: A Polysystems Approach. *New Comparison. A Journal of Comparative and General Literary Studies* 3:83–103.

———. 1994. *The Irish Ulysses*. Berkeley, Calif.: University of California Press.

Yeats, William Butler. [1907] 1952. *Deirdre*. In *The Collected Plays of W. B. Yeats*. London: Macmillan.

Part Three

Interrogating Patriarchy

6

Between the Tariqa and the Shari'a

The Making of the Female Self

Amila Butorovic

This essay discusses the ways Muslim women have configured their spirituality within the Sufi tradition of Islam. While it agrees with previous studies that argue that Sufism allows for a much more individualistic spiritual growth than mainstream religious teachings, the essay attempts to problematize these mainly phenomenological views of Sufi inclusiveness that do not take into consideration the historical complexities associated with the emergence and development of the Sufi path. The essay argues that Sufi practices have always been in a dialectical relationship with the dominant religious discourse and, as such, have reflected many of its social ambiguities and practices, including those concerned with gender relations. Therefore, Sufi women's participation in the mystical path has never been a simple one: rather, it has been predicated on their ability to navigate through the social constructions—Sufi and non-Sufi alike—of gender and public/private space. In that process, women mystics have left a powerful legacy that adds to the Sufi path a new metaphoric depth and a great symbolic diversity yet does not effect in any transformative way Muslim women's social status.

It has been a commonplace to treat Sufism—the mystical branch of Islam—as the most inclusive teaching within Islamic tradition. Its appeal to the unity of creation and its tendencies to reach out in dialogic terms to other religious traditions have rendered Sufism (*tasawwuf*) an important trajectory for interreligious dialogue in medieval as well as contemporary times.[1]

Indeed, from a phenomenological perspective, Sufism is an alternative voice in Islam. It personifies its message by positing every human being at the beginning and end of creation. "God created Adam in His own image," states a holy tradition. This individualized cosmogony predicates a cosmology in which every soul reflects the perfect modality of the universe. Hence a backward movement to the purity of being. Hence a personification of macrocosm through a return of each individual soul to its source of origin. As such, *tasawwuf* negates mediation and affirms cognition in sensory and/or gnostic terms.

A necessity to know—oneself primarily—emanates from the very act of creation, as confirmed by a holy saying: "I [God] was a hidden treasure and I wanted to be known, so I created the world." According to Nasr's interpretation, "the Universal Man [*sic*] is the mirror in which the Divine Names and Qualities are fully reflected and through which the purpose of creation itself is fulfilled" (1994:138). In other words, the epistemic relationship between God and the world is maintained by the world's existential continuity: as long as God makes us be, he wants us to know him/ourselves according to our state of creation. Michel de Certeau's observation in the context of Christian mysticism can be usefully applied to its Islamic counterpart:

> For mysticism, unlike theology, it is not a matter of reconstructing a particular, coherent set of statements organized according to "truth" criteria; and, unlike theosophy, there is no interest in letting the violent order of the world reveal itself in the form of general account (which makes personal experience irrelevant), but it is a matter of dealing with ordinary language (not the technical sectors) from an inquiry that questions the possibility of transforming that language into a network of allocutions and present alliances. . . . I and *thou*: two terms whose difference, regained and maintained, will be lost in the relation that posits them. (1986:90)

Ideally, then, Sufism denounces the categories of social differentiation as objectified through Islamic legal thinking: there are no slaves or orphans, no elite or uneducated masses, no male or female roles. It is humanistic insofar as it bypasses the authority of the religious institutions and identifies all human beings as the loci of divine essence. Homocentrism is a touchstone of theocentrism. The former precedes the latter, ontologically as well as epistemically. The Sufi demand on its followers, then, is the process of re-cognition of the divine pith stored in the innermost fibers of our body. "When you seek God, seek Him in your heart," said the fourteenth-century Anatolian poet Yunus Emre (d. c.1320), "He is not in Jerusalem, nor in Mecca, nor in the hajj." (Schimmel 1975:106). Similarly, the great master of Islamic Spain Ibn ʿArabi (d. 1240) speaks of the insignificance of the outward form—that is, institutionalized religion—in relation to the purity of inner love shared by the unity of creation (Shah 1968:80):

> Now I am called the shepherd of the desert gazelles
> Now a Christian monk
> Now a Zoroastrian.
> The Beloved is Three, yet One:
> Just as the three are in reality one.

If the Sufi teachings were set to challenge the established categories of social differentiation—and in many way this is indicated by the fact that Sufi orders often bring together people coming from different economic, ethnic, or racial backgrounds—what is relevant here is their effect on gender as a social category. In other words, as a social phenomenon, Sufism was bound to renegotiate the place and role of women within its teachings and practices. Its dynamic dialogue with the scriptural sources—the Quran and the *hadîth* (the sayings of Muhammad)—opened new possibilities for articulating alternative, spiritually based frameworks for gender relations. New demands and commitments were made with respect to the Quran. Lings writes:

> If it be asked, with reference to our basic symbolism, what form does the tidal wave take, the answer is that it takes above all the form of a book, namely the Qur'ân. The Sufis speak of "seeking to be drowned" (*istighraq*) in the verses of the Qur'ân which are, according to one of the most fundamental doctrines of Islam, the Uncreated Word of God. (1977:25)

The drowning in the Book implies completeness, an unbroken confirmation of one's spiritual commitment. The Quran makes such a demand on both men and women in equally explicit terms: in the chapter on women (33:35), the Quran says the following:

> For Muslims men and Muslim women
> for believing men and believing women

for devout men and devout women
for truthful men and truthful women
for men and women who are patient and constant
for men and women who are humble
for men and women who give in charity
for men and women who fast and deny themselves
for men and women who engage much in praising God
for them all God has prepared forgiveness and great reward.

Thus the Quranic revelatory paradigm clearly binds, not only in ethical but in ritual terms, both men and women in a profound, unquestionable manner, rendering their merits in accordance with inner/outer submission. The private and the public, the inner and the outer, are considered equally relevant sites for the attainment of knowledge. Yet this kind of bifurcated functionality, leaving profound effects on gender relations, had been associated with the Quran even before Sufism readdressed it. Knowledge, Foucault has taught us, is a discursive category that cannot be dissociated from power. Laying claim on knowledge about divine messages was the Islamic polity's strategy of control and governance. The "outer" of the Quranic was appropriated and objectified by the male learned élite—the *ulama*—in the centuries following Muhammad's revelations. Though one should by no means underestimate the pedagogical power that women may have possessed in the confined spaces of their homes—the "inner" practice—the fact remains that they had no prescriptive participation in the legal and theological discourse of the male élite (Mernissi 1991).

Furthermore, Sunni law espouses the community consensus (*ijma*) in an attempt to extend the boundaries of divine ethics beyond the explicit rules and regulations mentioned in the sacred sources (the Quran and the Prophetic Sunna). The legal history is thus shaped as an interplay between divine authority and human (male) intervention, that is, between the transcendental truth as embodied in revelation and historically determined, male reasoning. It is a product of centurieslong debates of the *ulama* on how to objectify the universality of divine ethics in the particularities of human conduct. The existing social patterns were not ignored: thus, as Leila Ahmed argues (1991), the legal discourse on gender represents a triumphant validation of the patriarchal order, despite the Quranic attempts to introduce corrective practices into the Arab society of the time.

On the other hand, as Barbara Stowasser points out, the legal tradition could not erase the influence that the women of the Quran exerted on the popular lore and imagination (1994:22). The stories of the wives and mothers of different prophets and notable leaders occupy much space in the exegetical and hagiographic literature in medieval Islam. Among them, Eve (who, incidentally, is not blamed for the Fall according to the Islamic teaching), Mary, and Zulaykha perhaps take the most central roles. Likewise, what we know of Muhammad's mother Amina; his wives, primarily Khadija and Ayesha; and his daughters, especially Fatima—all of whom we know through the fragmented narratives of the sacred texts—serve as examples of righteous behavior, devoted, supportive and kind. The stories about them are laden with didactic intent, so much so that their symbolic foregrounding and backgrounding aims to determine the social responsibilities for Muslim women of all times and places. Thus, though women are never bearers of divine message or active agents in its doctrinal articulations, women's roles are, in discursive terms, quite heavily charged.

It is therefore necessary to view the emergence of Sufism as dialectically bound to this mainstream climate in Islamic practices and ideals. To assume, then, that the Sufi path wiped out gender biases would be simplistic. Medieval Islamic polity was strongly patriarchal, and even though one cannot but acknowledge the ability of women to reach spiritual fulfillment in the privacy of their homes or partake in spiritual and religious education of themselves and others, history is largely silent on these matters. As Stowasser writes:

> While the pairing of specific key Qur'ânic concepts as antonyms or metonyms and tropes of each other led to mutually enforced semantic extensions of the concepts' original meaning, women's secluded space, concealing clothing, and unfitness for public activity emerged as three powerful determinants in the medieval Islamic paradigm on women's societal role. (1994:98–99)

On what grounds, then, can we hypothesize that Sufism opened new grounds for women to worship and love God? Was Sufism indeed, to borrow de Certeau's phrase, "a new space with new mechanisms?" Intimately related to this is the question of sources that mediate between us and the women mystics, particularly in light of the fact that our knowledge is mostly based on accounts about women by men rather than accounts by women themselves. In that process of mediation, what criteria in hagiographic literature were operative so as to acknowledge, to put it in Bruneau's terms, "individual resistance and attempts to assert subjectivity within the dominant definitions of 'femininity' " (1998:17)? In reading and interpreting the medieval sources one can hypothesize the following: rather than introducing "a new mechanism,"

Sufism allowed women to transform their homebound "orthopraxy" into a symbol of Sufi "orthodoxy." In other words, Sufism imbued women with the power to treat their socially constructed space as the principle site of mystical devotion and, in turn, remetaphorize the meaning of *islam*—submission. The transformation was therefore experiential, not societal. As Judith Bennet argues in her reading of European history, maintaining a critical distinction between history-as-continuity and history-as-transformation allows us to problematize women's experiences without losing sight of the patriarchal equilibrium (Bennet 1997: 73–4). In the Sufi tradition, women mystics' participation signaled a widening of the interpretive scope of both mainstream and Sufi teachings but did not generate a gender-based disruption in the social order of either.

In that sense, no specifically female history of Sufism can be outlined. Instead, there is a general history of this tradition within which women, by pushing and changing the limits of personal piety, were sufficiently empowered to act as agencies of reinscription of the traditional symbols of belief.

In his study on early Islamic mysticism, Michael Sells (1996) succinctly identifies three main phases in the historical development of Sufism: the early phase of the eighth century in which spirituality grounded in the Scriptural tradition gains a new ascetic momentum antithetical to the corruption and wealth of the expanding Islamic empire; the formative period of the ninth and tenth centuries, which saw the rise of Sufi literature and a gradual systematization of Sufi thought; and the eleventh century, the period of institutionalization of Sufi followers in the so-called *tariqa* orders and an increasingly speculative nature of Sufi thought as exemplified in the writings of al-Ghazali (d. 1111), Rumi (d. 1273) and Ibn 'Arabi.

Characteristic of the mystical tradition, then, is its progressive systematization, its shift from being a cry of individual piety to becoming a competing discourse and an institutionalized movement—the *tariqa*—credited with cementing the faith as well as spreading the word beyond the existing boundaries of the Islamic empire. Another facet of bifurcation occurred: though originally perceived as antithetical, the *tariqa* (the Sufi path) and the *sharia* (the legal/social path) evolved to be complementary and, in combination, reflected the inward and the outward manifestations of Truth (the *haqiqa*).

Ironically, from the perspective of gender relations, this kind of historical progression is not unlike the classical history of Islam: a spiritual emancipation as a renegotiation of social inequalities gradually giving in to more institutionalized forms of worship and the formation of strict patriarchal hierarchies. Though not exclusively, the *tariqas*, in centering around the spiritual authority of a sheikh through the principle of *ta-wajjuh* (mutual concentration), became increasingly male-oriented as fraternities par excellence. Occasionally we do read about *tariqas* that allowed the participation of women, like the Bektashi order in Turkey (Birge 1965:200–202) or some that were headed by female sheikhs in Mamluk Egypt (Schimmel 1975:432), but the great majority had an-drocentric foundations: so much so that the popular imagination thrived on stories about the formation of erotic and spiritual bonds among the participating men (Schimmel 1979:140).

Yet with its initial thrust to view the microcosmos as a reflection of the macrocosmos, the Sufi path provided a necessary alternative for the spiritual empowerment of Muslim women. It encouraged them to ad-dress the issues of divine transcendence and inner purification without necessarily challenging the established norms. Hence, women mystics negotiated their way through these norms by testing the symbolic limits of the private/public realms. There where seclusion characterized their social space and confined them to isolated—but not solitary—spiritu-ality, female mystics, as Sells points out, opened a dialogue between the visible and the invisible, the veiled and the unveiled (1996:153). As hag-iographic sources suggest, this propensity rarely generated tension. Al-though we are occasionally told stories about the women mystic's de-fiance of various social demands, these stories are narrated in a clean, trouble-free manner (e.g., Ibn ʿArabi). They are presented as hymns of triumph, as a collective validation of female asceticism. Of course, this form of authentication is external: it is mediated by the hagiographer's authorial voice. We have no stories told in the first-person form, no access to the inner turmoil and compromises to which these women were likely to be subjected as a consequence of challenging the social norms. The women's voices, then, are mediated voices that resonate with genuine commitment to spiritual self-betterment.

Therefore, caught up in a paradox of living at the intersection of *tariqa* and *sharia* modalities, women mystics maneuvered their way through the discursive ambivalence toward the socially weaker sex, ex-pressed as both affirmation and negation, rejection and infatuation, en-chantment and disenchantment (see Sabbah 1984; Andrae 1987:33–54). As male mystics struggled between obtaining sexual gratification through marriage and leading celibate lifestyles, the debate over sexu-ality continued to be directed against female companions and their role in a Sufi man's life. Yet her presence in the Sufi scheme of things could not be denied. Such male ambivalence is quite potently illustrated by the great Muslim thinker al-Ghazali in the following quotation:

Consider the state of the God-fearing women and say (to your own soul), "Oh my soul, be not content to be less than a woman, for a man is contemptible if he comes short of a woman, in respect of her religion, and (her relation) to this world." So we will now mention something of the (spiritual) states of the women who have devoted themselves to the service of God. (Cited in Smith 1994:166)

This conflictual view of woman can be read as constructive of a move toward an increasingly feminine symbolization of the mystical path. Historically as well as experientially, Rabi'a (d. 801), the greatest female saint in Islam, whose role I discuss in greater detail later is likely to be the culprit of this shift: her courageous stress on unconditional love, that is, her integration of emotional and somatic experiences, started this trend. Metaphors associated with female symbols and duties as stipulated by the Quran and the Sunna gained a prototypical function for the mystic's relationship with God: the metaphors of (un)veiling, impregnation, weeping, longing, dependence, submission entered the vocabulary of great Sufi masters, from Niffari to Ghazali, from Ibn 'Arabi to Rumi (Schimmel 1979:136–41), essentializing further the prevailing assumptions about woman's "biology" and its cultural purpose. For example, Ibn 'Arabi writes:

God cannot be seen apart from matter, and He is seen more perfectly in the human *materia* than in any other, and more perfectly in woman than in man. For He is seen either in the aspect of *agens* or in that of *patiens* or as both simultaneously. Therefore when man contemplates God in his own person in regard to the fact that woman is produced from man, he contemplates God in the aspect of *agens*, and when he pays no regard to the production of women from himself he contemplates God in the aspect of *patiens*, because as God's creature he is absolutely *patiens* in relation to God, but when he contemplates God in woman he contemplates Him both as *agens* and *patiens*. God manifested in the form of woman is *agens* of virtue of exercising complete sway over man's soul, and causing man to become submissive and devoted to Himself, and He is also *patiens* because inasmuch as He appears in the form of women He is under the man's control and subject to his orders: hence to see God in woman is to see Him in both these aspects, and such vision is more perfect than seeing Him in all the forms in which He manifests Himself. (Cited in Schimmel 1975:431)

Similarly, the mystical quest itself was frequently poetically gendered as a relationship between the (female) lover and the (male) beloved. Thus, as Anne Marie Schimmel points out, Mary and Zulaykha were both allegorized in mystical literature as models of feminine yearning. Similarly, the devotion of Khadija, Muhammad's first wife, to her husband was represented as an expression of ultimate devotion and piety. Fatima, the daughter of Muhammad and the mother of Hasan and Hussain, the second and third imams of the Shi'i tradition, has been venerated as the biological-cum-spiritual vector of divine guidance. As in medieval Christian tradition, in which weeping, devotion, submission, and silence marked a progressive feminization of mysticism (Bruneau 1992:17), similar tropes appeared in Muslim mystic writings to express unconditional submission and piety. The Muslim woman's social condition—the privacy of her space, her veil, her devotion to family as required by the tradition—acquired a symbolic function in the mystical dictionaries. Her socially invisible spiritual practices were thus made manifest, albeit in desocialized, or dehistoricized, terms.

Medieval hagiographic sources—our prime references to women in Sufi tradition—understandably reflect this ambivalence. While asceticism was not a recommended norm for either sex, female ascetics underwent a greater social scrutiny. A married life was a religious duty after all—a matter of orthopraxy. In redirecting their desire from men to God, the ascetic women posited their bodies as a site of social hiatus. There where the law disempowered her, the mystical path allowed for reempowering. The complementarity of the *sharia* (law) and the *tariqa* (Sufi path) in the attainment of the *haqiqa* (Truth) gained a new momentum in female asceticism. A story is told about the encounters of one Fatima of Nishapur (d. 849) encounters with the famous mystic Bayazid Bistami (d. 874). While she never wore veil in his presence, on one particular occasion Bistami noticed a beauty mole on her white complexion. His remark, a sign of rupture in their otherwise spiritual relationship, put an end to their communication (Schimmel 1975:427).

In historiographical terms, such women seemed to be remembered in greatest detail if the extent of their asceticism bordered with, or crossed into, the "paranormal." The mimetic/didactic intent of the hagiographic knowledge is highlighted by the overwhelming number of stories about out-of-the-ordinary experiences and practice associated with female ascetics (e.g., ʿAttâr, Ibn ʿArabi). The emphasis on performative austerity is quite ironic: after all, asceticism, ideally, necessitates a degree of social isolation and solitude in order to be spiritually gratifying. In the stories about women ascetics, however, the voyeuristic participation of the public in their ascetic practices seems to have elicited stronger hagiographic approval.

To be sure, the "paranormal" is not associated with female mystics only: many male mystics are remembered for out-of-the-ordinary capacities and practices as well. However, in Islamic hagiographic literature, this appears to be the true landmark of female asceticism. The fascination with their physical stamina, miracle work, quaint social habits, and emotional devotion/deprivation feature as symbols of spiritual sincerity and dedication.

Thus, the most famous woman saint, Rabi'a al-'Adawiyya is remembered by a series of legends that point to her extrasensory perceptiveness: she is said to elevate her rug while praying; she made a glowing lamp hover over her without being attached to the ceiling; she made Ka'ba come to her when she had to cut short her voyage to Mecca; her wishes always materialized through prayer; wild animals flocked to her in admiration. Similarly, Maryam al-Basriyya is said to have died in ecstasy; Bahriyya al-Mawsuliyya wept herself blind; while Tohfah neither slept nor ate (Schimmel 1997:34–54; Sells 1996:151–70; Nurbakhsh 1990:15–77, 103–16, 173).

But Rabi'a al-'Adawiyya stands out as the perfect example of this trend. Not only is Rabi'a the most famous Sufi woman but she is also, as history remembers her, the first true saint of Islam.[2]

Rabi'a's life has been told far and wide in the Islamic world, and her fame has earned her respect among the most prominent Sufi thinkers and writers.[3] One of them, Farîd al-Dîn 'Attâr, says the following about Rabi'a (cited in Nurbakhsh 1990:15):

> No she was not a single woman
> But a hundred men over:
> Robed in the quintessence of pain
> From foot to face, immersed in Truth
> Effaced in the radiance of god
> And liberated from all superfluous excess.

To honor Rabi'a's merit in piety, self-denial, and love of God, later Sufi masters attached the title "The Crown of Men" to her name, generously exalting her above any male Sufis of previous generations.

Having become an orphan at an early age, Rabi'a was sold into slavery for an insignificant sum of money. Suffering through slavery marked her youth. Though she was later manumitted, this period left a profound impact on her philosophy of life. Loneliness led her to God, and the lack of emotional intimacy made God her only object of love. In mystical terms, love for God became her "taste," that is, the most salient feature of her asceticism. Indeed, she is credited with having injected the otherwise dry diction of early Sufis with a powerful dose of emotionalism.

Love of God overwhelmed Rabiʿa's being and became the sole driving force of her existence. To the dismay of a number of people who cared for her and a number of men who offered her marriage, this love for God was exclusive and absolute. Once she was asked "Do you love God?" "Yes," she replied. "Are you then an enemy of Satan?" was another question. To this she said: "My love of all-Merciful God leaves me no room for hostility towards Satan."

Another common story associated with her tells that she used to carry a torch in one hand and a jug of water in the other. When finally asked why she was doing it, she replied: "I want to throw fire into Paradise and pour water into Hell so that these two veils disappear, and it becomes clear who worships God out of love, not out of fear of Hell or hope for Paradise." Drawing on the Quranic verse 5:59 which says "God loves them, and they love God," Rabiʿa geared her "submission" (islam) to loving and being loved by God in an absolute way, and her "excellence" (ihsan) in not letting anyone stand between her and the object of her love. On this Quranic verse, "God loves them and they love God," she meditated as follows: "Love has come from Eternity and passes into Eternity, and nobody has been found in seventy thousand worlds who drinks one drop of it until at last he is absorbed in God."

Many later Sufi women would follow Rabiʿa's example in their amorous devotion to God, hoping to achieve the same ability of fusing through love two seemingly opposite forces: the one of power and the other of submission. While power and submission remained, by and large, mutually exclusive in the dominant Islamic discourse, in Rabiʿa's mystical contemplations they blended. According to the Islamic law, for example, a servant of God, that is, one who submits, consciously recognizes his/her own impotency before the omnipotent God. The familiar phrase used by most Muslims in daily conversation, *inshallah*, "if God wills," is psychologically a powerful reminder that nothing is in the believer's hands, unless God wills so. Furthermore, the confirmation of submission as represented by a ritualistic touching of the ground with one's forehead during the prayer embodies this sense of unconditional dependence on God's might.

In Rabiʿa's case, on the other hand, love—her personalized manner of submission—was defined as a two-way street. Her conceptualization of love echoed neo-Platonic teachings, insofar as she saw it as a continuous energy that flowed from God to his creatures and from his creatures back to God. The cycle is the main driving force of all exis-

tence, and without it, the world would be no more. As long as God will
love us, we will exist. If he ever stops it, we shall perish. Yet in order
to be absorbed by the full force of the divine love, we must uncondi-
tionally and exclusively love God. Only in this reciprocal loving can we
truly feel what submission means, but also what divine might means.
The Sufi quest for annihilation of the human self in the divine self is
thus conceived by Rabi'a as the annihilation of human love in the perfect divine love. In one of her poems, she said (Nurbakhsh 1990:74):

> I have loved you with two loves
> a selfish love and a love that is worthy of You.
> As for the selfish love, I occupy myself
> therein with remembrance of You to the exclusion of all others . . .
> As for that which is worthy of You
> therein You raise the veil that I may see You
> Yet there is no praise to me in this or that
> Because all praise is with You.

Yet despite the mention of numerous female ascetics in hagiographic
sources, as well as the symbolic legacy of Rabi'a's asceticism, it appears
that many women reconciled their piety with family life. Rather than
the choice of a lifestyle what seems to be most important to recognize
in the practice of female mystics is a dual pattern of islam and *ihsan*—
"submission" and "excellence." While the former is the name of the
religion itself, implying a total submission to one God, the latter adds a
strong Sufi coloring to it. "Excellence" refers to spiritual excellence that
is achieved through submission, "islam." There where the law prescribes
five prayers a day, for example, to all those who submit—that is, "muslims"—excellence prescribes much more: it requires a continuous remembrance of God and thus a complete spiritual submission. But the
road to excellence is paved with individual taste (*dhawq*). And since
"there is no accounting for tastes," a single modality of piety was never
targeted, at least not until the formalization of the spiritual path
through the *tariqa* orders. Through *dhawq*, women could strategize the
ways of administering their spirituality without rupturing their social
space: many elaborated their spiritual lineage to Muhammad's wives
and daughters, starting with his wife Khadija. As the first convert to
Islam and a powerful businesswoman, Khadija was well remembered
for both her piety and devotion as well as her worldly successes. Muhammad himself is reported to have included Khadija among "the best
women of the world" (Stowasser 1994:59).

But Khadija's life story is rather exceptional: for most women in
Islamic history whose social space revolved around families and house

chores, she, as well as other women venerated by the Quran and prophetic traditions, served as encouraging exemplar that showing that
family duties did not have to stand in the way of spiritual growth.
Consequently, one finds numerous stories about women mystics who
balanced their family responsibilities with their spiritual needs in a very
determined manner. For example, a story is related about Fatima Umm
Ali of the ninth century, when she traveled to the house of one of the
greatest Sufis of the time, Bayazid Bistami, in search for guidance. Upon
arriving at Bistami's house, Umm Ali took off her veil and proceeded
to converse with him about spiritual matters. Her husband, witnessing
the candid manner in which his wife addressed another man, became
uncomfortable and, upon leaving Bistami's house, asked: "How can you
be so impudent with Bayazid?" She replied: "You are my physical nature's consort, Bayazid is my spiritual confidant. I attain my physical
desire through you; through him, I reach God. The fact that he does
not need my company, but you do, demonstrates this." (Nurbakhsh
1990:93).

Taking these examples together, a single type of Sufi woman cannot
be sketched out: women varied in terms of social status, age, personal
preferences. Some viewed "excellence" as a continuous prayer, some as
silence, others as love or fear of God. There are also accounts of women
staging performances of spiritual music in popular and courtly circles
(Andrae 1987:84). Their orientations revealed creative, singular approaches to "excellence." A Sufi woman by the name of Rabi'a of Syria
(d. 850) is said to have come before her husband every night with the
same question: "Do you have any needs?" If he did, she would perform
them. Then she would separate from him, make her ablutions, and
remain in worship till morning (Nurbakhsh 1990:79–84). Another
woman, Umm Hayyan, was known never to speak to anyone between
dawn and evening, because she was engaged in the silent recitation of
the Quran. After the evening prayer, she would finally engage in her
worldly duties, conversation with her family, and household tasks (Nurbakhsh 1990:85).

Perhaps the most characteristic aspect of these women's quest is
their determined social presence. Even in the case of Rabi'a, solitude
within society was preferred over solitude for its own sake. It was a
relational solitude, drawn both horizontally, toward other human beings, as well as vertically, toward God. A continuous yearning for God
that could never reach completion seems to have been the norm for
women mystics. The enchantment with the "Wholly Other" (Otto 1950:
25) was nurtured through the acknowledgment of the "Un-wholly Self."
Unlike al-Hallaj (d. 922), who in the moment of ecstasy exclaimed "I

am the Truth," irrevocably challenging the separation of the two spaces—divine and human—women mystics found solace in treating the social/divine boundary as an aspect of spiritual challenge. A late-ninth century Sufi woman by the name of Umm Ayman explains: "Since my ultimate return is to You, how should I not always aspire to be with You? As I never saw any good from other than You, how should I not love You? Since it is you who have set yearning within me, how should I not yearn for You" (Nurbakhsh 1990:90).

The relationship with God, then, is never exhaustive, never consummated. Achieving the aim in explicit terms would mean repeating al-Hallaj's trap of self-glorification and overcoming the necessary submission. Without spiritual submission there is no spiritual strength or awareness of God's glory. Thus Rabi'a and her followers consciously created a meditative paradox so as to ensure that the tension between possession and dispossession, submission and excellence, never gave in to self-destruction before the deserved self-annihilation. So whether wives, mothers, or complete ascetics, Sufi women opted to nurture spiritual strength with submission, and submission with strength. A Sufi woman of the late ninth century, Tohfah, aptly illustrated the reasons for keeping the tension active in these verses (Nurbakhsh 1990:116):

> Do not wonder at those slain
> In the dust at the Friend's door
> Marvel rather how anyone can survive
> with their soul intact [when opening the door].

Although in discussing women mystics in Islam one cannot speak of a separate history in which women's voices can be unproblematically recuperated or dissociated from Islam's dominant male agency, it is important to acknowledge these women's skill in metaphorizing socio-ethical norms and placing them into the service of their spiritual empowerment. The dialectic between (spiritual) possession and (material) dispossession, femininity and masculinity, the inner and the outer realms, came to be the main modality through which women mystic experience was shaped. Despite the fact that its discursive power remained in the hand of the male élite, the mystical path proved to be a source of spiritual strength and betterment for numerous women, enabling them to direct their creative energy toward, rather than away, from orthopraxy.

Notes

1. See C. Ernst's introduction to Sells 1996; and J. Fenton's (1995) cross-cultural perspective on mysticism as a basis for dialogue.

2. The concept of sainthood in Islam is developed only in Sufism. The word "saint" derives from the Arabic word *wali*, which means "a friend of God," implying the mental closeness with the divine that some Sufis have experienced through their spiritual exercise.

3. The following discussion is based on Smith 1994; Sells 1996:151–70; Schimmel 1975:8, 38–40, 426–35; and Nurbakhsh 1990.

References

Ahmed, Leila. 1991. Early Islam and the Position of Women: A Comparative Interpretation. In N. Keddi and B. Baron (eds.), *Women in Middle Eastern History*. New Haven: Yale University Press: 58–73.

Andrae, Tor. 1987. *In the Garden of Myrtles: Studies in Early Islamic Mysticism*. Albany: SUNY Press.

Bennet, Judith. 1997. Confronting Continuity. *Journal of Women's History* 9, 3 (autumn): 73–94.

Birge, John. 1965. *The Bektashi Order of Dervishes*. London: n.p.

Bruneau, Marie-Florine. 1998. *Women Mystics Confront the Modern World*. Albany: SUNY Press.

Butorovic, Amila. 1997. Spiritual Empowerment through Spiritual Submission: Sufi Women and Their Quest for God. *Canadian Woman Studies* 17, 1 (Winter): 53–8.

de Certeau, Michel. 1986. Mystic Speech. In B. Massumi (trans.)., *Heterologies: Discourse on the Other*. Minneapolis: University of Minnesota Press: 80–101.

Farîd al-Dîn 'Attâr. 1966. *Muslim Saints and Mystics*. Trans. A. J. Arberry. Chicago: University of Chicago Press.

———. 1984. *The Conference of the Birds*. Harmondswordth: Penguin Books.

Fenton, John. 1995. Mystical Experience as a Bridge for Cross-Cultural Philosophy of Religion. In T. Dean (ed.), *Religious Pluralism and Truth: Essays on Cross-Cultural Philosophy of Religion*. New York: SUNY Press: 189–205.

Ibn 'Arabî 1971. *Sufis of Andalusia*. Trans. R. W. J. Austin. London: Allen & Unwin.

Lings, Martin. 1977. *What Is Sufism?* Berkeley: University of California Press.

Mernissi, Fatima. 1991. *The Veil and the Male Elite*. Reading, Mass.: Addison-Wesley.

Nasr, Seyyed Hossein. 1994. *Ideals and Realities of Islam*. San Francisco: Aquarian.

Nurbakhsh, Javad. 1990. *Sufi Women*. London: Khaniqahi-Nimatullahi.

Otto, Rudolf. 1950. *The Idea of the Holy*. New York: Oxford University Press.

Sabbah, Fatna A. 1984. *Woman in the Muslim Unconscious*. New York: Pergamon Press.

Schimmel, Annemarie. 1975. *Mystical Dimensions of Islam*. Chapel Hill: University of North Carolina Press.

———. 1979. Eros—Heavenly and Not So Heavenly—in Sufi Literature and Life. In A. L. al-Sayyid-Marsot (ed.), *Society and the Sexes in Medieval Islam*. Malibu, Calif.: Undena: 119–43.

———. 1997. *My Soul Is a Woman*. New York: Continuum.

Sells. Michael. 1996. *Early Islamic Mysticism*. New York: Paulist Press.

Shah, Idries. 1968. *The Way of the Sufi*. New York: Dutton.

Smith, Margaret. 1994. Rabiʿa: *The Life and Work of Rabiʿa and Other Women Mystics in Islam*. Oxford: Oneworld.

Stowasser, Barbara. 1994. *Women in the Qurʾân; Traditions, and Interpretation*. Oxford: Oxford University Press.

"Merely a Love Poem"?

Common Sense, Suspicion, and the Song of Songs

Mary Dove

In medieval Christendom, library catalogues typically begin with what their male compilers perceived to be the most significant, valuable and veracious of all books, the Bible. After copies of the Bible, or parts thereof, they list commentaries of the church fathers on biblical books, authoritative guides to apt interpretation. Little wonder that Western feminists have regarded the Bible with special suspicion, or that the biblical book that seems to twentieth-century readers the least overtly "religious" book of the canon, and therefore the least suspect, the Song of Songs, was chosen as the subject of the first volume in the series *The Feminist Companion to the Bible.* As the editor of the series, Athalya Brenner, says, this book "can be read from the outset as less biased ideologically . . . than other texts of the Hebrew [and Christian] Bible," since the subject matter of Shir haShirim, Song of Songs, is apparently "neither theological nor even religious" but rather "heterosexual love and its erotic manifestations" (Brenner 1993:28). Nor, apparently, does the heterosexual love voiced in these lyric poems composed some twenty-three centuries ago exclude the female perspective or privilege the male.[1] According to Phyllis Trible, "there is no male dominance, no female subordination, and no stereotyping of either sex" (1978:145). "Ecce tu pulchra es, amica mea, ecce tu pulchra, oculi tui columbarum" (Behold, you are beautiful, my beloved, behold you are beautiful, your

eyes are the eyes of doves, says the male lover) (Song of Songs 1:14).[2]
The female lover—neither speaker is named or identified in the text—
replies, reciprocating, "ecce tu pulcher es, dilecte mi, et decorus, lectulus
noster floridus" (Behold, you are beautiful, my beloved, and lovely, our
little bed is flowery) (1:15).

Trible reads the Song of Songs as a redemptive reversal of the relationship between Eve and Adam in the second and third chapters of
Genesis, a "love story [that] went awry" (1978:159). Her uninhibitedly
romantic classification of the biblical myth of the origin of male domination and her unabashed characterization of the Song of Songs as a
"symphony of eroticism" (1978:144) led Francis Landy to accuse her
of "breathless enthusiasm" about the Song of Songs (1983:185).[3] But
we should remind ourselves that Trible perceived herself to be the inheritor of a "rational" hermeneutic tradition in dire need of imaginative
and affective rescue. The need was the direr in that early "feminist"
interpretation of the Song of Songs had spoken from the cold heart of
this tradition. Elizabeth Cady Stanton, in *The Woman's Bible* (1895),
claimed that the Song of Solomon (the book's title in the King James
Bible) is "merely a love poem," which "the [Christian] church, as an
excuse for retaining this book as a part of 'Holy Scriptures', interprets
... as expressive of Christ's love for the church," whereas "the most
rational view to take of the Song is, it was that of a luxurious king to
the women of his seraglio" (Brenner1993:55). The lecherous king is
Solomon, supposed by Cady Stanton (in line with Jewish and Christian
tradition, and Song of Solomon 1:1 in the King James Bible) to be the
author of the Song of Songs.[4]

Brenner applauds the "tongue-in-cheek common sense" (Brenner
1993:31) of Cady Stanton, presumably out of a felt need to speak well
of *The Woman's Bible*. But what kind of common sense was it that was
so suspicious of the Bible in general and the Song of Songs in particular
that it chose to ignore the female voice in the Song of Songs, preferring
to abandon love poetry to male lust, more specifically to the polygamous
practices of an exoticized potentate? The common sense of *The Woman's
Bible* would classify the Song of Songs as erotica, relegating it to the
locked cupboard in the gentleman's library—Cady Stanton may well
have had in mind one of those many illustrated soft-porn editions. Let
us then once again praise the uncommon sense of the famous men,
rabbis and ecclesiastics, who in the first centuries of the common era
refused to remove the Song of Songs from the biblical canon,[5] thus
ensuring that it would always be available to anyone who had access
to the Jewish or Christian scriptures.

Until the later Middle Ages, however, in Western Christendom, that "anyone" with access to the scriptures was characteristically a man, literate in Latin, who spent the larger part of his life in a male ecclesiastical community, whether a religious order, an educational institution, or a clerical foundation (or some combination of these). The access of the laity to scripture was restricted and, as Alcuin Blamires says in "The Limits of Bible Study for Medieval Women," women were particularly "disenscriptured," even women religious (Smith and Taylor, 1993: 3).[6] Common sense told medieval *clerici*, clergy, male readers and interpreters of the Latin Bible, that the love expressed in the Song of Songs cannot be earthly love. The Franciscan friar Nicholas of Lyre, a highly influential biblical scholar, explains why one must be suspicious of earthly love, in the prologue to his commentary on the literal sense of the Song of Songs, c. 1330:

Frequenter habet amor talis aliquid inhonestum et illicitum adiunctum, propter quod descriptio talis amoris non uidetur ad libros sacre scripture canonicos pertinere, maxime quia huiusmodi libri spiritu sancto dictante sunt descripti.

[L]ove of this kind (carnal love) frequently contains some admixture of the unchaste and the illicit, on account of which the description of such love does not seem appropriate to the canonical books of sacred scripture written at the dictation of the holy spirit.[7]

Even if, Nicholas of Lyre continues, the love described in the Song of Songs were, *per impossibile*, earthly love without tincture of sin, the author, Solomon, would still have to be understood to be writing "from experience," not "through revelation." This understanding is in turn impossible for any educated man, knowing, as he must, that this book "has always been reputed to be canonical, both by Hebrew and Latin scholars," and therefore "written at the dictation of the holy spirit." This low view of human experience of love and high view of scholarly authorities is scholastic Nicholas of Lyre's version of a common-sense approach to the Song of Songs. His common sense concludes that the subject of the book is God's love for his people, first the synagogue and, afterward, the church instituted by Christ, an interpretation going back at least as far as the third-century Christian scholar Origen, who derived it from Jewish tradition.[8] Nicholas of Lyre's influence helped to ensure that this interpretation was handed on not just to the postmedieval Catholic church but to the Reformers as well.[9]

Lyre, following Augustine, maintained that his reading of the Song of Songs was literal, not allegorical, while Origen believed that at one level (albeit a low level) the book could be read in the historical-literal sense as an epithalamium composed by Solomon in the form of a drama (see Dove 1996:318–20). Medieval and modern debate about what constitutes an allegorical and what a literal interpretation of the Song of Songs is ultimately indeterminable, as I have argued elsewhere (1996).[10] Consequently, I shall avoid the terms *allegorical* and *literal* here. Instead, I shall term the tradition handed down by Nicholas of Lyre the presecular Christian tradition of interpretation of the Song of Songs. This presecular tradition is now characteristically perceived by scholars, female and male, as a long wrong turning, an erratic exegesis that was at long last reoriented by eighteenth-century German biblical criticism. *A Feminist Companion to the Song of Songs* refers to the presecular tradition only in passing, Brenner rightly observing that it awaits "comprehensive feminist research" (1993:30). Since the "comprehensive" must always originate in the particular, my discussion will focus on two interpretive moments: one at the heart of the presecular tradition, in the twelfth century, and one during the transition from presecular to secular, in the late eighteenth century.

To return to the lovers' voices—the male lover saying "behold, you are beautiful, my beloved, behold you are beautiful, your eyes are the eyes of doves" (1:14), and the female replying "behold, you are beautiful, my beloved, and lovely, our little bed is flowery" (1:15). How are the lovers' words interpreted in the Glossed Bible, that early-twelfth-century conflation of biblical text and commentary that later came to be called the *Glossa Ordinaria*, standard commentary?[11] The Glossed Song of Songs, compiled by Master Anselm at the School of Laon in Picardy, in the second decade of the twelfth century, has probably been the most widely read of all presecular commentaries on the Song of Songs.[12] In the Glossed Bible, the glosses, comprising interpretive commentary compiled from patristic, Carolingian, and later scholarly sources, are written between the lines of the biblical text and in the margins alongside it, and throughout the late medieval and early modern periods the Glossed Bible was readily available to anyone who could read Latin and had access to a library of Latin texts.[13] Again, of course, that anyone was far more likely to be male than female. None of the manuscripts of the Glossed Song of Songs I have located was owned by a female community, although sixteenth- and seventeenth-century women literate in Latin may have had access to printed copies, since the *Biblia Latina cum Glossa Ordinaria* was in print from 1480/81 until 1634.[14] (My edition of

the Glossed Song of Songs (1997) is the first modern edition of any part
of the Glossed Bible. In this instance, then, archival reconstruction of
the original text and feminist rereading of it are simultaneous activities.)

The Glossed Song of Songs recognizes, as *The Woman's Bible* does
not, that mutuality of the lovers that delights Trible and other contemporary scholars. In a marginal gloss derived from Bede of Northumbria,
the male lover's words "behold, you are beautiful, my beloved, behold
you are beautiful, your eyes are the eyes of doves" (1:14) are said to be
occasioned by the testimony the woman has given to the "dilectionis
pignora" (pledges of love) she has received from him, and "mox remu-
nerationis uice respondet: ecce tu pulchra es" (he soon repays her by
replying: "behold, you are beautiful"). Likewise, the female lover, in a
marginal gloss derived from Origen, "audiens sponsa se per dilectionem
sponsi meruisse ut ab ibso sponso laudaretur, sponso uicem in laudibus
tribuit" (hearing that through her love of the bridegroom she has deserved to be praised by the bridegroom himself, speaks in her turn the
praises of the bridegroom).[15] This "she," the *sponsa*, bride, the beloved
of Christ, is both the church and the individual Christian, for Origen
and the presecular tradition as a whole move very flexibly between the
two (see Matter 1990:28). Love, in any case, is answered by love.

Equals, however, these lovers in the Glossed Song of Songs are not.
The male lover's words "behold, you are beautiful" would not seem to
us to need any explanation, but Bede provides one, still in the bridegroom's voice: "ex hoc quod me diligis pulchra efficieris" (the very fact
of your loving me makes you become beautiful) (chapter 1, gloss 171).
Origen explains that the bride

> sponso uicem in laudibus tribuit, non quod ei quod non habet suo
> preconio largiatur sed intelligens decorem eius per quem et ipsa
> decora facta est, ait: ecce. (chapter 1, gloss 176).

> speaks in her turn the praises of the bridegroom, not in order
> that what he does not have may be given to him by her praising,
> but realizing the beauty of the one through whom she herself
> has been made beautiful she says: behold.

As often in the Glossed Song of Songs, a short interlinear gloss
sharply spells out what the marginal glosses express more diffusely. The
bride's "behold, you are beautiful" is glossed, in her own voice, "natur-
aliter per diuinitatem: ego ex te sum pulchra" (you are beautiful by
virtue of your divine nature: I am beautiful through you) (chapter 1,
gloss 179). This gloss derives from Anselm of Laon's own lectures on

the Song of Songs. The desire of the bride in the Song of Songs is for a desired who is, according to Origen and Bede and Anselm, perfect man as well as true God. The female's discourse about her own desirability, "I am beautiful," is always qualified by "through you."

Brenner terms the presecular interpretation of the Song of Songs "the romance of Jesus and the church" (1993:30). I am not sure how seriously she offers this characterization, but it is true that the patterning of the lovers' relationship in the Glossed Song of Songs is a romance paradigm. By that I mean that the lovers do not love with unconditional mutuality, Trible's "symphony of eroticism"; there is one who bestows and one who receives. In medieval secular romance, it is the man who desires and the woman who bestows (or withholds) favors. Any reversal of the pattern is shocking, as when the Fair Maid of Astolat, in Thomas Malory's Arthurian tales (written in the third quarter of the fifteenth century), desires the unrequiting Launcelot. "I myght," Launcelot says,

> have bene maryed and I had wolde, but I never applyed me yet to be maryed. But bycause, fayre damesell, that ye love me as ye sey ye do . . . wheresomever ye woll besette youre herte upon som good knyght that woll wedde you, I shall gyff you togidyrs a thousande pounde yerly . . ."
>
> "Alas! Than," seyde she, "I muste dye for youre love." (Vinaver 1971:638)

In the Glossed Song of Songs, by contrast, the male lover both initiates desire and bestows rewards; its male readers are invited to identify with the desired female to whom rewards are given.[16] Indeed, they are told that the "thousand" obscurely mentioned in Song of Songs 8:12, "mille tui pacifici" (a thousand [of/from?] your peaceful one), represents "quid sua relinquentibus in eternum conseruet," (the reward Christ lays up in eternity for those relinquishing their own possessions) (chapter 8, gloss 107). The most scholarly of its readers, "those who guard (the vineyard's, that is the church's) fruits" (8:12), by teaching and preaching, can expect to receive twice as much, Anselm asserts, "quia duplex meretur premium qui et se tuetur et alios lucratur" (because he who both looks after himself and gains others deserves a double reward) (chapter 8, gloss 114). If the male receiver is gendered female in this text, he is apparently—unlike the Fair Maid of Astolat—ready to understand money as standing for love, and his sense of fair play is to the fore, whereas she dies rather than negotiate with Launcelot. In the romance of the Glossed Song of Songs, written by and for men, there is at least as much hard head as soft heart.

But what were the implications of the presecular Song of Songs for female spirituality, for the value women placed upon themselves? Barred from ecclesiastical office, they could not even look forward to the rewards promised in Song of Songs 8:12. They must, surely, have felt themselves invited to say: "I have a truly grateful spirit; and so I ought to have; for I have nothing but my love of him to value myself upon." These words were actually written about fictional husband, [earthly, not heavenly,] by Samuel Richardson's Pamela, in a letter she dates "the Fourth Day of my Happiness," that is, the fourth day of her marriage to Mr. B. (1980:400). The popularity of *Pamela* in 1740 the especially among female, readers, established a romance paradigm that can be read as a secular translation of the presecular Song of Songs: the female has nothing to bestow on the beloved male except her desire; in return, the male bestows on her everything, including, of course, his name. God becomes the earthly husband; the earthly husband becomes God.

Is this, then, how women read the Song of Songs when it was first coming to be understood as a secular text, during the mid to late eighteenth century? The answer is no, because those women who had access to biblical scholarship did not read the Song of Songs as romance, they read it as a text celebrating an actual Oriental marriage in the tenth century B.C.E., Solomon's. In common with all biblical scholars of the period and with Cady Stanton later, Ann Francis (1738–1800), writer of the annotated *Poetical Translation of the Song of Solomon from the Original Hebrew* (1781), follows the tradition that Solomon is the author of the Song of Songs; like most of her scholar contemporaries, she understands that the male voice is his and that the subject is his marriage to an Egyptian princess, and like her chief authority, Thomas Harmer (*The outlines of a new commentary on Solomon's song, drawn by the help of instructions from the East,* 1768), she understands the book to be a narrative in the form of a drama.[17]

Ann Francis was the daughter of an Anglican clergyman Daniel Gittins (1710–1761), who had a modest reputation as a scholar of biblical Hebrew. To his credit he taught her this language, as well as Latin and Greek, and when she visited Cambridge a quarter of a century after his death, her thoughts centered on the undergraduate he had been there—in King's College Chapel she experienced what she describes as a "vision" of him as a "smooth-cheek'd youth."[18] Perhaps it was this intense recollection of her paternal tutor that provoked her to begin reading Hebrew again. She tells us that in preparation for her annotated translation of the Song of Songs she read the Hebrew text "with the assistance of a learned friend" (1781:v), probably the Rev. John Parkhurst, to whom her book is dedicated.[19] Her husband was another clergyman, Robert Francis, rector of Edgefield, near Holt in Norfolk.[20]

Francis's translation of the Song of Songs, it has to be said, is not of the very highest quality (1781:17):

> Behold, thou'rt wond'rous fair! my love,
> Behold, thou'rt wond'rous fair!
> Thine eyes, than those of yonder dove
> More mild, more tender are.
>   Behold, my best-belov'd is fair!
>   Yea, pleasant to the sight!
>   Our carpet's green, by nature's care
>   With flowrets gay bedight.

The line-filler "by nature's care" prompts the cynical thought that the grounds of the Edgefield rectory were doubtless entrusted to the care of a nature improved by a disciple of Capability Brown, but the stage directions provided by Francis make it clear that she wants the reader to have in mind an altogether more exotic locale than a Norfolk garden. The male lover's words are spoken by "Solomon, meeting the Spouse, as they are conducting her into the royal Pavilion," meeting her, because all the words in female voices from Song of Songs 1:1–13 are understood to be "Processional Songs by the Virgins of Jerusalem" (1781:3), who are advancing from Solomon's camp to meet his new bride.

The opening words of the Song of Songs, "let him kiss me with the kisses of his mouth" (King James version) ("Let him on me the balmy kiss bestow/With ruby mouth, whence honey'd accents flow"), (Francis 1781), are, according to Francis, sung by one of the virgins "personating the Bride." Bold words like these, she explains, cannot be understood as being spoken by the bride in her own voice, for

> [b]rides, even in *our own country*, are seldom *talkative*; polite and prudent brides, *never so*. Those of the Asiatics are *extremely reserved*. . . . [O]our sacred bard, who adheres invariably to *nature*, describes persons and things, customs and manners, such as they were in his time, and such as they, pretty nearly, appear to be *at present* among the *Orientals*. (1781:ix)

Just before the bride finally speaks for herself, Francis notes that when Solomon says to her "thou hast dove's eyes," he implies "eyes full of love, benignity, and gentleness; rendered more *soft*, more *amiably engaging*, by some degree of doubt and youthful diffidence" (1781:17). Any suggestion of mutual desire is erased in advance from the bride's words; she is praised for showing lack of confidence and for perceiving herself to be the legatee of Solomon's superior age, wisdom, and sexual experience. In the Latin Bible and the King James Bible, the female lover boldly speaks of "our bed"; here, on the authority of Harmer, the "bed" becomes a "carpet."

Taking another suggestion from Harmer, Francis finds a way to conserve the silence of the new, young bride. Wherever she gauges that the female speaker is impassioned, Francis attributes the words to another person of the drama. This is familiar "madwoman in the attic" territory, and, like Bertha Rochester, the impassioned woman in Francis's drama is a former bride of the master-male; she is a Jewish queen displaced from her position as Solomon's principal wife by the gentile princess, though still, of course, *a* wife. "The language of the royal *bridegroom*," says Francis, "is ardent—eloquent: that of the Jewish Queen, plaintive—inquisitive—arguing *distrust*—now expressive of resentment—then relenting, and melting into love—then again declarative of *violent* anger and chagrin" (1781: viii).

The new bride, by contrast, "speaks but little; just enough to *convince* her royal partner of the preference her heart gives him." Francis allows just one exception. When the Jewish queen demeans the bride as "a little sister" who "hath no breasts" ("no dawning beauties glow,/On swelling hills of animated snow," 1781:97, 8:8, King James Bible), the "*woman* is awakened" (1781:ix). This accounts for the bride's reply to her envious rival, which, warns Francis, is "*strong*, even for the *mouth* of an *Asiatic*" (1781:98):

> I am indeed a guardian wall,
> Adorn'd with turrets fair and tall,
> For here, behold, twin beauties glow,
> On hills of animated snow.

As the primary object of male desire, the new bride is an unawakened woman; what provides the context for her arousal is the Asiatic seraglio. Rivalry for affection stimulates affect and self-esteem.

For Francis, this dramatic love story with three principal players is the literal meaning of the Song of Songs, and it is the text's literal content, that is, its literary-historical content, with which her annotated translation is concerned. Nevertheless, she insists that the text has an other-than-literal meaning: "that *a sublime allegory is couched beneath this description of conjugal love, there cannot* (I think) *with a Christian, remain a doubt*" (1781:xiii).[21] Here in 1781, as the presecular era of interpretation of the Song of Songs draws to a close, allegory is coming to be perceived as a specialized meaning supposed by the believing Christian to shore up the "real" text, which is the text available for discussion in literary-historical terms. Such a reduction of allegory was to guarantee the text's secularization. Francis herself, however, does not separate herself as Christian from herself as literary historian, for she both supplies an allegorical theme (a "description of conjugal love") and provides her literal narrative (which, in her view, *is* the literal narrative of the Song of Songs) with an allegorical counterpart. The three persons, she says, are Christ, the Jews, and the gentile church: "Christ calls in the *Gentile* world, the *Jews* in consequence thereof fly from the Messiah, and still remain distinct, distant, irreconcilable" (1781:v).

Had the Song of Songs not been, in her view, a canonical text with a divine meaning, this late-eighteenth-century laywoman, the scholarly daughter of one scholarly clergyman and wife of another, would have been bound to think both it and her project indelicate—she suspected that in any case the ignorant would deem her work "unfit for the exercise of a *female* pen" (1781: i). In common with other eighteenth-century gentlewomen, she relished the passionate verses of a contemporary Turkish potentate to his intended bride her translation of which was included in Lady Mary Wortley Montagu's published letters, verses aptly compared by the letter-writer to the Song of Solomon, but in those verses there is no answering female voice.[22] Both safety of cultural distance and canonically secured purity were prerequisites before Francis could give her wholehearted scholarly attention to the voice of female passion.

Even then, for a woman to publish on the Song of Songs demanded considerable courage, a courage no doubt derived at least in part from the fact that she had all those things to value herself on that Pamela lacked—class, connections, education, money. If she had been primarily interested in her reputation as a biblical scholar, she would certainly have chosen a less problematic text: the Psalms, for instance, were traditionally recommended as suitable for female study (Blamires 1993:4). Instead, having lived all her life among male clerical biblical scholars, she chose, as a laywoman, the one book that enabled her to write from her female experience as well as her acquired knowledge. What feminists may perceive as paradigms of patriarchy in her text—the split between the passionate and the passionless woman, the nexus of female affect and rivalry for male affection—Francis perceived as truths of female experience, the more recognizable for being written by "an *inspired penman*" (1781: ii) and in a language incomparably more passionate than polite English.

We may not like the Song of Songs Francis writes; we may be uneasy about her need, in a time of transition, to cling to a presecular interpretation, but her insistence on bringing together learning and feeling, what she knew as male and female worlds, makes her Song of Songs an oustanding feminist moment. A century later, Cady Stanton resigned the Song of Songs to the male world, to the "luxurious king" serenading his seraglio, a world a woman would do well to leave well alone. Trible wants the Song of Songs to transcend any possible cultural context: if neither the third century B.C.E. nor the end of the second millennium C.E. has enabled equal and mutual love-relations between men and women, this text offers us something to aspire toward, a "symphony of eroticism." Yet the Song of Songs invites us not to separate off in our minds the lover's gentle and desired despoliation of the garden [5:1] from the watchmen's savage stripping of the wandering lover [5:7]" (Dove 1990:73). Both the Glossed Song of Songs and Ann Francis understand that the Song of Songs is not "merely a love poem," that love is both personal and public. For us, thinking in the aftermath of *A History of Sexuality*, it may perhaps be the text to bridge the gap between Foucault's East and West, his suspiciously feminized *ars erotica* and suspiciously masculinized *scientia sexualis*.

Notes

1. The current scholarly consensus is that the Song of Songs is a collection of ancient love lyrics (see Cross & Livingstone 1997:1517); on the nature, origin, and language of these lyrics, see Falk 1982 and Fox 1985). The date of the Song of Songs (like most aspects of this problematic text) is disputed; arguments for dating as early as the tenth century B.C.E. and as late as the third century B.C.E. are discussed by Pope [1978:22–33]. On linguistic grounds I incline towards a late dating (c. 300 B.C.E.), but of course individual poems, or originals of them in other languages, may be earlier.

2. The Latin text is from the Vulgate, edited by Weber (1975); the literal translation is my own. Chapter and verse numbers refer to the Vulgate text.

3. Landy took back his criticism later, arguing that Trible's imaginative insights erase "generations of pedantic biblical scholarship" (Brenner 1993: 260). He had excepted from his 1983 accusation Trible's 1973.

4. On some of the implications of Solomon's supposed authorship, see Dove 1990:67.

5. Whether its canonical status was ever seriously in jeopardy among Jews or Christians is still debated (see Cross & Livingstone 1997:1517). Rabbi

Aqiba's assertion at the end of the first century C.E. that the Song of Songs was the holiest of the holy books of the Jews may imply that its holiness had been questioned: see Rowley 1952:189–90.

6. The only exceptions, Blamires argues, were some royal and aristocratic women, and there was a decline in female scholars of Latin between c. 1100 and c. 1300 (1993:4).

7. *Sweynheym* & Pannartz (1471–72); there is no modern edition. *Canticum Canticorum* is in vol. 3: there are no quire or folio numbers, and there is no *postilla moralis* on the Books of Solomon in this edition. I discuss Nicholas's *Postilla Litteralis in Cantica Canticorum* in (forthcoming)

8. On Origen's writings on the Song of Songs, see Matter 1990:20–48.

9. On early modern readings of the Song of Songs, see Engammare 1993. Pope's bibliography (1978:233–80) can be supplemented for the sixteenth through the nineteenth centuries by Ricciotti's annotated bibliography (1928:178–89).

10. I take as my starting point E. D. Hirsch's statement "allegory has more or less gone away" (1994:549).

11. On the *Glossa Ordinaria* as a whole, see Smalley 1983:46–66, 1984: 452–7. The text of the Song of Songs in the *Glossa Ordinaria* differs in certain details from the Vulgate text of Canticum Canticorum, edited by Weber (1975:997–1002); the verse-divisions and numbering given here, which both post-date the *Glossa Ordinaria*, follow Weber.

12. For evidence of Anselm of Laon's authorship of the Glossed Song of Songs, and its date, see Dove 1997:33–40; on Anselm, see also Smalley 1983:49–51.

13. In manuscript, the Glossed Bible is a multivolume work, and libraries rarely contained the entire Bible glossed. Margaret T. Gibson points out that typically the contents of manuscripts of Glossed books reflect Cassiodorus's division of the Bible into nine volumes, *Biblia Latina cum Glossa Ordinaria* (1992: vii).

14. On the printed editions, including J.-P. Migne's incomplete edition, *Patrologia Latina*, vols. 113–14, see Froehlich 1992.

15. Text from chapter 1, glosses 171 and 176 (Dove 1997:130–4); full references to the Bede and Origen original are provided. On Bede's commentary, see Matter 1990:97–101.

16. For a Jungian reading of the identification of the male reader with the bride, see Astell 1990:89–104.

17. On the interpretation of the Song of Songs in the eighteenth century, see Pope 1978:130–2, 250–1. Francis argues, against Johanna David Michaelis (d. 1791), who was "inclined to look no farther than the *literal* meaning," that the Song of Songs is a poetic drama, not an epithalamium (as Origen had claimed) or a pastoral (Francis 1781: xii–xv).

18. "A Vision Occasioned by my visiting Cambridge, Nov. 1787" in Francis 1790:31–6.

19. This was her only venture into biblical scholarship: she published three volumes of poetry: *The Obsequies of Demetrius Polyorcetes: A Poem* (1785); *A Poetical Epistle from Charlotte to Werther* (1788), and *Miscellaneous Poems* (see note 18).

20. The information about Ann Francis in the *Dictionary of National*

Biography, c. 1890, is derived from James Dallaway 1819:57, 193. I am indebted to my friend and colleague Sybil Oldfield for drawing my attention to Ann Francis.

21. See p. 17 for context see also Pope 1978:131.

22. See Jack (1993:76–9) for letter of April 1, 1717 (extracted from *Letters . . . written during her travels in Europe, Asia and Africa*, 3 vols. [London, 1763]); Francis describes these verses (1781: xi-xii.)

References

Astell, Ann. 1990. *The Song of Songs in the Middle Ages*. Ithaca, N.Y.: Cornell University Press.

Biblia Latina cum Glossa Ordinaria 1992. Turnhout: Brepols. Facsimile reprint of the editio princeps. Strassburg: Adolph Rusch, 1480–81, 4 vols.

Blamires, Alcuin 1993. In Smith and Taylor 1993:1–12.

Brenner, Athalya (ed.). 1993. *A Feminist Companion to the Song of Songs*. Sheffield: *Journal for the Study of the Old Testament*.

Cross, F. L., and E. A. Livingstone (eds.). 1997. *The Oxford Dictionary of the Christian Church*. 3rd ed.Oxford: Oxford University Press.

Dallaway, James 1819. *A History of the Western Division of the County of Sussex. Including the Rapes of Chichester, Arundel, and Bramber, with the City and Diocese of Chichester*. Vol. 2. London: T. Bensley.

Dove, Mary. 1990. *Amor Vincit Omnia*: The Human in the Song of Songs. In (ed.), Venetia Nelson *On Being Human*. Melbourne, Australia: Lovell: 65–75.

———. 1996. Sex, Allegory and Censorship: A Reconsideration of Medieval Commentaries on the Song of Songs. *Literature and Theology* 10:317–28.

———. 1997. *Glossa Ordinaria in Canticum Canticorum*. Turnhout: Brepols. Corpus Christianorum Continuatio Medievalis, 170 pars 22.

———. 2000. "Literal Senses in the Song of Songs." In *Nicholas of Lyra: The Senses of Scripture*, ed. Philip Krey and Lesley Smith, Leiden: Brill; Studies in the History of Christian Thought: 129–46.

Engammare, Max. 1993. *Qu'il Me Baise Des Baisiers de Sa Bouche: Le Cantique des Cantiques à la Renaissance. Étude et Bibliographie*. Travaux d'Humanisme et Renaissance 277. Geneva: Droz.

Falk, Marcia 1982. *Love Lyrics from the Bible*. Sheffield, England: Almond.

Fox, Michael V. 1985. *The Song of Songs and Ancient Egyptian Love-Lyric*. Madison: University of Wisconsin Press.

Francis, Ann. 1781. *A Poetical Translation of the Song of Solomon from the Original Hebrew*. London: n.p.

———. 1790. *Miscellaneous Poems by a Lady*. London. n.p.

Froelich, Karlfried. 1992. *The Printed Gloss. Biblia Latina cum Glossa Ordinaria*. Turnhout: Brepols. Facsimile reprint of the editio princeps. Strassburg: Adolph Rusch, 1480–81: vol. 1, vii–xi.

Gibson, Margaret T. 1992. *The Glossed Bible*. Biblia Latina cum Glossa Ordinaria. Turnhout: Brepols. Facsimile reprint of the editio princeps. Strassburg: Adolph Rusch, 1480–81: vol. 1, xii–xxvi.

Hirsch, E. D. 1994. Transhistorical Intentions and the Persistence of Allegory. *New Literary History* 25 (3):549–567.

Jack, Malcolm (ed.). 1993. *Vathek and Other Stories: A William Beckford Reader*. London: Pickering.

Krey, Philip and Lesley Smith. eds. 2000. *Studies in the History of Christian Thought*. Leiden: Brill.

Landy, Francis. 1983. *Paradoxes of Paradise: Identity and Difference in the Song of Songs*. Sheffield, England: Almond.

Matter, E. Ann. 1990. *The Voice of My Beloved: The Song of Songs in Western Medieval Christianity*. Philadelphia: University of Pennsylvania Press.

Migne, J.-P. 1852. *Patrologia Latina*. Vol. 113, cols. 1125–68. Paris: n.p.

Pope, Marvin H. 1978. *The Song of Songs: A New Translation with Introduction and Commentary*. New York: Doubleday.

Ricciotti, Giuseppe. 1928. *Il Cantico dei Cantici*. Turin: n.p.

Richardson, Samuel. 1980. *Pamela; Or, Virtue Rewarded*. London: Penguin Books.

Rowley, H. H. 1952.*The Servant of the Lord*. London: Lutterworth.

Smalley, Beryl. 1983. *The Study of the Bible in the Middle Ages*. 3rd ed. Oxford: Blackwell.

———. 1984. *Glossa ordinaria. Theologische Realencyclopädie*. Vol. 13. Oxford: Oxford University Press: 452–7.

Smith, Lesley, and Jane H. M. Taylor (eds.). 1993. *Women, the Book and the Godly*. Cambridge, England: D. S. Brewer.

Sweynheym, Conradus, and Arnoldus Pannartz (eds.). 1471–72. *Postilla litteralis et moralis in Vetus et Novum Testamentum*. 5 vols. Rome: n.p.

Trible, Phyllis. 1973. Depatriarchalizing the Biblical Interpretation. *Journal of the American Academy of Religion* 41:42–8.

———. 1978. Love's Lyrics Redeemed. In *God and the Rhetoric of Sexuality*. Philadelphia: Fortress: 144–65.

Vinaver, Eugène. 1971. *Sir Thomas Malory: Works*. Oxford: Oxford University Press.

Weber, R. 1975. Biblia Sacra Iuxta Vulgatam Versionem Emendata. 2 vols. Stuttgart: Wurttemberische Bebelanstalt.

8

Mother, Maiden, Child

Gender as Performance in *The Book of Margery Kempe*

Clare Bradford

*T*he *Book of Margery Kempe* (1438) is frequently characterized as the first autobiography in English. The subject of the *Book*, however, is not the "I" of first-person narration but is referred to by way of third-person narration, in the introduction as "a synful caytyf" (Windeatt 1985:1)[1] and throughout the *Book* as "this creatur." This feature enacts a gap between Margery Kempe and her *Book*, prohibiting any simple or unproblematic identification of Kempe the author with the Margery Kempe constructed through the narrative of the *Book*.[2] In another distancing strategy, the process of writing the *Book* is self-consciously present within it, since the narrative is, in part, about Margery's difficulties in producing a narrative: finding trustworthy scribes; persuading them to invest their time in transcribing her narrative; convincing them that they will suffer no ill effects through association with her; quite simply, getting the task done. For Margery Kempe is represented in the proem to the *Book* as illiterate but educated, a combination difficult to imagine in our century, when knowledge is identified with literacy, but not in the late fourteenth and early fifteenth centuries, when there existed a robust tradition of oral transmission of instruction and stories through sermons, mystery plays, liturgical forms, and the practice of reading aloud to an audience.[3]

When the *Book* was discovered in 1934,[4] it was seen, in the words

of David Knowles, "at once as a godsend and as a disillusionment"
(1961:139). That is, the *Book* was thought to constitute an autobio-
graphical work of historical and social interest, featuring an English
eccentric, a noisy, self-promoting and hysterical woman who could not
be taken seriously as a writer on spirituality and doctrine and who was
commonly compared (always to her disadvantage) with her contemporary, Julian of Norwich.[5] The recuperation of Kempe as the author
of an important and complex work has been due in large part to feminist scholars who have examined the gendered nature of Margery's
spirituality and its relationship to traditions of feminine mysticism (see,
for example, Beckwith 1986; Partner 1991; Lochrie 1991; Petroff 1994).
Another useful line of inquiry has focused on the double-voiced and
hybrid nature of the *Book;* for example, Sarah Beckwith's Bakhtinian
reading (1992) of authority and agency in the language of the *Book*
and Schklar's discussion (1995) of its blurring of the lines between
orthodoxy and heterodoxy. Many feminist readings of the *Book* have
identified its writer with the figure of Margery as she appears in its
pages, viewing the work as the expression of an "authentic" (and sometimes essentialized) female identity, but Lynn Staley's *Margery Kempe's
Dissenting Fictions* (1994) offers a different interpretation: that *The Book
of Margery Kempe* is "best understood, not as an autobiography, but as
a biography, a 'treatise,' written by someone about an exemplary person" (1994:37).[6] While Staley's reading avoids the trap of ascribing to
Margery Kempe a fixed and static subjectivity, it nevertheless runs the
risk of transferring a similar kind of unproblematized identity to Kempe,
as the shaper of Margery's character and the world of the *Book.* My
reading follows Staley's lead in viewing the *Book* as an exemplary narrative that traces Margery's pilgrimage from sinner to holy woman, but
I believe that the dynamics of narrative and discourse in the *Book* are
more complex than the term "exemplary narrative" suggests. Rather,
I see in *The Book of Margery Kempe* a web of meanings, inscribed in
the language and narrative structure of the *Book* and manifesting
what Norman Fairclough calls the "traces of the productive process"
(1989:24): the constraints, conventions, ideologies, and sociohistorical
factors that impinged on its production. My reading thus foregrounds
the performative nature of the *Book* and of Margery as an exemplary
figure.

One of the *Book*'s central concerns is the problematic relationship
between women writers and traditions of writing in the late medieval
period, and by inserting Margery's scribes as characters within the text,
Kempe dramatizes some of these tensions. Far from being mere tran-
scribers of her narrative, the scribes of the *Book* are depicted as actively

intervening in its production: they argue with Margery, strike bargains with her, delay the work of transcription, testify to her holiness. The presence of these male scribes constructs a world in which practices of literacy are still dominated by men; more important, it foregrounds the predicament of the holy woman who desires to participate in discussion and debate on spirituality and doctrine but whose gender marginalizes her by placing her outside institutional structures such as the priest-hood, and clerical and religious orders, and who is subject to prohibi-tions against women speaking publicly on religion. When Kempe de-scribes Margery's interactions with scribes and their interventions in the writing of the book, she discloses the subterfuges and strategies a woman had to employ in order to write on religious topics, and the dangers that attend public utterances on doctrine and spirituality.

Indeed, Kempe's narrative is built on stories involving spoken utter-ances: Margery's speeches when she is accused; the many exchanges in which she confounds her accusers; her "krying & roryng" (Windeatt 1985:68); the words she hears when Christ, Mary, and the saints are "spekyng in hir mende [mind]" (Windeatt 1985:230); her own prayers, recorded as direct address to Mary or Christ; her interactions with her fellow Christians (hostile or friendly). Thus, while Kempe's account of the writing of the *Book* dramatizes Margery's entrapment within a pa-triarchal order, the narrative itself is focused on the production of a vocal, outward-looking, and frequently resistant subjectivity that refuses the socially sanctioned role of feminine passivity, meekness, and silence. This disjunction (between entrapment and resistance) is replicated in a number of ways throughout the *Book* and works against interpretations that see Kempe either as straightforwardly subversive (see Petroff 1994; McEntire 1992; Mahoney 1992) or as a pawn of the patriarchy (see Beckwith 1986; Lochrie 1991; Szell 1992).

During the fourteenth and fifteenth centuries, those speaking on re-ligion had good reason to take particular care with words, since a care-less or imprecise expression might easily be construed as heresy. In 1401, when, according to the temporal scheme of the *Book*, Margery was in her late twenties and living with her husband at Bishop's Lynn in Norfolk, a local clergyman, William Sawtre, chaplain of St. Mar-garet's Church, was publicly burnt as a Lollard; between 1428 and 1431, more than sixty women and men were tried for heresy by the episcopal court at Norwich.[7] Kempe's *Book* abounds with incidents in which Margery's fidelity to Church doctrine is tested and questioned by bishops, monks, friars, and priests and occasions when she is accused of Lollardy and threatened with burning at the stake.[8] For the *Book* plots Margery's attempts to live a life both public and spiritual, a dan-

gerous and difficult project at a time when women who devoted themselves to spiritual matters commonly lived in convents or anchorages,
where they were supposedly more readily controlled by bishops and
clerics than were women living "in the world." More than this, Margery's demeanor and very clothing make her a public personage. A
married woman who has borne fourteen children, she dresses in white,
the color associated with virginity. She is given to extravagant displays
of devotion: at her local church, at churches throughout England, and
at places of pilgrimage in Europe and the Holy Land, she cries loudly
and at length, especially when she is about to take Communion; frequently she "fel down & wrestyd wyth hir body & mad wondyrful cher
& contenawns wyth boystows [violent] sobbyngys & gret plente of
terys" [She fell down and twisted her body about and made astonishing
gestures and facial expressions with violent sobbing and abundant
tears.] (Windeatt 1985:40).

Judith Butler's distinction between expressive and performative gender attributes (1990:134–41) is a useful starting point for the interrogation of some of the contradictions that characterize the representation of Margery as an exemplary figure. On the one hand, Kempe's
descriptions of Margery's encounters with clerics, which typically focus
on her attempts to receive validation for the way she lives out her spirituality, construct gender as a stable identity in which masculinity is
expressed both by the binding nature of clerical authority and by the
actual judgments and statements by which clerics manifest their power.
On the other hand, Margery's quest for masculine validation centers on
her performance of actions that undo the binary frame (active/passive;
subject/object; intellect/feeling) dominant within her time and culture.
That is, she seeks from men approval for practices that undermine the
dominance of masculine authority. Butler's concept of a gendered self
"structured through repeated acts that seek to approximate the ideal of
a substantial ground of identity, but which, in their occasional *discon*-
tinuity, reveal the temporal and contingent groundlessness of this
'ground' "(1990:141), thus accords both with Margery's performance of
repeated and public acts and with the inconsistencies evident in her
depiction of these acts.

The most striking aspect of Kempe's narrative is its insistence on the
materiality of religious experience and especially her deployment of discourses of maternity and sexuality. The *Book* begins with an account
of Margery's experience of a period of insanity that followed the birth
of her first child and that lasted over six months, ending with a vision
of Christ "in lyknesse of a man, most semly, most bewtyuows, & most
amyable that euyr mygth be seen wyth mannys eye" (Windeatt 1985:

8), who sits "upon her bedside" and consoles her with comforting words. This semierotic representation, set within the intimate space of Margery's bed when she is alone, constructs Christ as *fin amor* lover, a role that provides for the interpellation of Margery as loved maiden and paves the way for her mystical marriage to Christ. The terms in which this marriage is described mingle discourses of sexuality and maternity; Christ is depicted as saying:

> Therfore most I nedys be homly [familiar] wyth the & lyn in thi bed wyth the . . . & thu mayst boldly, whan thu art in thi bed, take me to the as for thi weddyd husbond . . . & as for thy swete sone, for I wyl be lovyd as a sone schuld be lovyd wyth the modyr. . . . [T]hu mayst boldly take me in the armys of thi sowle & kissen my mowth, myn hed, & my fete as swetly as thow wylt. (Windeatt 1985:90)

Other medieval women mystics, notably Julian of Norwich, represent Christ as simultaneously lover and mother;[9] in the *Book*, Christ is rarely referred to as Margery's mother, but more often as her tender lover and helpless child. This image of Christ as Margery's child is built on Kempe's construction of a protagonist who has borne fourteen children and who therefore possesses an intimate knowledge of the fragility and dependence of children's bodies. Following an episode in which Margery is mystically married to Christ, Kempe describes her as affected equally by the sight of women carrying male infants, a sight that causes her to weep and to snatch babies out of their mothers' arms and kiss them "in the stede of Criste," and by seeing handsome men, who also cause her to weep and sob "ful sor in the manhod of Crist" (Windeatt 1985: 86). The multiplicity of subjectivities in Margery's roles here as lover of Christ, as archetypal mother (including Mary), and as Christ himself resonates with contemporary feminist concerns with the performance of gender.

But these acts of devotion to the manhood and childhood of Christ are complicated by another set of acts, through which Margery rejects male sexuality. Her conversion and calling to follow Christ is constituted in part as a rejection of sexual activity, and here Kempe's writing of the female body touches on some of the most vexed and complex questions in medieval theology. Bernard of Clairvaux, whose teachings on the body were especially influential at the time the *Book* was written, associated women with the flesh, or the principle of sexual desire and appetites; the body, as distinct from the flesh, was thought to be not in itself evil but easily corrupted by the will, which was dominated by the desires of the flesh. The female body, being fissured, and thus susceptible to attack and defilement, was regarded as the inverse of the male body (which was, of course, the "normal" or "standard" body) and was identified with the flesh and its dangers. The ideal female body was therefore the virginal, intact body, ideally situated within the sealed confines of convent or anchorage. It followed that marriage was considered a state inferior to widowhood and far inferior to the celibacy of clerics and nuns, unless both parties within a marriage vowed to live chastely. The *Book* draws on these schemata of the female body by describing in some detail the obstacles and difficulties Margery experiences in her project of living the life of a holy woman.[10]

Following her conversion, Margery attempts to persuade her husband that they have together "dysplesyd God be her [by their] inordynat lofe [love] & the gret delectacyon that thei haddyn eythyr of in vsyng of other [the great delectation that each had experienced in using the other's body]" (Windeatt 1985:12) and that they should live chaste lives; but at this stage John Kempe is reluctant to take a vow of chastity, arguing (reasonably enough) that he has received no divine calling to do so. Here, as well as later in the *Book* when Kempe describes Margery's early relationship with her husband, the language of the narrative has a curiously double effect. On one hand, sexuality is represented as displeasing to God and as disgusting; Margery would rather "etyn or drynkyn the wose, the mukke in the chanel [the ooze, the muck in the gutter]" (Windeatt 1985:12) than have intercourse with her husband. On the other hand, the terms used to represent the sexual pleasures of Margery's youth ("lofe," "delectacyon," even "lust," which at this time carries the meanings "desire" and "pleasure") are terms of romance and "lofe-talkyng" and are not themselves displaced by signifiers of disgust. This disjunction speaks of tensions between the deployment of discourses of sexuality to encode the female mystic's relationship with Christ and cultural and theological unease concerning the fissured flesh of the female body.

These unresolved tensions find expression in two descriptions of temptations experienced by Margery following her conversion. The first of these, which occurs during a period when she is still (though unwillingly) having intercourse with her husband, involves a man "whech sche lovyd wel," who asks her to come to him "befor evynsong," when he would "ly be hir [lie with her] & have hys lust of hys body" (Windeatt 1985:14). Margery can think of little else but the man's words and is persuaded by the devil that God has forsaken her; otherwise she cannot be so tempted. In this frame of mind, she goes to the man "that he xuld haue hys lust, as sche wend [believed] he had desyred." But the man rejects her, telling her that he "had levar ben hewyn as smal as flesch to the pott [he would rather be cut into pieces as small as meat for the pot]" (Windeatt 1985:15). In this instance, the man who tempts Margery is an enigmatic figure, his motivations and actions being outside the narrative frame, and the incident appears to constitute a proof of her weakness and instability, her susceptibility (as a woman) to the temptations of the flesh. It is what is unsaid in this incident that is of most interest: Kempe's refusal to ascribe motivation to the man and the contrast between Margery's determination to live chastely and her willingness to engage in sexual activity. Here, as elsewhere, Kempe engages in a strategic silence concerning masculine sexuality, a silence that speaks of the constraints experienced by women who wrote about men in the late Middle Ages. Similarly, the contradictory representation of Margery in this episode carries the traces of Kempe's entrapment between the misogynist view of women that prevailed and the *Book*'s representation of Margery as a powerful woman.

The most startling of Margery's temptations occurs after she rejects certain revelations from God—those in which she is told which of her fellow Christians will be saved and which will be damned. Margery's rejection of this knowledge, which she represents as both the mark of her privilege and a cause of pain (since the thought of the damned distresses her), results in a bizarre and telling form of punishment: she is besieged by "fowle thowtys & fowle mendys [imaginings] of letchery" (Windeatt 1985:144), the worst of which involve a vision in which "men of religyon, preystys, & many other, bothyn hethyn & Cristen comyn be-for hir syght . . . schewyng her bar membrys un-to hir [showing their naked genitals to her]" (Windeatt 1985:145), after which the devil tempts her to prostitute herself to these men. These visions are represented as God's way of persuading Margery of the veracity of those visions of the damned that she formerly rejected. In this way, the narrative suggests that when such privileged knowledge is accorded a woman, it is dependent on her rejection of sexuality; at the same time, the vision constructs male sexuality as a highly complex site of meaning, where the drama of attraction and repulsion mingle, just as human and divine are uncomfortably associated.

If gender in *The Book of Margery Kempe* were a "stable identity or locus of agency from which various acts follow" (Butler 1990:140), the distinctions between the various roles women play (especially maiden and mother) would be clear and obvious, manifested through such physical signs as clothing and way of life. But Margery's performance of her identity as a woman resists such distinctions and calls for a redefinition of categories. Following her conversion, she is convinced that she is called to live chastely within marriage, but she obtains John Kempe's agreement only after they have lived as man and wife for twenty years, and this crucial agreement is reached as the two walk, "in rygth hot wedyr" (Windeatt 1985:23) on the road from York to Bridlington, she carrying a bottle of beer and John Kempe bearing a cake beneath his clothes. These homely details introduce negotiations that center not only on marital intercourse but on the habitus associated with the domestic and familial life of Margery and John Kempe. John Kempe's first ambit is to seek a somewhat ambiguous compromise: his wife should pay his debts, and eat and drink with him on Fridays as she used to before she began a regimen of fasting, and in turn they should "lyn stylle to-gedyr in o bed [still lie together in one bed]" (Windeatt 1985:24). To "lyn . . . to-gedyr" is not necessarily to have intercourse, and it seems that John Kempe is seeking to maintain the habitus of married life while conceding the possibility of a chaste (though still intimate) relationship. Margery, torn between the obligations of two kinds of abstinence, is told by Christ that she is not bound by her vow to fast on Fridays, and so she is encouraged to drive home the bargain; but in comparison with her husband's articulation of a (possibly) chaste marriage, she is both explicit and uncompromising. She will pay his debts, and eat and drink with him on Fridays, and in exchange he will "not komyn in my bed," nor will he "askyn no dett of matrimony [demand the obligation of matrimony] aftyr this day" (Windeatt 1985:25).

The white clothes Margery chooses to wear from this point undo the distinction between maiden and wife and break down the hierarchy of values that separates virgins from sexually experienced women, a bold move rationalized in a passage in which Margery, during an interchange with Christ, laments the fact that she is not a virgin. Christ reassures her, "thu art a mayden in thi sowle . . . & so xalt thu dawnsyn [shall you dance] in Hevyn wyth other holy maydens & virgynes" (Windeatt 1985:52). The whiteness of Margery's clothes is their most obvious signifying feature, but in fact they are multivalent signifiers and carry several other meanings, political as well as religious. Their austerity and simplicity contrast both with the clothes Margery wore prior to her conversion (elaborate head dresses, garments slashed and with bright fabric underlaid beneath the slashes) and with the stylish clothes of worldly clerics such as the "eld monk" she meets at Canterbury, who has been the queen's treasurer and who is "a riche man, & gretly dred of mech [many] pepyl" (Windeatt 1985:27). Such reaction against the wealth and corruption of the institutional church is a mark both of Lollardy and of the broader cultural movement evident in the anticlericalism of the *Canterbury Tales* and *Piers Plowman*; in this way, while

Margery's clothes do not identify her as a Lollard,[11] they make a clear political statement about the desirability of a return to Gospel simplicity.

But more than any other meaning, her clothing constitutes an affront to gendered notions of authority, since, together with her loud and prolonged weeping, it makes her conspicuous as a holy woman, inviting both laypeople and clerics to question her as to her opinions and beliefs, and (most important) to seek her advice. This is audacious behavior indeed, transgressing church and secular law at a time when prohibitions against women as preachers and teachers betray the unease of the patriarchy at the prospect of learned women. The prelate and scholar Jean Gerson, for example, writes; in 1423

> [t]he female sex is forbidden on apostolic authority to teach in public, that is either by word of mouth or writing. . . . All women's teaching is to be held suspect unless it has been examined diligently and much more fully than men's . . . And why? Because they are easily seduced and determined seducers, and because it is not proved that they are witnesses to divine grace. (Cited in Colledge & Walsh 1978:151)

It's worth considering one instance of Margery's public performance of her identity as holy woman, a visit to Leicester, where she is interrogated by civic and religious authorities. The *Book*'s account of this event is a telling instance of Kempe's strategic deployment of discourses of sexuality and gender and is presented as a drama in three acts: in the first Margery is arrested by the mayor of Leicester and taken into custody for a night; in the second she is interrogated by the steward of Leicester and again taken into custody; in the third she is formally arraigned "be-for the hy awter [high altar]" of All Saints Church in the presence of the abbot and dean of Leicester, many friars and priests, and so many lay people that "thei stodyn up-on stolys [stools] for to beheldyn hir & wonderyn up-on hir" (Windeatt 1985:114).

The account of Margery's trial inevitably evokes the dramatic representations, in various mystery plays, of the trial of Christ. The figure of the innocent, wrongfully accused and appearing before secular and religious authorities;[12] the presence of a crowd before whom the action takes place; interchanges between accused and accusers; the representative nature of characters; all these elements appear both in Margery's trial and in the trial of Christ depicted in mystery plays. But Margery's trial is of a gendered nature, as the narrative indicates from the outset, when the mayor, having heard of her loud and public crying in one of the churches of Leicester, summons her to him and demands, in a none-too-gentle reminder that women derive their identities from men, to know "whos dowtyr sche was" (Windeatt 1985:111). Margery's response, a wholly orthodox one, is to claim respectability by virtue of two respectable men—her father, five times mayor of Lynn, and her husband, also a burgess of this town. In comparison with the mildness of her answer, the mayor's accusation of doctrinal and sexual deviance appears hysterical and extreme: "thu art a fals strumpet, a fals loller [Lollard], & a fals deceyver of the pepyl, & therfor I xal have the in preson [prison]." But the city jailer and his man, metonymically representing "the pepyl," are shown, in an inversion of social hierarchies, to be capable of distinguishing truth from falsehood: they do not believe that Margery is a criminal and refuse to place her in prison "a-mong men" (Windeatt 1985:112), where she will be in physical danger, and instead she is lodged in the jailer's own house and permitted to go to church.

The second act of the drama is syntagmatically connected with the first and heightens the sense of Margery's bodily danger at the hands of men, this time when she appears before the steward of Leicester, "a semly man" (Windeatt 1985:112) who is no image of Christ. Again, traditional gender binaries are inverted: Margery's reasonable, restrained demeanor and speech against the steward's irrational and uncontrolled behavior. And again, the danger she highlights (that of sexual assault) is calculated to undermine the charges of immorality laid against her: "Than the Stywarde toke hir be the hand & led hir in-to hys chawmbyr & spak many fowyl rebawdy [ribald] wordys un-to hir, purposing & desyryng, as it semed hir, to opressyn hir & for-lyn [violate] hir" (Windeatt 1985:113).

The third act relates to the first two paradigmatically: the place of Margery's trial is now, crucially, in a church and before powerful clerics, so that it is constituted as a test of her religious orthodoxy; while the first two acts were conducted in the private rooms of the mayor and the steward, the third is public and open. The mayor is again a key player, but he is himself to be tested against the same standards that are applied to Margery. Margery is first required to deliver a statement concerning her belief in the Articles of the Faith and (to determine whether she is a Lollard) her understanding of the Eucharist. Her clerical questioners are satisfied with her responses, but the mayor, "hir dedly enmy," returns to his previous charges of hypocrisy, and the ground of argument now changes to that of Margery's sexually transgressive behavior: "Than the Meyr alto-rebukyd [severely rebuked] hir & rehersyd many reprevows [reproving] wordys & ungoodly, the whiche is mor expedient to be concelyd than expressyd" (Windeatt 1985:115)

Margery now claims an identity calculated to strike at the heart of the mayor's argument: she is, she says, bound to her husband by marriage, but she loves God "a-bovyn al thynge" and "al men in God & for God" (Windeatt 1985:115). From this position as chaste wife and chaste lover of humans, she levels at the mayor the accusation that he is not merely too corrupt to be mayor but that his corruption is of a specifically sexual kind: "for owr Lord God seyde hym-self er [before] he wolde takyn ven-iawnce [vengance] on the cyteys, 'I xal comyn down & seen,' & yet he knew al thyng" (Windeatt 1985:116). The scriptural reference Kempe deploys here was a staple of medieval sermons and religious instruction: "the cyteys" are Sodom and Gomorrah (Genesis 18:21), synonymous in Kempe's time as in ours with sexual depravity, so that Margery's retal-iation to the mayor's insult takes the form of an accusation more serious than his, being loaded with scriptural authority and with the implica-tion that Margery, like the Yahweh of Genesis, can see beyond the sur-face to what is in people's hearts.

The mayor now resorts to a coded accusation of Lollardy, centered on Margery's white clothes and associating them with a subversiveness that, he claims, will result in the destruction of marriage itself: "I wil wetyn [I want to know] why thow gost in white clothys, for I trowe [be-lieve] thow art comyn hedyr [hither] to han a-wey owr wyvys fro us & ledyn hem wyth the [to lure our wives away from us and lead them off with you]" (Windeatt 1985:116). The most obvious significance of this complaint concerns female solidarity and its capacity to undermine masculine authority, but Ruth Shklar (1995:296–7) suggests that an-other, concealed message is encoded in the mayor's speech: an accusa-tion of homosexuality (a charge frequently used to vilify Lollards) by which the mayor returns her coded accusation of sodomy. Margery's fi-nal move is to refuse to explain to the mayor the circumstances in which God called her to wear white clothing, on the grounds that he is "not worthy to wetyn [know] it" (Windeatt 1985:116), but she undertakes to provide an explanation to three high-ranking clerics—the abbot, the dean, and a friar. The mayor is symbolically disempowered, required to leave the clerics' seats and to join the laypeople, after which Margery satisfies the clerics that she has indeed been called by God to wear white clothes, and the closure of the episode is constituted by a displacement of roles in which Margery is vindicated and the mayor publicly humili-ated. The narrative is thus built on a strategic arrangement of incidents: Margery, accused of sexual and religious transgression, is saved by her orthodoxy; the mayor's deployment of accusations of Lollardy is turned back upon him to reveal his sinfulness; and Margery's claim of a divine call (revealed by her clothing) is approved by powerful clerics. The gender politics of this episode underline Margery's dependence on the authority of abbot, dean, and friar, so that her role as holy woman is contained within a schema of masculine power. At the same time, Margery's victory over her enemy the mayor works as a critique of the incursion of secular power into matters pertaining to belief and doctrine; and it overturns two common gender stereotypes (passive, silent women and garrulous, irrational women) by representing Margery as a public figure and an eloquent, quick-witted, and tactical speaker.

Kempe's descriptions of Margery's frequent outbursts of "krying & roryng" and of displays of devotion, such as throwing herself on the floor and stretching out her arms in the shape of the cross, were pathologized from the time of the *Book's* discovery, characterized as the symptoms of hysteria or (in the case of the episode following the birth of Margery's first child) postpartum depression or psychosis. Such gendered judgments, which always had the effect of undermining the significance of the *Book's* treatment of spirituality, mask the significance of episodes such as Margery's trial at Leicester, where her identity as holy woman is performed quite differently; in addition, they underrate the degree of reflexivity that Kempe interpolates into her descriptions of Margery's behavior. In the absence of her regular confessor, Margery confesses her sins to another priest, and on her confessor's return she criticizes his replacement as follows: "He . . . is rygth scharp un-to me. He wyl not levyn [believe in] my felyngys; he settyth nowt by hem; he heldyth hem but tryfelys & japys [trifles and follies]" (Windeatt 1985: 44). Margery's feminine affectivity and emotion ("felyngys") are here set in opposition to her confessor's masculine rationality; since, by this point in the narrative, Margery's "felyngs" about people and events have been shown to be accurate and reliable, this priest's suspicion of the feminine is clearly intended to be read as shortsighted and uninformed. To say as much explicitly would, of course, have constituted too direct a slur on masculine rationality at the time of the *Book's* writing, and Kempe defuses Margery's complaint by representing her regular confessor as advising her that, while he believes his replacement to be mistaken, he is nevertheless destined to be her "scorge" (Windeatt 1985: 68), occasioning a trial through which Margery will be purified and cleansed.

Margery's most acute episodes of crying and roaring occur when she contemplates Christ's passion (see Windeatt 1985:67–73, 167, 174, 184–7). Like the writings of Julian of Norwich, the *Book* mobilizes discourses of maternity within its representation of the suffering Christ, but there are important differences between the two books. Julian sees before her a feminized body whose long labor on the cross brings forth

Christian souls and who feeds his young not with mother's milk but "with himself . . . with the Blessed Sacrament, that is the precious food of true life" (Walsh 1961:164). In the *Book*, Margery is herself represented as enduring the "gostly labor" (Windeatt 1985:69) that is marked by her cries and tears. In this way, her identification with the suffering Christ redeems the fissured female body, which is now sanctified through association with the body of Christ, "al-to rent [severely rent] & toryn wyth scorgys, mor ful of wowndys than evyr was duffehows of holys [dovecot with holes]" (Windeatt 1985:70). While the relationship of Christ to Margery is here represented by way of familial and social roles (he is her spouse, lover, and child), another strand of imagery depicts Margery as an efficient, bustling servant within what Sarah Beckwith terms "the Holy Family Romance" (1986:46). Emerging social norms concerning family and social life are played out within this domestication of relations between God and humans and are manifest in the *Book* during a sequence in which Margery, deep in meditation, imagines herself to be the servant, first of Saint Anne and then of Mary. In these roles she cares first for the young Mary, providing her with "good mete & drynke, wyth fayr whyte clothys & whyte kerchys" (Windeatt 1985:18); later, she imagines herself as Mary's servant, arranging bedding for the infant Christ, begging food for Mary and her son, swaddling his infant body while she recalls the "scharp deth that he schuld suffyr for the lofe of synful men" (Windeatt 1985:19).

In Kempe's depiction of Margery's trial at Leicester, the jailer and his wife, unlike the city's corrupt officials, recognize her as truthful and pious; the crowd who attend her arraignment constitute a silent presence, observing the mayor's humiliation. In similar ways, the presence of the community of Christians adumbrates many of the events in which Margery shows herself to be a holy woman. Episodes of misrecognition commonly reflect the deficiencies of observers and participants, since Margery is constituted as "a merowr [mirror] amongys hem," at once a reflection of Christ's sufferings and a model of true repentance. Of those who misrecognize Margery, many are shown to be blinded by undue regard for status, money, and reputation, so that in a period when a growing mercantile class was emerging from the wreckage of the feudal system, Kempe proposes a quite radical resistance to bourgeois values. Thus, when Margery travels, with other English pilgrims, to Jerusalem and Rome, she annoys her companions by fasting from meat, weeping publicly, and talking of spiritual matters, whereas they are intent upon "makyn[g] mery" (Windeatt 1985:65). Those who recognize her as a holy woman are, in contrast, frequently poor, outcast, or of low status: in the Holy Land, for example, she is assisted by a

Saracen, and in Venice a poor, humpbacked man from Ireland befriends
her and accompanies her in her pilgrimage.

The two strands of imagery that manifest in Kempe's descriptions of
Margery's contemplation are played out as well through her relations
with her fellow Christians. Her identification with the suffering Christ
offers Christians a model for contemplating the Passion; but in her relations to her fellow Christians, Kempe frequently constitutes Margery's
actions as maternal, or as validations of maternity. In a telling exem-
plum, she is told of a young woman who, in an echo of the events
surrounding the birth of Margery's first child, has become insane following childbirth. Margery visits the woman, who is "bowndyn handys
and feet wyth chenys of yron that sche xulde smytyn no-body" but who
becomes quiet and calm when she sees Margery. Eventually the woman
is cured of her illness and is "browt to chirche & purifijd as other women
be" (Windeatt 1985:178); that is, Margery's capacity to heal is ratified
through the public and communal actions involved in the ritual of
"churching."

The most poignant exemplary story of the *Book* concerns Margery's
husband and occurs late in his life, when he is "a man of gret age
passying thre scor yer" (Windeatt 1985:179). Kempe's explanation of
the domestic arrangements of Margery and John Kempe points to the
problems they have encountered following their vow of chastity. When
they live chaste lives in the same dwelling, people accuse them of un-
chastity, and when they go on pilgrimages together, they are accused
of going, not to places of worship, but to "woodys, grovys, er [or] valeys
to usyn the lust of her bodijs that the pepil xuld not aspyin it ne wetyn
it." The implication of the narrative is that the narrowness and pruri-
ence of their community prohibits Margery and John Kempe from en-
acting a marriage different from other marriages, forcing them to live
apart, in separate lodgings. When John Kempe falls down some stairs
and is seriously injured, however, Margery is told by Christ that she
must take him to her home and care for him. Finally, he "turnyd chil-
disch . . . & lakkyd reson," becoming incontinent, so that Margery had
to spend much of her time not in contemplation but in "waschyng &
wryngyng" (Windeatt 1985:180). Two strands of narrative here inter-
sect: John Kempe's body, the occasion of "delectabyl thowtys, fleschly
lystys, & inordinat lovys" during Margery's youth, is now her penance;
and his helplessness and childishness makes him a representative figure,
a metonym for the sick and poor in whom Margery serves "Crist hym-
self" (Windeatt 1985:181).

In discussing how the devotional literature of the late Middle Ages
mobilizes and sanctifies domestic and social roles within the bourgeois

family structure developing during this period, Sarah Beckwith reads this literature as "both a response to the potentially subversive nature of female desire and a way of domesticating and internalizing it" (1986: 46). *The Book of Margery Kempe* works in a more complex way than this. For while it is powerfully informed by discourses of social and domestic life and represents Margery's inner and outward lives in relation to schemata of marital and family relations, the *Book* represents Margery as performing a public and active role, played out in spaces associated with the structures and practices of masculine power. Further, Margery appropriates the very strategies of her male opponents, so subverting the idea of fixed gender identities: Kempe's account of her trial at Leicester foregrounds Margery's capacity to defeat civic and religious authorities at their own political game. This dialogic interplay between discursive practices produces a text of great complexity, which bears the traces of its production at a period when the Lollards and other groups offered powerful resistance to civic and religious authority. The *Book*'s construction of gender is thus double-voiced: in its representation of Margery as exemplary figure, it offers grounds for readerly resignification of female spirituality; but, at the same time, it draws on doctrines that insist on the weakness of the female body and its susceptibility to temptation. The very ambivalence with which Kempe alternates between indirection and directness, and between radicalism and traditionalism, disrupts the norms that govern medieval representations of female spirituality, showing them to be implicated within political structures and discourse, but at the same time offers contemporary readers a historically grounded and dramatic example of prefeminist resistance.

Notes

1. All quotations are from the Middle English text, 1940. Where necessary, I have translated words and phrases, and I have replaced the thorn and yogh letters with their modern orthographic equivalents. An excellent translation is available, by B. A. Windeatt (1985).

2. Throughout this article, I follow the practice of Lynn Staley (1994), who refers to the author of the *Book* as "Kempe" and the constructed figure within the book as "Margery."

3. The *Book* mentions a young priest in Lynn who "red to [Margery] many a good boke of hy [high] contemplacyon & other bokys, as the Bybyl wyth doctowrys ther-up-on, Seynt Brydys boke, Hyltons booke, Bone-ventur, Stimulus Amoris, Incendium Amoris, & swech other [others of a similar kind]" (Windeatt 1985:143).

4. Although some excerpts from the *Book* had been printed, around 1501, by Wynkyn de Worde, in a seven-page pamphlet, the *Book* itself was

not discovered until 1934, in the library of a Catholic family, the Butler-Bowdons.

5. Julian, who lived as a recluse in Norwich for much of her life, and whom Margery visited to obtain spiritual advice, wrote an account of her own visions and her reflections on them, published in Middle English as Colledge & Walsh 1978 and in translation as Walsh 1961.

6. Very little is known about Margery Kempe as a historical figure, apart from her admission to the Trinity Guild of Lynn in 1438. Her father, John Brunham, is mentioned in the records of the town of King's Lynn as a mayor, alderman, and public official; her husband, John Kempe, is also named in civic records. The *Book* relates many of the incidents of Margery's life to historical events, well-known contemporary figures, and geographical and civic locations; this specificity of reference, which has convinced many readers of the "truth" of Kempe's writing, serves to underline the relationship of the exemplary figure of Margery to institutions and cultural practices.

7. Lollardy was a movement that had its beginnings in the teachings of John Wycliffe and that constituted a reaction against the corruption and venality of powerful figures in the Church. It rejected doctrines not based on scriptural authority and called for a return to Gospel principles. One of its principal "heresies" was the rejection of the doctrine of transubstantiation, but its main threat to the institutional Church was its scepticism concerning the authority of the pope. The term "lollard" derives from the Middle Dutch verb *lollen*, to mutter or mumble, and was applied first as a derogatory term to Wycliffe's followers because of their commitment to the vernacular as opposed to Latin in church worship. This also earned them the appellation "dullards."

8. Ruth Shklar (1995:277–304) argues that Kempe simultaneously deploys and rejects the doctrines and practices of Lollardy, so establishing a form of dissent "neither strictly orthodox nor heterodox, but rather rooted in her performance of Lollardy as critique" (1995:304).

9. See Walsh 1961:150.

10. For an illuminating discussion of Kempe's writing of the female body, see Lochrie, 1991.

11. Lollards eschewed ostentation and promoted simplicity of life, and so Margery's clothing alludes to their dissent but carries it further and places it in a gendered context.

12. The secular authorities were, of course, Herod and Pilate; the religious authorities Annas and Caiaphas. Mystery plays commonly represented Annas and Caiaphas as bishops, dressed in the scarlet gowns, tabards, and mitres associated with the bishop's office and surrounded by learned clerics.

References

Beckwith, Sarah. 1986. A Very Material Mysticism: The Medieval Mysticism of Margery Kempe. In David Aers (ed.), *Medieval Literature: Criticism, Ideology and History*. Brighton, Sussex England: Harvester Press: 34–57.

———. 1992. Problems of Authority in Late Medieval English Mysticism: Language, Agency, and Authority in *The Book of Margery Kempe*. *Exemplaria* 4 (1): 171–99.

Butler, Judith. 1990. *Gender Trouble: Feminism and the Subversion of Identity.* New York: Routledge.

Colledge, Edmund, and James Walsh (eds.). 1978. *A Book of Showings to the Anchoress Julian of Norwich.* 2 vols. Toronto: University of Toronto Press.

Fairclough, Norman. 1989. *Language and Power.* London; New York: Longman.

Knowles, David. 1961. *The English Mystical Tradition.* London: Burns and Oates.

Lochrie, Karma. 1991. *Margery Kempe and Translations of the Flesh.* Philadelphia: University of Pennsylvania Press.

Mahoney, Dhira B. 1992. Margery Kempe's Tears and the Power over Language. In Sandra J. McEntire (ed.), *Margery Kempe: A Book of Essays.* New York: Garland: 37–50.

McEntire, Sandra J. 1992. The Journey into Selfhood: Margery Kempe and Feminine Spirituality. In Sandra J. McEntire (ed.), *Margery Kempe: A Book of Essays.* New York: Garland: 51–69.

Meech, Sandford Brown, and Hope Emily Allen (eds.). 1940. *Book of Margery Kempe.* Oxford, England: Oxford University Press.

Partner, Nancy F. 1991. Reading the Book of Margery Kempe. *Exemplaria* 3 (1): 29–66.

Petroff, Elizabeth Alvilda. 1994. *Body and Soul: Essays on Medieval Women and Mysticism.* New York: Oxford University Press.

Shklar, Ruth 1995. Cobham's Daughter: The Book of Margery Kempe and the Power of Heterodox Thinking. *Modern Language Quarterly* 56 (3): 277–304.

Staley, Lynn 1994. *Margery Kempe's Dissenting Fictions.* University Park: Pennsylvania State University Press.

Szell, Timea K. 1992. From Woe to Weal and Weal to Woe: Notes on the Structure of *The Book of Margery Kempe.* In Sandra J. McEntire (ed.), *Margery Kempe: A Book of Essays.* New York: Garland: 73–91.

Walsh, James (trans.). 1961. *The Revelations of Divine Love of Julian of Norwich.* London: Burns and Oates.

Windeatt, B. A. (trans.). 1985. *The Book of Margery Kempe.* Harmondsworth: Penguin Books.

9

Helen and Hermes' Conceit

Stephen Curkpatrick

B usy? Can I talk to you?"

"Yes, come in Helen. Good to see you. It's been a while since we've had a chat."

"You haven't got a sermon to prepare?"

"No, not at all. That can wait till Saturday. How's the doctoral thesis going?"

"Actually, that's what I want to talk to you about."

"Me? What can I tell you about 'heretics' . . . what's your thesis called again?"

"Marginalized movements in the history of Australian Churches."

"That's right. Well, how's it going?"

"Do you remember your denominational history?"

"Just. Not my best subject, I'm afraid."

"Ah, yes, but that's because history is seldom taught well."

"So how do you think it should be taught?"

"Well, history is about discourse, politics and rhetoric . . . it's about power, gender, ideology, disjunctions, discontinuities, and suppressed anomalies . . . what we call 'history' is usually *the winner's story*, but it's 'effectively' only ever half the story."[1]

"Like the absence of indigenous *Australian* histories, until very recently."

"That's right. Your generation was thoroughly imbued with a *winner's* perspective."

"And not yours?" ·

"*Everything* is under intense reevaluation at the present."

"Hence your interest in 'marginalized movements,' but I'm not aware of any in our denomination."

"Exactly! But there are traces and fragments of alternative stories."

"So how can I help you?"

"Well, there is an aspect of my research about which you may know something."

"I'm all ears."

"I'm researching a freelance journal published within our denomination during the 1890s."

"What was the name of it?"

"*Hermes' Conceit.*"

"Never heard of it. Sounds intriguing. Why *Hermes' Conceit?*"

"Hermes, messenger of the gods, always interpreted the messages. The gods could never speak without being interpreted."

"*Hermes* . . . ah yes, *hermeneutics*! But tell me about *Hermes' Conceit.*"

"It was produced by a group of women who wanted to take our rootedness in biblical tradition seriously . . ."

"I thought we *did!*"

"That's the rhetoric. They were convinced we didn't nearly enough."

"They were fundamentalists then?"

"No. Precisely the opposite. They believed that taking biblical tradition and especially the New Testament seriously forced us to wrestle with issues of Christian theology such as equality, justice, and ecumenical dialogue."

"Sounds reasonably healthy to me."

"Yes. *Hermes' Conceit* was fascinating really, full of issues that the source texts themselves raise."

"Have you got copies of this journal?"

"No, they are only in the archives of the University history department."

"Not even in the archives of our denominational Historical Society?"

"No. Apparently not. They were expunged from the records. There are archives and archives."[2]

"Why? I thought we valued diversity and freedom of opinion. 'In our *essentials*, agreement, in things peripheral, diversity, but in all things . . .'"

"Yes I know the rhetoric."

"Rhetoric? Oh yes, your view of history."

"Let me pose a question. What if one of the *essentials* could never be stated without dissonance, disjunctions, and aporias, even in the New Testament?"

"I guess we'd have a theological crisis on our hands."

"Not necessarily. According to *Hermes' Conceit*, we'd have a normal New Testament issue on our hands."

"What do you mean?"

"Precisely this. The New Testament tradition is thoroughly diverse in its expressions of faith, and so to adhere to *New Testament tradition*, any particular Christian tradition must necessarily encompass the abyss of indeterminacy . . . or *mystery*."

"Yes, but with a few *essentials* though, wouldn't you think?"

"Such as?"

"The resurrection, for example. That's central to Christian faith."

"Indeed it is, but even here there is great diversity in the New Testament as to how resurrection is understood."

"The tradition is basically quite homogeneous, that's obvious, otherwise we wouldn't have a New Testament."

"Not according to the writers of *Hermes' Conceit*."

"So you mean they're questioning the resurrection?"

"Did I say they *questioned* the resurrection? Just the opposite. They affirmed the intrinsic diversity of resurrection witness in the New Testament, which leads to diverse theologies of Christian confession and *spirituality*."

"What was their evidence?"

"Reverend. I'm surprised! The source texts, of course."

"You mean the Gospels?"

"Yes, and other source traditions too. I assume you're preparing your sermons for Easter from these texts?"

"Eventually. So what did these people . . . the writers say?

"Well, firstly, they demonstrated the diversity and even, well dare I say . . . nonchalant discrepancies of Gospel tradition itself."[3]

"Oh yes, such as?"

"Appearances, movements, gender . . ."

"Gender?"

"Yes. Was Peter or Mary Magdalene first to encounter . . ."[4]

"Yes I see the ecclesiastical implications."[5]

"Even if you do, listen to your quick dismissal . . ."

"My apologies. I can't begin to explain the difficulties this issue has created for us."

"Theologically? Or in tenure and appointments?"

"Now you're being cynical. I'm sure there are legitimate changes to be made . . . but not too quickly."

"Oh, and why not?"

"Think of the legal labyrinths we might get into if we let this issue unravel too far, not to mention the theological difficulties it has already created."

"You seem to be uncomfortable with the unsettling particularities of resurrection tradition."

"Helen, resurrection tradition is permeated with different modes of perception, that much I will concede."

"Paul, for example."

"Paul? He doesn't have a resurrection narrative."

"Paul is the *first* New Testament witness to interpret resurrection. Although writing of an event that occurred years later, his *encounter* with the risen Christ is qualitatively the same as others, giving us a clue to his interpretation of resurrection."[6]

"Yes. 'Have I not seen Jesus our Lord?' "[7]

"Paul is the *only* New Testament apostle and writer to claim such a personal encounter. He has no tomb tradition. There is none until Mark, forty years after Jesus' execution. Even then, there is no appearance, only an enigmatic ending."[8]

"So, you've been doing some research on Paul. What else?"

"According to *Hermes' Conceit*, Paul's encounter with the risen Christ is also couched in terms of 'revelation,' which he describes in the mode of a prophetic calling."

"Yes, Galatians. Go on."[9]

"Paul's type of *encounter* was not an issue with Peter, even if commensality between Jewish and Gentile constituents of the Church was."[10]

"Yes, it's Paul's 'your faith is futile if Christ hasn't been raised'?"[11]

"Precisely. If you follow his arguments carefully, Paul pointed to confessional communities 'in Christ' as the tangible reality of resurrection."

"Helen, I must admit I'm a bit rusty on all this, but that comes from thirty years in busy parish life . . . one does lose touch with all that 'seminary jargon,' but let me ask you a simple question, Helen, . . . what about historicity . . . of the resurrection?"

"Resurrection is a disruption of history . . ."

"Disruption?"

"Yes, a disruption of continuity, of the possibility of assimilation into categories we can comprehend, by analogy . . ."

"By analogy?"

"Yes, resurrection as a symbol of transcendence . . ."

"That disrupts assimilation by analogy?"

". . . a disruption that shows the possibility of totally 'other' ways of perceiving reality. It is a reversal of Troeltsch. You did study Troeltsch didn't you?"[12]

"Yes, the only thing I can remember is, er . . . 'history is always being rewritten or renegotiated in the light of new information' . . . but a 'reversal of Troeltsch,' you say? What do you mean? And what 'other ways of perceiving life'?"

"I'm referring to his belief that any event must have a correlation with other events, so that 'analogies will be found,' as it were, for the seemingly unique or anomalous event, even if we have only known such events through symbols."

"That makes sense. Otherwise, how would we understand anything?"

"Perhaps there are aspects of reality we cannot assimilate. Surely there are perspectives on life that will elude our repertoire of analogies?"[13]

"So you feel an analogy might violate something unique?"

"It can. You see, we are always faced with the presence or face of 'the other,' the nonassimilable that is a lacuna in our tidy ways of propounding and presenting reality, even a *confessional* Christian reality."[14]

"Yes, I see, but let me pose a more tangible issue. Paul does speak of the resurrection of believers. How does *Hermes' Conceit* deal with this?"

"Paul used diverse metaphors such as seed and plant, tents and houses, labor and birth . . ."[15]

"I'd forgotten that last image."

"Many do. All constructions of theology are expressed in metaphors of some kind . . ."[16]

"Yes I'm aware of that."

"Ah, but the problem is that the metaphoricity of some metaphors is *forgotten*, while other metaphors are eclipsed and *never* remembered . . . perhaps because they seem incongruous, even dangerous . . ."[17]

"Run that one past me again, Helen."

"Some metaphors assume the status and currency of 'facts'—while others, especially those that privilege the experiences of women, are forgotten."[18]

"Now, now Helen . . . you're not going to try and convince me to pray 'Our Mother who art in heaven,' are you?"

"You may well protest, but even in theology, the metaphors you use come to legitimate their own constructed 'reality'. There are other

metaphors. For example, being 'in Christ' and 'in the Spirit' are inter-
changeable for Paul. The destiny of creation, 'in the Spirit,' and the
Spirit in the womb or body of creation, is as conceptually elusive as
Paul's own encounter with Jesus, whom God exalted in the terms of an
ancient martyr vindication tradition."[19]

"You, or should I say, *Hermes' Conceit*, seems to suggest that resurrection is a changing tradition."

"Yes. They proposed that the whole New Testament tradition is a
wrestling with the *who, what, how, why* of the Jesus tradition, including
his ignominious death, in an emerging belief in his exaltation, even if
expressed mythically after the Jewish eschatological tradition. It was an
adventurous scenario in their time."[20]

"Go on."

"One script of Easter was barely written when the drama took on a
new twist, generating new scripts. These were the earliest Christian
theologies of faith in the risen Christ, expressed in hymn, confession,
liturgy, and narrative."[21]

"Phew! But do you really think we can accept an evolving Easter
tradition and remain Christian? That's loaded. It sounds like New Age
talk. Besides, if there is something in what you say, what's the point of
unsettling most of the faithful?"

"Resurrection *is* unsettling. It's a radical discourse of disruption.
Consider the pervasive presence of women in the resurrection
traditions."[22]

"Yes, and the 'radical' significance of this?"

"They *knew* resurrection in their bodies."

"How, Helen?"

"Resurrection was that experience of discovering they could be socially inscribed, or *written up*, differently, their bodies no longer a palimpsest of pejorative abuse."[23]

"Helen, I don't follow you. Resurrection is something that happens
to Jesus' body, surely. Are you suggesting it happened to *their* bodies.
That's absurd."[24]

"That's where you and I begin from different premises. You believe
the site of transcendence is somewhere else . . . somewhere other than
bodies."

"Yes, that does seem obvious, doesn't it?"

"What if all bodies are sacred sites of transcendence, bodies like
mine, but that they become sites of pejorative graffiti, generation
after generation . . . until the graffiti, not the bodies, was all that was
read."[25]

"Yes, I think I follow you, but what sort of graffiti?"

" 'Bitch,' 'nigger,' 'slut,' 'old bugger,' 'retarded idiot' . . . anything that is used pejoratively to denigrate or scribble on their human dignity."

"I see what you mean by graffiti."

"Do you know what that graffiti does to people?"

"It might make them angry, passive, or it might destroy them."

"Yes, and if they should really discover their own bodies, their own sensations, pain, or struggle . . . not as these are described for them . . . they might discover their own bodies as sacred . . . sacred sites of transcendence."[26]

"That would no doubt be liberating."

"So much so, that if it happened in their experience in a context of social change that recognized the body as a site of transcendence, they would be challenged to engage in compelling, poetic explorations of the character of this disclosure."[27]

"What do you mean?"

"They would be compelled to create new stories, stories with textures of freedom and struggle, but struggle allied with hope in the emergence of alternative realities."[28]

"*Realities* plural?"

"Yes, plural. We construct our worlds by *wall-papering* them with words."

" 'Wall-papering with words'? Helen I don't follow you."

"We experience life through bodies. We interpret our sensations through language, in fact we configure our bodily sensations through language . . ."[29]

"Are you suggesting there is nothing outside language?"

"The world is wall-papered with language. The world has always been wall-papered with languages. Babel did not happen. Babel always happens."[30]

"That's an interesting twist on an old story."

"Language configures the flux of life. This process is culturally specific, and through it, we can 'make our way' in the basic demands of life. 'Reality' is linguistically configured, specifically within cultures. This linguistic configuration precedes us and our 'consciousness' of life, let alone 'meaning to life'."

"So you are saying our 'truths' about life are arbitrary?"

"Not so much arbitrary, but culturally specific. We are born into an existing linguistically wall-papered world, which shapes 'reality' in a certain way. We receive this 'reality' tacitly, as being natural, obvious, or self-evident."[31]

So what you are saying is that women create the resurrection narrative from their own experience of transcendence, in their own bodies?"[32]

"Against a palimpsest of pejorative scribble . . ."

"What a metaphor! You do have a way with words, Helen."

"They saw the possibility of an alternative world . . ."

"An alternatively *wall-papered* world?"[33]

"Yes, and with it, a new palimpsest on their bodies."

"When we talk about resurrection, Helen, we can only return to our written sources, the texts. You now seem to suggest otherwise."

"The point is, and let me read you a quote from *Hermes' Conceit* . . ."

"At last, some hard data from your mysterious journal!"

"Here we are. 'These slippery, divergent, evocative texts show us what the textures of resurrection are—the open possibility of life itself.' The implicit testimony of these traditions is that 'he is not here . . . ' at least not in the texts."

"Then where, Helen, where?"

"Reverend! *He is risen* into life, and is in the textures of the world in which you and I can encounter her in *others*."[34]

"Helen, are you sure you are talking about God now?"

"One writer says that *God, Being, the origin of origins* is always under erasure. Neither predicate or subject but copula . . ."

"The verb 'to be' . . . you say?"

"Yes. The verb 'to be' is also under erasure in every combination of words and reality we might make . . . leaving an ancient tear in the quest for the representation of *essence* or *Being*, even if we use words and the verb 'to be' in making many such representations in the tactile world."[35]

"I haven't a clue what you're on about."

"No, I don't suppose you do. Perhaps I could put it like this—do we really know what we are talking about when we talk about God, and if we think we do, by whose criteria?"

"The old Kierkegaard paradox you once reminded me of!"

"Yes. We must commit ourselves to a position without the requisite evidence for our taking a position on life, this being an impossible commitment."[36]

"Few people can live with that kind of tension, Helen."

"Perhaps we have no choice. Perhaps that is why we must return to tactile bodies, poetry, and the very materiality of *the Other* . . . which includes women, and respond to their bodies as sites of transcendence—

and write poetry and stories that metonymically affirm the textured mysteries of life. After all, there are only *textured* mysteries."[37]

"Textured mysteries?"

"Mysteries are embodied and textured with interpretation, even if indeterminate."

"Ah, until scientific evidence proves such mysteries to be perfectly explicable natural phenomena."

"Transcendence or otherness will always exist, despite our modern empirical attempts . . ."

"To colonize difference? I'm beginning to read your mind, Helen."

"If you think so. Our neat conceptual systems throw up anomalies— of difference and mystery."

"Such as?"

"Whales!"

"Whales?"

"Yes. Dolphins and whales are not fish, but they swim like fish, and are wet with the same water. They confuse categories. Whales are aquatic divas with sonorous bones, not feathers. If 'deep calls to deep,' we should call on Bach as well as Attenborough, fugues as well as facts. Pavarotti not Pavlov might be a better interpreter of the cultural behavior of whales. The cultural mystique of whales cannot be ascertained in an empirical fishbowl, without reduction of their difference or otherness."

"I must say, I don't know much about Puccini or Verdi, but I'll remember that the next time I watch a program on whales."

"There is an alterity in whales we cannot assimilate into human perceptions. If there is always a chink of difference and therefore alterity in phenomenological reality—sea, fish, wet, dry, mammals, singing, feathers, culture, divas—how much more in constructed social perspectives!"[38]

"Yes, quite. Intriguing to say the least, but let's get back to what we were discussing. You said the New Testament tradition was fundamental to *Hermes' Conceit*."

"Yes. The texts provide us with a subtle repertoire of ways in which we may recognize God's transcendence in our world . . ."

"Through a prism of Jesus tradition, I take it?"

"Yes, if one is *confessionally* Christian. Listen, I'll read you some more of this. 'Cling to the texts as if we control them, and we will lose the poetry of such "presence" and the capacity to "recognize" the risen One. Allow these narratives to nestle seductively in open minds, rejuvenated bodies, and they will continue to speak and vigorously challenge us, enabling us to meet the transcendent one in the most surprising ways.' "[39]

"So what exactly happened to this *maverick journal* and its perpetrators?"

"The journal was declared, through various euphemisms, *heretical.* It lapsed through lack of funds, and its advocates were ostracized."

"So why don't we have any record of it, apart from your University archives?"

"Because alternative, *subversive* histories are often erased, expunged within their cradle of nurture. As I said, there are *archives,* and there are *archives.*"

"So what did you want clarified? You seem to know all there is to know."

"It's not my thesis. It's my faith in the church."

"I'm not surprised. One shouldn't pursue religious concerns at secular universities!"

"You're teasing, but I suspect you really do think that . . . you see, I have grown up in the church . . . it's part of me, but I'm not sure whether . . ."

"You've outgrown it . . . isn't that a little presumptuous!"

"No, that's not what I feel. No, what I really want to know is whether the Church . . ."

"Which means the people who lead it . . . like myself, isn't that what you mean by 'the Church'?"

"I want to know if the Church . . . is really prepared to wrestle with the implications of *New Testament Christianity,* which is grounded in the elusive confession, 'Christ is Risen'."

"Wrestle? Isn't that what we've been doing? And look, I really must get back to work now. I'm afraid you . . ."[40]

Notes

1. Foucault's "effective history" is disruptive to the quest for continuities in history, introducing discontinuities, disjunctions, and anomalies, in contrast to historians who want to "confirm our belief that the present rests upon profound intentions and immutable necessities." "Effective history" also seeks to demonstrate that all history is perspective-contingent (1984: 86–90). "Not only is history *written* by the winners, it is also made by them" (Schüssler Fiorenza 1983:80; 1993:173).

2. This is a play on Foucault's concept of *archives.*

3. Galilee represents the future: "go and tell my brothers to go to Galilee; there they will see me."(Matthew, Mark [John: "Jesus showed himself again to the disciples by the Sea of Tiberias"]) while in Luke, Galilee represents

the past (Luke: "Remember how he told you while in Galilee"). There are appearances to "the eleven" only in Galilee (Matthew [Mark?]), while in Luke there are appearances to "the eleven" only in Jerusalem; John has an appearance to the disciples and Thomas a week after the first, yet in Luke the ascension occurs on "Easter day," and forty days later in Acts; women encounter the risen Jesus (Matthew, John), while women do not encounter the risen Jesus (Mark, Luke); men are responsible for the preburial anointing (John), while women undertake the postburial anointing (2, 3, many women?) (Mark, Luke).

4. Compare Luke 24.34 and Mark 16.7 with Matthew 28.9–10 and John 20.11–8. In Luke the women remember (24.8), and interpret this memory to the disciples (9), who disbelieve them (24.11), and two of these disbelievers are later rebuked for not heeding (remembering) the Word (24.25–6). For Luke, witness is interpretation, and the women are pivotal to this witness. The writer endorses the trustworthiness of the women's report or message, even if some of the disciples do not. Indeed, Luke portrays the men as tardy in belief, but the women are ready interpreters as witnesses of resurrection (Seim 1994:154–7; Plevnik 1987:90–103; Karris 1994:14–9).

5. On ecclesiastical implications of "first encounters," see Schüssler Fiorenza 1992:80–1; 1993:162–4.

6. 1 Corinthians 15.5–8; Galatians 1.15–16. Appearance (1 Cor. 15.8 "made to see"; *ophthe* passive) and revelation (Gal. 1.15, 16, *apokalypsai . . . en emoi,* "to reveal [his son] in me") speak of the same experience. In his Corinthian account, Paul speaks of being "untimely born" (1 Cor. 15:8, NRSV *ektromati*). Romans 16:7 would suggest that Paul's Christophany experience occurred some time after the "first apostolic experiences of Christophany," with apostles Andronicus and Junia being "in Christ" before Paul. Was Paul's reference to *ophthe* visual, mystical, metaphorical or numinous? The usage of *ophthe* (made to "see") indicates a variety of religious experiences that are nuanced heavily toward epiphanies of divine presence: in the Septuagint; the appearance of Moses and Elijah in the Transfiguration scene (Mark 9:4); the appearance of tongues of fire at Pentecost (Acts 2.3), Carnley 1987:227–9). These occurrences of *ophthe* in the Transfiguration and Pentecost stories indicate postresurrection Christophanies, the first read back into the ministry of Jesus, and the second depicting the birth of a multicultural community.

7. 1 Corinthians 9:1.

8. Mark 16:8. The alternative endings are later attempts to ameliorate the abrupt ending.

9. Galatians 1:15–16 "to reveal his Son *in me.*" The same phrase is used in Galatians 2:20: "it is Christ who lives *in me*" *(en emoi),* indicating an inner revelatory experience. Compare 2 Corinthians 4.6 "For it is the God who said, "Let light shine out of darkness," who has shone in our hearts to give the light of the knowledge of the glory of God in the face of Jesus Christ" (NRSV).

10. Galatians 1:18–2.2.

11. 1 Corinthians 15:12–19.

12. Troeltsch advocated the relativity of social and cultural phenomena, which, he noted, is always historically contingent, with values relative to

time, place, circumstances within cultural matrices. He advocated relativism in faith—Christianity being a faith relative to our cultural context (albeit for Troeltsch, the quintessential expression of religion in Western culture), while other religious traditions are phenomena relative to different cultures. Troeltsch's *historicism* also included understanding history by analogy, in which not all events can be known but all events can be incorporated analogously to what is known. Claims outside analogy are to be rejected, for any event has some correlation with other events; therefore, history is continuity. See Macquarrie 1981:141–4.

13. Against Troeltsch, Moltmann argues that the "fallacy of analogy" is an eclipse of aberration, the different and strange. Analogy is a form of conceptual colonialism, integrating only what is analogous with a particular horizon of experience and perception and suppressing, rejecting, what is "other" or outside this horizon. Analogical colonialism is a form of historical homogenization that destroys the diverse, polymorphous textures of history and closes off genuine perception of diversity and difference (Moltmann 1990:227–45). Eschatology, in this instance, resurrection, is the language of discontinuity, disruption, and otherness and is resistant to analogical colonialism (Winquist 1995:62–83).

14. According to Emmanuel Levinas, a response to the "face" of the Other is a response to the singular experience of the Other in the Other's difference. This response is not an assimilation of otherness but an opening to the otherness of the Other. The face of "the other" demands our response (1979:187–219).

15. 1 Corinthians 15:35–41; 2 Corinthians 5:1–5; 1 Thessalonians 5:1–3 is used in the apocalyptic context of resurrection and parousia.

16. See McFague 1982; 1987.

17. Schüssler Fiorenza 1995:97–128.

18. Nietzsche pointed out that language is permeated with metaphors, even if we do not recognize or have forgotten this: "What then is truth? A mobile army of metaphors, metonymics, anthropomorphisms: in short, a sum of human relations which became poetically and rhetorically intensified, metamorphosed, adorned, and after long usage, seem to a nation fixed, canonic and binding: truths are illusions of which one has forgotten that they *are* illusions; worn-out metaphors that have become powerless to affect the senses; [die abgebützt und sinnlich kraftlos geworden sind], coins which have their obverse [Bild] *effaced* and now are no longer of account as coins but merely as metal; Derrida 1982:217, quoting Nietzsche, F., "On Truth and Falsity in their Ultra moral Sense," in Levy, D. (ed.), *Collected Works*, vol. 2 (London T. N. Foulis, 1911), 180.

19. Romans 8:31–9. See Perkins 1984.

20. Schüssler Fiorenza 1995:111–5; Schillebeeckx 1991:518–32.

21. This is a perennial issue of epistemology, even in the late New Testament era. That is, what do Christians mean when they claim to *know* the risen Christ? How do they know that what they experience spiritually and claim theologically relates to Jesus of Nazareth? Peter Carnley deals extensively with this issue (1987)

22. Mary Magdalene and "the other Mary" (either the mother of James and Joseph or the mother of James and John: Matt. 27:56, 28.1–10); Mary

Magdalene, Mary the mother of James, Salome (Mark 16:1–8); Mary Magdalene, Mary the mother of James, Joanna (Luke 24.1–11); Mary Magdalene
(John 20.1–18).

23. See Sawicki 1994:185–241.

24. Paul suggests this eschatological reality in 2 Corinthians 4:7–18,
5.16–17.

25. See Sawicki 1994:185–241. On language and subjectivity, see Fulkerson 1994:61–116 and Weedon 1987:74–135.

26. Kasper notes that the human person is characterized by "*individuality*, in the sense of uniqueness" and "*spirituality*" and therefore "infinity"
or transcendence (1989:27).

27. The vocative, prophetic summons to just relationships with neighbor
is a pervasive and primary site of revelation in biblical narrative and poetics.
That is, I am addressed, vocatively, from beyond myself (transcendence/
otherness), through the prism of neighbor at the limit of human dignity. A
profound endorsement of human dignity occurs in the Judeo-Christian tradition, through the Hebrew scriptures, the Jesus tradition, and the genuine
Pauline epistles. Each endorses a paradoxical theology of God's embodiment
in the lives and narratives of people, while proclaiming a God of mystery
and transcendence, whether through a burning bush or eschatological resurrection. Indeed, transcendence (Yahweh) siding with fragile, often oppressed embodiment (widow, orphan, stranger) takes precedence over cultic
"truth-telling." The "truth" of religion, according to Isaiah, is abominable
when it denies human dignity to the embodied other.

28. According to Elisabeth Schüssler Fiorenza, biblical narratives can be
recreated through "historical imagination, artistic recreation, and liturgical
ritualization . . . from a feminist perspective, to reformulate biblical visions
and injunctions in the perspective of the discipleship of equals" (1984:20–
1).

29. See Kerr 1986, [1997].

30. This is a variation of Crossan's statement: "Emmaus never happened. Emmaus always happens" (1994:197).

31. Wittgenstein proposed that language is culture and culture is language, with no one language able to provide the benchmark for osten-
sive meaning in human discourses. Literal correlations between words
and referents are conventional, not essential (1967 [1953]: no.26, 12
no.28, 14e, no.371, 116e, no.496, 497, 138e, no.355, 113e). We are generally unaware of this until we encounter a "different world" in another
language. Conventional meanings exist within the context of particular language use: "The meaning of a word is its use in the language." (no.43,
20e).

32. According to Sawicki, Gospel narratives are the poetic production of
Church communities seeking to delineate modes and practices for "seeing
the Lord" in the face of the epistemological issue of correlating the claim
to encounter the risen Lord with Jesus of Nazareth. This occurs in the texts
and praxes of bodies as much as written texts. Indeed, marginalized bodies
contesting cultural texts become sites of poetic production of Gospel texts.
For Sawicki, the combination of body language and the epistemological

issue of recognition provides the central impetus for the production of Gospel narrative, as the poetics of "seeing the Lord" (1994).

33. This raises a significant contemporary question: "How do we gain ethical and political traction while allowing for both difference and perspective-contingent values or *wall-papered worlds?*" An important recognition needs to be made here: the demand of the Other pressed to the limits of human dignity—is not linguistically constructed but an embodied reality. The Other can be taunted or tortured, go hungry and cold, become sick, or die. The empirical experiences of hunger or homelessness and their impact on human bodies are not linguistically constructed, even if the "social realities" precipitating such conditions often are. It seems that the body and its need for dignity is where we touch a striking consensus of values, whatever the culture, language, or *wall-papered* worldview. Hence a place of dialogue between different perspectives with their contingent ethical values is possible, even if this dialogue presupposes hard work in highly particular situations.

34. Schüssler Fiorenza points out that "Christhood," being a theological confession, is not gender specific (1995:50).

35. See Derrida (1978:64–78).

36. Existence carries with it the need to decide and act on truth claims, and therefore a paradox: one cannot know the truth, yet one must live the truth. One must live with "objective uncertainty" as an "existential paradox" regarding truth. For Kierkegaard, objective uncertainty combined with subjective passion and commitment is made through "risk" or a "leap of faith." This is an "absolute paradox." God is unknown, nonanalogical, infinite. Yet faith in God is "an existential leap of faith." This is not nonsense. However, to prove it is not nonsense is impossible. Existential commitments and passions are not assimilable to rational judgment, yet they consist in making contingent judgments (Sikes 1968:111, 117).

37. In contrast to metaphorical theories designating two modes of discourse—literal and nonliteral, ordinary and quasi-transcendental—language is always grounded in sensual materiality, from which its metaphors are derived. While a trope designates an unanticipated turn or change from one mode of reception to another, this need not create a dichotomy between "literal" and "nonliteral" language. Rather, language is metonymic, always oscillating between literal and nonliteral reference, depending on context. This metonymic character of language can intensify images metaphorically, while affirming that language still has its reference in the opaque, embodied complexities of life. If metonymy, according to Derrida, is turning a sensible part of a metaphorical image (signified) into yet another metaphor (signifier) signifying something else (1982:227n. 32), it has not erased the sensuality of metaphor but expanded its possible reference (signification) further. A recognition of the metonymic nature of metaphor enables us to recognize the material effects of language by plotting the effects of "natural" metaphors in human behavior and relationships. Such metaphors are not so "dead" as is often assumed. "[S]ublimation"of the "literal" or sensual into nonliteral metaphorical images, even if the metaphoricity of these images has been forgotten, is a repression of the material (usually marginal).

Hence for Bal, "metaphors . . . carry the traces of what they have repressed"(1993:185, 204–6).

38. In contemporary parlance, *alterity* refers to difference, otherness (i.e., *alter*native), and can include paradox, mystery, and even transcendence. Mark Taylor provides extensive discussion on alterity in *Altarity* (1987).

39. Theological exploration of the resurrection through metaphor, story, and confession in epistles and Gospels is evocative, not prescriptive, for integral belief in the Easter event and its ongoing effects in human life. The confession is simple, even if the primary data are subtly complex and diverse and authenticated only by life-giving and liberating practices in the human community. Thankfully, the Gospels compound this mystery with irreconcilable accounts of postresurrection appearances or Christophanies. They resist both crass fundamentalist and smug reductionist interpretations by generating diverse readings of resurrection that point to the mystery of alterity, or "otherness," embodied in life.

40. This replicates the enigmatic ending of the Gospel of Mark.

References

Bal, Mieke. 1993. Metaphors He Lives By. *Semeia: an experimental journal* 61: 185–207.

Carnley, Peter. 1987. *The Structure of Resurrection Belief*. Oxford: Clarendon Press.

Crossan, Dominic. 1994. *Jesus: A Revolutionary Biography*. San Francisco: HarperCollins.

Derrida, Jacques 1978. Edmond Jabès and the Question of the Book. In *Writing and Difference*. Trans. A. Bass. London: Routledge and Kegan Paul.

———. 1982. White Mythology: Metaphor in the Text of Philosophy. In *Margins of Philosophy*. Trans. A. Bass. Chicago: The University of Chicago Press.

Foucault, Michel. 1984. Nietzsche, Genealogy, History. In P. Rabinow (ed.), *The Foucault Reader*. New York: Pantheon: 76–100.

Fulkerson, Mary 1994. *Changing the Subject: Women's Discourses and Feminist Theology*. Minneapolis: Augsburg Fortress.

Karris, Robert. 1994. Women and Discipleship in Luke. *Catholic Biblical Quarterly* 56:1–20.

Kasper, Walter. 1989. *Theology and Church*. London: SCM Press.

Kerr, Fergus. 1986[1997]. *Theology after Wittgenstein*. London: SPCK.

Levinas, Emmanuel. 1979. *Totality and Infinity: An Essay on Exteriority*. Trans. A. Lingis. The Hague: Martinus Nijhoff.

McFague, Sallie. 1982. *Metaphorical Theology: Models of God in Religious Language*. Philadelphia: Fortress Press.

———. 1987. *Models of God: Theology for an Ecological, Nuclear Age*. Philadelphia: Fortress.

Macquarrie, John. 1981. *Twentieth-Century Religious Thought: The Frontiers of Philosophy and Theology, 1900–1980*. 2 rev. ed. London: SCM Press.

Moltmann, Jürgen. 1990. *The Way of Jesus Christ: Christology in Messianic Dimensions*. Trans. M. Kohl. London: SCM Press.

Perkins, Pheme. 1984. *Resurrection: New Testament Witness and Contemporary Reflection.* New York: Doubleday.

Plevnik, Joseph. 1987. The Eyewitnesses of the Risen Jesus in Luke 24. *Catholic Biblical Quarterly* 49:90–103.

Sawicki, Marianne. 1994. *Seeing the Lord: Resurrection and Early Christian Practice.* Minneapolis: Fortress.

Schillebeeckx, Edward. 1991. *Jesus: An Experiment in Christology.* New York: Crossroads.

Schüssler Fiorenza, Elisabeth. 1983. *In Memory of Her: A Feminist Theological Reconstruction of Christian Origins.* London: SCM Press.

———. 1984. *Bread Not Stone: The Challenge of a Feminist Biblical Interpretation.* Boston: Beacon Press.

———. 1992. *But She Said: Feminist Practices of Biblical Interpretation.* Boston: Beacon Press.

———. 1993. *Discipleship of Equals: A Critical Feminist Ekkle-sia-logy of Liberation.* London: SCM Press.

———. 1995. *Jesus: Miriam's Child, Sophia's Prophet: Critical Issues in Feminist Christology.* London: SCM Press.

Seim, Turid. 1994. *The Double Message: Patterns of Gender in Luke-Acts.* Edinburgh: T. and T. Clark.

Sikes, Walter. 1968. *On Becoming the Truth: An Introduction to the Life and Thought of Kierkegaard.* St. Louis, Mo.: Bethany Press.

Taylor, Mark. 1987. *Altarity.* Chicago: University of Chicago Press.

Troeltsch, Ernst. 1974. Historiography. In *Encyclopedia of Religion and Ethics.* Ed. James Hastings with the assistance of John A. Selbic and Louis H. Gray. Edinburgh: T. & T. Clark, Vol 6: 716–23.

Weedon, Chris. 1987. *Feminist Practice and Poststructuralist Theory.* Oxford: Blackwell.

Winquist, Charles. 1995. *Desiring Theology.* Chicago: University of Chicago Press.

Wittgenstein, Ludwig. 1967 [1953]. *Philosophical Investigations.* Trans. G. E. M. Anscombe. Oxford: Blackwell.

The Heavenly Woman and the Dragon

Rereadings of Revelation 12

Dorothy A. Lee

[1]Now a great sign appeared in heaven, a woman clothed in the sun, the moon beneath her feet and on her head a crown of twelve stars. [2]She was pregnant and crying out in labor, struggling in agony to give birth. [3]Then there appeared another sign in heaven: a great fiery-red dragon with seven heads and ten horns and on each head seven diadems! [4]His tail dragged a third of the stars from heaven and flung them to the earth. The dragon stood before the woman who was about to give birth, ready to devour her child when it was born. [5]She gave birth to a male child, a son, whose destiny it was to shepherd all the nations with a staff of iron. And the child was snatched up to God and to his throne. [6]Then the woman fled into the wilderness, where she has a place prepared for her by God, so that there she might be nourished for one thousand, two hundred and sixty days.

[7]War broke out in heaven, Michael and his angels in combat with the dragon. The dragon with his angels fought, [8]but he did not prevail, and no longer was a place found for them in heaven. [9]The great dragon was flung out—the ancient serpent, the one named "Devil" and "Satan," the deceiver of the whole world. He was flung to the earth and his angels were thrown down with him. [10]Then I heard a great voice in heaven proclaiming:

Now salvation and power have come,
the reign of our God and the authority of his Christ!
For the accuser of our brothers and sisters has been cast out,
the one who denounces them before our God day and night.
[11]They have conquered him through the blood of the Lamb
and the word of their testimony,
for they did not love their lives even to death.
[12]For this rejoice, O heavens, and those who dwell in them!
But woe to the earth and the sea
for the devil has come down to you, furiously angry,
knowing he has but little time.
[13]When the dragon saw that he had been cast down to
earth, he pursued the woman who had given birth to the
male child. [14]But she was given the two wings of the great
eagle to fly from the face of the serpent into the wilderness
to her own place, where she might be nourished for a time
and times and half a time. [15]Then the serpent spewed water
from his mouth like a river after the woman, to sweep her
away in the torrent. [16]But the earth came to the woman's
help, opening its mouth and swallowing the river which the
dragon had spewed from his mouth. [17]Then the dragon became enraged with the woman and went away to make war
on the rest of her offspring—those who guard the com-
mands of God and hold to the testimony of Jesus. [18]Then the
dragon stood on the shore of the sea. (Revelation 12)

Ancient Myth and Women's Contemporary Context

The myths of socioreligious groups are not peripheral but central to
culture, spirituality, and identity. Myths reveal the beliefs as well as the
sufferings and dreams of those who shaped and handed down the sacred stories, operating at the level of symbol that precedes yet also
includes the cognitive (Ricoeur 1967:1–18, 161–70). Feminist religious
studies has seen in recent years a revival of interest in the mythology
of the ancient world (e.g., Spretnak 1978; Christ 1987; Downing 1988;
McLean 1989; Gimbutas 1989; Carmody 1996). As active participants
in these stories, women in ancient cultures shared in their transmission
and possibly also their composition. A contemporary rereading of mythology animates women's recovery of an efficacious past, becoming a
means of entering the world of "holy dreaming" where past and present
coalesce. The multivalence of these ancient stories allows them to be
read by women in changing circumstances. After all, much of the great

literature of the past that has survived represents a reinscribing of even more ancient myths within new frameworks, reflecting changing times and new understandings of the world.

Contemporary women's rereading of ancient myth is complicated by the alien worldview of the stories, enshrining values that women, since the Enlightenment, have been extensively reshaping. The issue is critical within the Judeo-Christian tradition, where myth provides a sacred canopy for socioreligious structure, giving narrative framework to its life and buttressing its teaching and ritual. The question is whether and how we can revalorize ancient stories formed in an androcentric haven where every aspect of a woman's life—occupation, religious and political status, moral characteristics, relationships—was laid down by the socioreligious system and supported by its mythology.

Feminist exegesis in biblical studies begins with a "hermeneutic of suspicion" that seeks to unlayer textual misogyny and expose the way texts are used to authorize male precedence (Schüssler Fiorenza 1984: 15–22; 1992:39–62). A "suspicious" reading is necessary in the hermeneutics of myth because mythology operates intuitively at the unconscious as well as conscious levels. Suspicion is a tool that aims to thwart patriarchal meaning—where it assaults and where it insidiously co-opts the reader. The task of recognizing the troublesome aspects of ancient myth can then make room for new readings and deeper understandings, in dialogue with contemporary women's experience (Tolbert 1990:5–23; and Schneiders 1993:34–7). Biblical mythology is thus "a record of [women's] oppression as well as a source for the reconstruction of a useable past and of images of hope" (A. Y. Collins 1987: 91). With this two-sided hermeneutic we approach the myth of Revelation 12, asking the pertinent question of whether it offers women today "a useable past" and "images of hope" for the future.

Structure, Context and Intertextuality in Revelation 12

The story of the heavenly woman and the dragon occurs in a series of visions through Revelation 6 to 16, structured around the mystical number seven (seven seals, 6:1–8:1; seven trumpets, 8:2–11:19; seven bowls/plagues, 15:1–16:21). The narrative of Revelation 12 is part of an intermediate section (12:1–14:20) that includes the coming of the two beasts (13:1–18), the redemption of the 144,000 (14:1–5), and the prophecy of the destruction of "Babylon" and judgment on those who have worshiped the second beast (14:6–20). In literary terms, the narrative of Revelation 12 forms a neat and simple chiasmus in three sections, in which the first and third scenes parallel one another (A, vv. 1–6, and A^1, vv. 13–8) and frame the central scene (B, vv. 7–12). Within the chiastic frame, the first and third scenes narrate the story of the heavenly woman's conflict with the dragon (Harrington 1993:129), while the middle scene, comprising the cosmic battle between the archangel Michael and the dragon (see 1 Enoch 6–13), is sandwiched between the two stages of that drama.

Behind the intercalation, it is possible to detect two different sources, manifest in the awkwardness of the seams that join them together—for example, in the way the time-frame works unevenly from one episode to the next.[1] Nevertheless, the sources have been stitched together in a felicitous way, forming a new narrative through literary juxtaposition. The dragon is the common element in both, his aggression spanning the spheres of heaven and earth, uniting them in the same conflict and struggle, the same longing for peace. Moreover, the story of eschatological victory in heaven, inserted into a narrative of tumultuous earthly events, aims to set those events within an intelligible and hopeful frame of meaning.

Reading the narrative in its sociocultural setting, this cosmic myth functions as "parenesis"—that is, moral encouragement and motivation—for a hard-pressed community that identifies its own suffering with the mythological trials and tribulations of the heavenly woman (Schüssler Fiorenza 1985:35–67).[2] The fundamental issue here is political as well as religious, relating particularly to the cult of emperor worship in the Roman Empire, which sprang up during the reign of the Emperor Augustus (*imperator*, 27 B.C.E.–14 C.E.) in Asia Minor—the geopolitical setting of Revelation (Schüssler Fiorenza 1991:80). Over the next century the imperial cult rapidly became the test of political allegiance for peoples subject to the Roman imperium. The first altars were raised to the goddess Roma, personification of the city of Rome, and her "son" Augustus in Pergamum and Nicomedia—Pergamum (Rev. 2: 12–7) being the third church mentioned in the epistolary frame of Revelation (Rev. 1:4–3:22, 22:6–21). It is quite possible that Revelation itself was written during the reign of the emperor Domitian (81–96 C.E.) who used for himself the Latin title *Dominus et Deus noster* ("our Lord and our God"; see ὁ κύριος μου καὶ ὁ θεός μου, John 20:28).

The communities of the seven churches addressed in Revelation appear to be in a context of impending, if not actual, persecution, the problem being their refusal to participate in the imperial cult. For the author of Revelation, John the Seer, the underlying theological issue concerns where the ultimate source of sovereignty lies. To participate in the imperial cult means idolatry for the Jewish and Christian mind, giving an absolute authority to that which is, by definition, relative and derivative. In the worldview of the Hebrew prophets, moreover, idolatry usually manifests itself in sociopolitical injustice and oppression (e.g., Isa. 1:2–31; Amos 2:6–8, 5:10–24; Mic. 2:1–3:12). Similarly, the community of Revelation sees itself as confronting not merely the threat of religious intolerance but the equally terrifying menace of political and economic injustice.

The heavenly woman becomes a powerful symbol of a community under threat from the sociopolitical and religious power structures of the Roman Empire, as represented by the dragon. Within this sociopolitical and religious context, the protection afforded by God at each attack of the dragon encourages the embattled communities of Revelation with the knowledge of divine favor and the promise of eschatological deliverance. The battle between Michael and Satan plays a cathartic role, reassuring the community that the dragon, evicted from heaven, "is an enemy already defeated" (Talbert 1994:50; also A. Y. Collins 1984). The myth explicates the suffering and persecution of the community as the consequence of the dragon's furious yet limited time on earth (Boring 1989:159–60).

Like the Book of Revelation as a whole, the mythology of the narrative draws on Judeo-Christian apocalypticism, which originated in Jewish communities that interpreted their historical experience as that of religious and political oppression (Reddish 1990). For them, the present age has nothing to offer but humiliation and pain. The only hope lies in God's future, in the "new age," where the persecuted will be vindicated and freedom will flourish (Rowland 1982; J. J. Collins 1984a, 1984b:1–24; also J. J. Collins & A. Y. Collins 1992:279–92). Thus, as with other Jewish apocalyptic writings, the cryptic language and imagery of Revelation serve as a mask to hide a dangerous and subversive message against the oppressors that is as much political as religious.

The mythology of Revelation 12 also operates intertextually in comparable mother-son myths in the ancient world that follow a similar pattern of threat, escape, rescue, and vindication. The Egyptian myth of Isis and the birth of Horus, and the Greek myth of Leto giving birth to Apollo (and Artemis) before the Python, are two cogent examples. In both narratives, the mother-goddess (Isis, Leto) is attacked to prevent her giving birth to a powerful son; mother and child subsequently receive divine protection and the son grows up to overcome the adversary (A. Y. Collins 1993:20–3). Furthermore, the same mythological form has immediate historical and political ramifications, being enacted on the political stage in the form of the goddess Roma and the emperor. These intertextual parallels are important because they suggest historical and archetypal underpinnings that make links between otherwise disparate mythological material. The parallel symbolism opens up fields of reference across cultural, sociopolitical, and religious traditions—an important area of concern for women's studies, with its conviction of the commonality of women's experience within widely diverse contexts.

The same symbolic associations are found similarly in Hebrew literature, where the serpent-dragon Leviathan is a symbol of cosmic chaos associated with the sea (e.g., Isa. 27:1, 51:9–14, Jer. 51:34–37, Ezek. 32:1–6). The first creation account presents the overcoming of chaos in an ordered pageant of creativity and vitality (Gen. 1:1–2:4), while the second account describes the enmity between the first woman Eve and the serpent, who leads her and her consort astray in the garden (Gen. 3:15; also Ps. 74:13–14; Isa. 27:1; Song Sol. 22:5; see Minear 1991: 71–7; Sweet 1990:194–6).[3] Behind these images from the Hebrew scriptures lies ancient Near Eastern mythology in which creation comes to birth in the overpowering of the dragon-monster representing chaos: Tiamat in the Akkadian *Enuma Elish* is killed and dismembered by Marduk, and in the Ugaritic Ras Shamra tablets, the god Baal kills the sea-serpent/dragon with seven heads and asserts his lordship over creation.[4]

First Reading: Androcentrism and Suspicion

We do not need to probe far to discover the androcentric contours of the Roman-Hellenistic and Jewish worlds from which the myth of Revelation 12 derives. There are a number of aspects to this. In the first place, the heavenly woman is encompassed by male figures on every side, good and bad. Opposite her, ready to devour the offspring when her laboring is done, is the male δράκων μέγας πυρρός, the "fiery-red dragon," who stands as the symbol of evil and "parody of God the Creator" (Boring 1989:155, 164–7; Talbert 1994:49); he is implacably hostile to the woman and her infant.[5] The child to whom she gives birth is male (υἱὸν ἄρσεν, v. 5a) and the narrative of his birth is followed immediately by the disclosure of his coming rule, which is to be one of cosmic power and breadth ("to shepherd all the nations with a staff of iron," v. 5b; Ps. 2:9). The child is to have cosmic authority, which to the Jewish mind recalls the sovereign rule of God (e.g., Pss. 93, 145) but to the Roman-Hellenist mind strikingly recalls the Roman imperium and the cult to which it was attached.[6]

Threatened by a powerful male dragon while giving birth to a male child marked out for a powerful destiny, the woman is rescued by the protective power of a deity who is depicted throughout Revelation in male language and imagery. God takes on the role of the father, snatching the newborn child into heaven and setting him beside the divine throne, thus ensuring his physical well-being and future dominion. No deity, however, seizes the mother: instead, she is compelled to flee the dragon within moments of giving birth.[7] Here, in harsh and lonely terrain, she is afforded divine protection for a specific period of time (v. 6)[8] but still remains in danger, the object of the dragon's hostility (v. 17). The woman is powerless and exposed, serving the interests of the male symbols of power that seem to enclose her; even her body is precarious, subject to control and invasion. Vulnerable to physical assault, she requires male protection from male violence. Nor can her offspring escape: mother and children together represent the most vulnerable and least protected group within the structures of the ancient world. No earthly paterfamilias sheds his protection around her; the mother is dependent entirely on the heavenly Pantocrator (παντοκράτωρ) whose primary concern seems to be not her but the child.[9]

In the central scene set in heaven, symbols of masculine power predominate, substantiating the use of violence to overcome evil. The militarism of the heavenly forces is the cause of violence on earth (v. 9): "woe to the earth and the sea for the devil has come down to you, furiously angry, knowing he has but little time!" (v. 12b) The narrative concludes with the ominous picture of the dragon standing on the seashore (v. 18), awaiting the rising of the beast from the sea (13:1–10) and the beast from the earth (13:11–18), who will receive the dragon's authority to "make war on the rest of her offspring" (12:17). The combat myth presupposes a world where women and children are perpetually at risk of violence.

The woman herself (ἡ γύνη) is depicted in maternal terms, her role complementing and completing, though in a proleptic way, that of the victorious bride whose marriage to the Lamb is celebrated at the end of the apocalypse (19:7, 21:2, 9, 17). Marriage and motherhood— though curiously in reverse order in Revelation—represent the primary roles assigned to women in the ancient world. The only woman in Revelation who is an exception is condemned for the content if not actuality of her prophetic ministry (2:20–23a). Significantly the "heretical" nature of her teaching in Thyatira, and its consequent punishment, are delineated in disturbingly violent sexual terms (see Pippin 1992a: 67–82; Schaberg 1992:219–26), as her namesake "Jezebel" implies (1 Kings

16:31–34, 18:1–19:10; 2 Kings 9:30–37). Adultery and fornication as images of idolatry preempt the personification of Rome as the "great whore" who has sold herself to the "kings and merchants of the earth" in order to gain power and wealth (17:2; 18:3, 9). She too is called "the woman" (τὴν γυναῖκα, 17:6), reflecting a dualistic anthropology in which women are either demonized or idealized (Garrett 1992:382; Pippin 1992b:67–82; Schüssler Fiorenza 1991:13; A. Y. Collins 1993:33). In Revelation, the prophet Jezebel is presented as corrupting the authentic and austere teachings of the church by her permissive ethical stance (2:20; see 2:14).[10] Anxiety about female power, it would seem, blends with anxiety about the boundaries of female sexuality, as portrayed in the Hebrew scriptures, where Israel is often described as whore and adulterous wife (Ezek. 16, 23, Hos. 1–3; see Bird 1989:119–39; Frymer-Kensky 1989:92–4; Lee 1996:1–15; also Garrett 1992:378). It also reflects Greco-Roman misogyny directed at married women's supposed sexual infidelity and promiscuity (e.g., Apuleius 1989:9.16–28). The modern reader of Revelation might well question whether power of any kind is admissible to women.

These telling points reveal the difficulty for the contemporary reader in reading the myth of the heavenly woman and the dragon: a simple and direct rendering is no longer possible. We are left with a number of compelling questions about the gendered nature of the myth. The authentic Christian woman, for John the Seer, seems on first reading to be one who endorses male power and seeks no status of her own outside prescribed roles. So far the myth seems to function only as "a record of oppression"; the question still remains whether other readings are possible. Is the problem with the myth itself or its interpreters? To frame an answer to this question, we must revisit the myth, probing tentative conclusions and searching out possibilities of new renditions. The myth of the heavenly woman may yet have something to offer.

Second Reading: Sovereignty, Hope, and Resistance

Like symbols, myths are not exhausted by one reading. Ideas of polyvalence and the "surplus of meanings" draw attention to the implicit openness of myth and symbol and their adaptability to new dimensions of signification (Ricoeur 1976:45–69). It is therefore difficult to maintain essentialist meanings that rule out, in advance, further readings. Moreover, the reader is an active partner, not a passive recipient, in the unfolding of meaning; mythic and poetic forms animate dialogue be-

tween reader and text.[11] These notions are important as we explore
trajectories for revisioning the myth. Suspicion need not be the last
word.[12]

There are several points in the narrative from which such a rereading may proceed. In the first place, we note the strong role that identification plays in reader response. The actual reader of the text
(whether male or female, ancient or modern) is encouraged throughout
the narrative to accept the ideological framework set up by the myth,
including its symbolism, characterization, and theology. In literary
terms, we might say that the real reader is enticed in subtle (and sometimes unsubtle) ways to blend with the implied reader who is a literary
construction of the text itself. The crosscurrents flowing between implied reader and female hero are embedded within the story, their aim
being to evoke common experience and therefore empathy and identification between the actual reader and the heavenly woman. This is
aided by the reader's knowledge of the world behind the text, for the
woman's suffering echoes, in mythic form, the experience of the community and, in particular, as I have noted, its refusal to render allegiance to Rome. The empathy of the implied reader—and hopefully the
real reader—with this beleaguered group is assured by the terrifying
description of the dragon-monster (v. 3), his cosmic powers of destruction (v. 4), his loathsome intention of devouring the newborn baby (v.
5), and his unappeasable lust for revenge. In the woman's experience
of torment, loss, flight, and terror the real reader is summoned to perceive the contours of her or his own suffering and to receive the message of hope and eschatological deliverance, however different the
reader's context might be. Whatever else we say about the myth, the
hero is undeniably female and the intended readers (male or female)
are invited to see themselves, collectively and individually, in female
guise.

Second, since gender identification cannot itself go far, it is important
to observe that a major concern of the myth is that of power—or better
the struggle between competing systems of power. Both the woman and
the dragon bear symbols of power and authority in their physical appearance: garments of sun and moon and a crown of stars compete
with seven crowned heads and ten horns (17:10, 12; Dan. 7:7c, 20,
24).[13] As the "great sign" (σημεῖον μέγα) appearing in heaven, the
woman's garments and cosmic locality are not decorations adorning
her beauty but rather indications of sovereignty and of the heavenly
powers she holds (v. 1). The rays of the sun—the greater light—bathe
her body in a dazzling garment, light being the first symbol of the
created world and primordial signifier of life (Gen. 1:1–5; John 1:4–5),

associated with divine power and guidance (see Ps. 27:1; Isa. 9:2). The woman also stands on the full moon—the lesser light—with authority to direct it, treading her way through the pathless realms of the dark, disseminating a pale, subtle light over the dim earth. Her sovereignty is thus associated with the sun which rules the day, and the moon and stars, which reign over the night (Gen. 1:14–18; Ps. 136:7–9). In the Classical world, the woman's clothing embraces the distinctive yet complementary spheres of Apollo and Artemis—Apollo, the male deity, associated with the sun and thus, by extension, civilization and culture, and Artemis, his sister, linked to the moon and the hunt, symbolizing the mystery of the feminine, her virginity guaranteeing independence from the male world.

In the Hebrew scriptures, the stars are a kind of divine script written in the sky for the inhabitants of the earth to read. In Genesis, for example, the numerous stars are a sign for the aged Abraham and Sarah that barrenness will become fertile, life will be irrepressible in the face of death, and isolation will flower into vibrant community (Gen. 15:5, 22:17, 26:4). In the early chapters of Revelation, the seven stars in the right hand of the "Son of Man" represent the seven angels who are the heavenly counterparts of the seven churches on earth (1:16, 20, 2:1, 3:1). In Hellenistic terms, there are also astrological implications: when the sun rises and sets within the constellation Virgo, the moon is at the foot of the constellation. The zodiacal overtones of the twelve stars are important, the diadem of stars representing the woman's regal control over human destiny. She is pictured, like the much-loved Egyptian goddess Isis, as "a cosmic queen who has power over the rhythm of night and day and over human destiny" (A. Y. Collins 1993: 21; see Pippin 1994:117–8).[14] Thus the heavenly woman presides over all that gives life meaning, direction, and guidance.

These powerful images may seem to stand in tension with the vulnerability of the woman's status noted earlier. Yet the precariousness of the woman's existence does not belie her strength. On the contrary, it is precisely this strength that the dragon—his crowned heads signifying both intelligence and formidable power (Prévost 1993:100)—seeks to overpower. The struggle for power, moreover, is not simply a battle between equivalent and warring factions. There is a striking disparity between the two competing powers. The creativity of the woman's pregnancy and her powerful birthing contrast with the wholesale destruction of the dragon's power, threatening the very power—the stars—with which she is associated. The fecundity of her strength compares with the barren wasteland formed by his (see Dan. 8:10). The reader is confronted by two radically different kinds of power, the one associated with light and life, the other with vandalism and death. Through narrative rhetoric the reader is enticed to embrace the one and repudiate the other.

At the beginning of Revelation, the household of faith is described as a priestly people (ἱερεῖς τῷ θεῷ καὶ πατρὶ αὐτοῦ) possessing divine βασιλεία (rule or sovereignty, 1:6; also 5:10). Similarly, at the end of the book, the servants of God who dwell in the new Jerusalem will paradoxically "reign for ever and ever" (βασιλεύσουσιν, 22:5). The real reader is intended to recognize the symbolic number of the stars as pointing to Israel-Zion-church, the people of God and messianic community (Schüssler Fiorenza 1991:81), and to perceive the other signs associated with the woman as symbols of Israel's authority. Awareness of the Roman-Hellenistic mythological background—powerful and courageous goddesses giving birth in horrifying circumstances—also serves to facilitate this reader response. In identifying with the woman, the reader can identify, both personally and communally, with cosmic symbols of sovereignty. Combined with the gender identification outlined earlier, the heavenly woman confronts the reader as a striking example of female authority. The wondrous power of the heavenly woman accrues to the sympathetic reader.

There is a further dimension to the issue of identification. Throughout the narrative the dragon-serpent is the aggressor and the woman the victim of his aggression. In the third scene, the language of the woman's flight recalls Classical myths where a female deity or mortal is sexually pursued by a male deity.[15] In each case, rescue is granted the terrified woman, often through the agency of nature (e.g., Daphne is turned into a tree to escape Apollo, Io is transformed into a cow to escape Hera's anger, resulting from Zeus's desire for her, while Persephone is given respite from the dreaded Hades and reunited with her mother Demeter during the fertile months of the year). Though sexual assault is not mentioned in the story in Revelation, the dragon's violent intent is at least reminiscent of this mythological motif, underscoring the way female generative capacities can give rise to male hostility and dominance. It represents another aspect of women's suffering, portrayed in the suffering of goddess figures on an amplified mythic stage. The reader finds, in this aspect of the myth, a channel of identification for gendered forms of abuse.

Third, the ideological structure of the myth authenticates at some level the created world and the human struggle to flourish within it. While the origin of both kinds of power is heavenly, the earth is the place where each is enacted. All things fall to earth: the dragon and his angels, filled with rage, the woman in her pregnancy and flight.

Here the battle will be fought; here it will be won. Both the wilderness (τὴν ἔρημον, vv. 6, 14) and the earth (ἡ γη, v. 16) are hospitable to the woman's plight, creating a place of refuge, a safe house where she can shelter from violence—the wilderness having biblical overtones of exodus and refuge (Harrington 1993:129; Roloff 1993:147; Sweet 1990: 197–8). God's rescue/salvation comes through the agency of natural forces, in the form of eagle's wings, on which the woman flees to the wilderness (v. 14; Exod. 19:4; Deut. 32:11), and in the (feminine) personified figure of earth that swallows the flood caused by the dragon (v. 16; Exod. 15:12; Num. 16:32–34; see Boring 1989:153; Roloff 1993: 151). In the end, the dragon is as frustrated by the earth as by the woman and her children (v. 7). In the cosmology of the myth, earth as well as heaven belongs in the divine provenance; both are subject to the power of evil and both will gain final victory. Nor are earth and wilderness in opposition to history and civilization; each is victim of the dragon's destructive powers.

At the same time, while parts of nature are hospitable to human life, other parts are inimical, witnessed in raging waters and wild seas. Whereas the earth provides stability and nurture, the symbol of water is ambivalent in the ancient Near East, where floods and sea-storms signify the threat of overwhelming chaos (Pss. 32:6, 107:23–29, 124: 4). For John the Seer, nature and civilization are both conflict zones, though it is important to observe that the dualism of the conflict is ethical and eschatological rather than dualistic and denying of the body. The yearning for renewal thus extends to every level of existence, spiritual and corporeal—a yearning that comes to fruition only in the final vision of the new Jerusalem in which nature and history converge in the garden-city (21:9–22:5). The new Jerusalem receives its true ethos from heaven, but it is fundamentally a renewal of earthly existence: there is no denial of matter or bodily existence. The vision of the city that embraces wilderness (the river, the grove of trees) paves the way for an ecological theology that interprets nature and civilization, from an eschatological perspective, in congenial rather than competing terms.

Fourth it can be argued that in the framework set up by Revelation 12 the community's opposition to idols is a form of resistance, both religious and political. The strict monotheism of Revelation (e.g., 9:20) leads to a focus on worship throughout, not just as ritual enactment but as a way of proclaiming where, for the author of Revelation, true sovereignty belongs (M. M. Thompson 1992:45–54). This conviction is manifested in the testimony (μαρτυρία) of those who have held to their convictions, remaining faithful to God as Pantocrator and ultimately conquering (vv. 11, 17). John the Seer encourages the community to hold out against the imperial cult, arguing that resistance to an oppressive political system is vital despite the hard cost: economic poverty and hardship (marginalization in the market-place built on pagan sacrifice), persecution and even martyrdom (Rev. 6:9–11, 13:16–17).

Feminist theologians in the Judeo-Christian tradition have defined the critical theological problem of patriarchal religion as one of idolatry—the idealizing/idolizing of an élite group above others, forming a pyramid that disempowers, to varying degrees, those beneath (e.g., Johnson 1993:17–57). Both women and nature are victims of this framework, as also are those men who are disadvantaged by the same structures. The heavenly woman is persecuted for her refusal to negotiate with the forces that surround her; in this mythology, they are idolatrous (placing the emperor at the pinnacle of the pyramid) and destructive (devouring those who refuse to pay allegiance). Like Jesus in the wilderness in the Synoptic tradition (Matt. 4:1–11/Luke 4:1–13), and unlike those who worship the beast in Revelation (13:4, 14:9–11), the woman does not turn and worship the dragon. Such refusal becomes a powerful symbol of opposition to the narcissism of those who demean others and exploit the earth. For contemporary women—living in a very different context—the myth endorses a stance of resistance.

The central place of the victory hymn within the narrative assures the reader of the heavenly woman's ultimate triumph (Roloff 1993: 149), the archetype of which is the death and resurrection of the Lamb (v. 11; see Laws 1988:24–35). The symbols of cosmic sovereignty with which the myth began will finally be restored to the woman; her victory over the dragon represents the fulfillment of the reign of God and the dawning of the new age. Embedded in this narrative of struggle and resistance (scenes 1 and 3) is thus the eschatological hope of triumph (scene 2). Those who have struggled are assured of a glorious victory, knowing that they will prevail. The woman and her children, victims of violence and domination, will be eschatologically vindicated along with the values for which they have suffered (7:13–17). Her raiment proclaims her triumph over darkness, suggesting an apocalyptic advent that will suffuse the earth in radiance and fecundity. In the framework of the myth, the longing for a new age is proleptic of its realization.

In this way, the myth can be read in relation to women's struggle against injustice. While propelling the imagery in new directions, such an interpretation is congruent with Judeo-Christian apocalypticism. The vision of Revelation "challenges the notion that injustice and oppression are at the center of the universe" (Schüssler Fiorenza 1991:120). The seven-headed, ten-horned dragon as a symbol of evil represents the economic and political power that exercises unlawful sovereignty over others, bringing a trail of devastation in its wake. In today's context, it is an image of patriarchal power and exploitation that has reified women and dangerously depleted the earth's resources.

The symbolism of the myth of Revelation 12 can also be interpreted in terms other than the political. In the realm of relationships, for instance, the redemptive self-sacrifice demanded of women for the good of others becomes a burden of drudgery and servitude that leaves them, again and again, feeling empty and forlorn. The same imagery can also be turned inward to address women's struggle for self-esteem and authentic selfhood. The androcentrism of the male world finds its correspondence in the inner landscape, where women's invisibility is mirrored in their lack of ontological substance, identity, and self-esteem. Even allowing for class difference, male identity for the most part is substantiated to a far greater degree than female identity, through ubiquitous symbols (external and internal) on every level of culture: sociopolitical, psychological, aesthetic, spiritual, physical, and so on. The resultant heightening of self-confidence and self-esteem is something men perhaps take for granted; yet it is not readily available to women in anything like the same way. Female identity does not receive comparable spiritual or psychological confirmation. The deadly "accuser" of Revelation (ὁ κατηγορῶν, 12:10) who "denounces them before God day and night" is an enemy that resides, for women, within as well as without, corroborating what is already a deficit in women's ontological identity with harsh internal self-recrimination. The image is a powerful symbol for an evil that burrows from the outside into the center: from the sociopolitical to the personal and spiritual. From this perspective, the pregnant woman in the throes of labor, threatened by the dragon, can be read as metaphorical of women's struggle and longing on the personal as well as political level. The same imagery embodies not only the suffering of undeserved self-judgment but also the eschatological hope of identity, self-esteem, and sovereignty.

Third Reading: Against the Grain

A further step is required, however, in directing a feminist hermeneutic to biblical myth. There are occasions when it is necessary to read against the grain: that is, to read both with and against the text in the same paradoxical movement. An example of this kind of reading is found in Revelation's anthropological dualism. It is both desirable and necessary to reconfigure the heavenly woman so that her portrait does not idealize one mode of being female while demeaning others that do not conform to "stereotyped feminine images" (Garrett 1992:377). Symbols of female sovereignty do not necessarily lead to a dualistic idealizing/demonizing of women. The resistance that Revelation endorses here can be opened up and pushed in new directions, in order to provide women with much-needed divine symbols of female identity and authority.

A second example in Revelation that requires reading against the grain is the masculine language and imagery for God. The reader can direct Revelation's critique of idolatry against the text's own androcentric language (see Wainwright 1995:100–119), since to identify the deity exclusively with maleness amounts to idolatry in the strict terms of Judeo-Christian theology. In this tradition, as feminist theologians have noted, God is ultimately incomprehensible and beyond all images or categories, whether gender or otherwise (LaCugna 1991:322–35; Johnson 1993:6–8, 54–6, 104–12, 241–5; McFague 1982:145–92; Carr 1990: 134–57). The imagery of the heavenly woman may here have something vital to offer in articulating a more nuanced language for God that acknowledges divine transcendence while expressing divine immanence in language that is gender-balanced and inclusive.

The problem with this, however, is that in the Catholic tradition, the heavenly woman has been interpreted narrowly as symbolic of the Virgin Mary, mother of the Messiah. Such an interpretation of the heavenly woman runs the danger of endorsing the androcentrism of much of the Christian tradition, where Mary represents the idealization of female identity (virgin-mother) and subordination of the feminine to masculine power (Carr 1989:8–14). It is not easy to perceive, moreover, how the Marian tradition relates to many of the elements of the narrative in Revelation 12, if read in a strictly allegorical way. While the child being snatched into heaven can be seen as an indirect parallel to the Ascension, the narrative of the mother's persecution by the dragon is almost unparalleled in the scant biblical traditions about Mary.[16]

On the other hand, like the mother of Jesus in the Lukan and Johannine traditions (Luke 1:26–56; Acts 1:14; John 2:1–12, 19:25–27), the heavenly woman is an ecclesiological figure, representing Israel in a single, continuous line extending from the ancient people of God to the Christian community (Prévost 1993:99–100). She is associated with the mythological figure of Eve, mother of all living, whose conflict with the serpent is part of the curse on her and her "offspring" yet who is also promised deliverance (Gen. 3:15; also Ps. 74:13–14; Isa. 27:1; Song of Sol. 22:5)—a promise of hope that later Christian exegesis interpreted in both christological and mariological terms. The heavenly woman is also suggestive of Zion as mother in the Hebrew scriptures, giving birth and suckle to her children (e.g., Isa. 26:16–27, 54:1, 66:7–11; Mic. 4:9–10). In other words, the heavenly woman suggests the mythological mother of the Judeo-Christian tradition, Israel-Zion-church, which is a symbolization of the messianic community persecuted by the serpent/dragon (Schüssler Fiorenza 1991:81). This tradition is closely associated with the figure of Mary—though a rereading of John and Luke-Acts demonstrates that, far from being a passive or subservient figure, she stands as an authoritative symbol of the Christian community. In these general terms, it is possible to argue that Mary, as representing Israel-church, is part of the symbolic association of the heavenly woman for the community behind Revelation.

A further step for Christian feminism, however, is to construe the heavenly woman as an image not just of Mary, or of women's experience in general, but also of the feminine divine, a reading inspired by the Bible's affirmation of women as well as men made in the image of God (Gen. 1:26–7). Without this further step, Revelation leaves intact the problematical biblical portrayal of God as divine husband and Israel/Church as dependent (and often erring) wife (e.g., Hos. 1–2; Eph. 5:22–33). In the later "wisdom" traditions, there is biblical precedence for a gender symbolism that is very different (Schüssler Fiorenza 1998:160–83). The portrait of *Sophia* (σοφία, wisdom) develops beyond early images of personification into a cogent female symbol of the divine, influenced undoubtedly by the figure of Isis (Johnson 1993:86–100, 124–87). The Book of Wisdom (7:25–6, 29–30) describes Sophia in a striking passage:

> She is the vapor of God's power
> and unpolluted stream of the glory of the *Pantocrator* . . .
> For she is the reflection of eternal light
> and the unstained mirror of God's energy
> and the likeness of God's goodness. . . .
> For she is more glorious than the sun
> and higher than every constellation of stars.
> Compared to light she is found superior;
> whereas night follows day,
> nothing evil can overpower *Sophia*.

Here and elsewhere in the wisdom tradition, Sophia is symbolized as the creative and life-giving manifestation of God's immanence in the world, bridging the gulf between Creator and creation and joining together spirit and matter. She is depicted as providing companionship and sovereignty to those who desire her, a sovereignty that is spelt out in love and knowledge, glory and honor within community (Wis. 8:10–16). There is an implicit, if not actual, parallel between this kind of symbolic language and Revelation's mythic depiction of the heavenly woman. Both female figures hold cosmic powers associated with the sun and the stars and both inhabit the earth as well as heaven, spanning the realms of divinity and humanity. The trajectory that connects the two figures—the divine Sophia and the heavenly woman—permits the latter to be construed not just as an image of community, as in Revelation 12, but also as a substantial icon for God in female form.[17] The heavenly woman represents the messianic community—with likely Marian overtones—yet also stands as symbolic of divine motherhood, a maternity that transcends the human realm entirely. Reading against the grain thus challenges female invisibility and subordination in the divine as well as human spheres. The symbols surrounding the heavenly woman are, in this sense, truly divine.

A Topography For Women

French philosopher and psychologist Luce Irigaray has captured vividly the dynamic of women's marginalization in an androcentric world, using images of envelope and place. Woman, who is defined by patriarchal culture as the "place" or "envelope" for the other (man or child), loses all sense of herself as a separate being. The result is a radical diminishing of her "self" (body and soul), in which she is permitted to exist only for the other but not—in contrast to the man—in and for herself. This damaging withholding of identity from the woman, according to Irigaray, entails both her own psychological demise and also the loss of the other within her undeserved suffering and fall into nothingness. It results, in other words, in the ultimate impoverishing of both female and male:

> As for woman, she is place. Does she have to locate herself in bigger and bigger places? But also to find, situate, in herself, the place that she is. If she is unable to constitute, within herself, the place that she is, she passes ceaselessly through the child in order to return to herself. She turns around an object in order to return to herself. And this captures the other in her interiority. . . . Passage from one place to another, for her, remains the problem of place as such, always within the context of the mobility of her constitution. She is able to move within place as place. Within

the availability of place. Given that her issue is how to trace the limits of place herself so as to be able to situate herself therein and welcome the other there. If she is to be able to contain, to envelop, she must have her own envelope. Not only her clothing and ornaments of seduction, but her skin. And her skin must contain a receptacle. She must lack

- neither body,
- nor extension within,
- nor extension without,

or she will plummet down and take the other with her. (Irigaray 1993:35)

Seen from this perspective, the myth of Revelation 12 acts as both mirror and window for women's existential dilemma (see Pippin 1994: 126–7), needing sovereignty on the one hand and rescue and protection on the other. This catches the ambivalent position of the heavenly woman, who is clothed in hopeful symbols of power and resistance yet is also the victim of a patriarchal and militaristic world, compelled into flight and danger, roaming the world with her children as refugees. In these inhospitable circumstances, the woman finds the envelope she needs—"a place prepared for her by God" (τόπον ἡτοιμασμένον ἀπὸ τοῦ, θεοῦ, v 6) which is "her own place" (τὸν τόπον αὐτῆς," v. 14)—and unexpected support from the earth, which provides refuge from the terrifying waters, a respite from the danger of plunging downward in an eternal narrative of "fall."

In this sense, what feminist theology is engaged with could be described as topography—literally, "the writing of place." The heavenly woman in the text of Revelation, set within a narrative of sovereignty, struggle, and vindication, envisions this much-needed sense of place to counter a violent and marginalizing world. Set in the wilderness in the midst of pain and grief, this place is given to the woman by God, providing her with both refuge and nourishment for the time of her tribulation. The symbolic narrative of Revelation 12 encourages feminist creativity in redefining women's place, taking seriously their struggle, identity, and need for nurture in an often hostile environment. For such topography to occur, however, the heavenly woman needs to be interpreted as a feminine icon of divinity. Women's renaming of their reality needs precisely this kind of symbolic framework, capable of spanning the realms: the writing of a place for women not just on earth but also in heaven.

The myth of the heavenly woman is set in the numinous space between the sixth and the seventh seals, caught in the eschatological tension between the "already" and the "not yet." The final vision of Jerusalem, to which the myth points, represents the defining of a place for women: no longer temporary, no longer under threat. Eschatology becomes "protology" in this understanding, where the longed-for End of all things is a return to the beginnings; thus Paradise is restored and woman and man belong together in harmony and mutuality, sharing stewardship of creation (Gen. 1:28–9).[18] The serpent-dragon is overcome, losing his usurped place in the cosmic order (οὐδε τόπος εὑρέθη, v. 8). In this reading, the heavenly woman/bride adumbrates women's longing for sovereignty, rescue, and an end to struggle. It represents the marriage of all that is divided, creating a true place, a refuge for the hunted, an end of suffering, a homecoming for those on the margins (22:17).

Notes

1. Further on the question of literary unity and possible sources behind Revelation 12, see A. Y. Collins 1976:101–45; see also Roloff 1993:142–5.

2. For a helpful account of the social context of Asia Minor and the communities of Revelation, see L. L. Thompson 1990:95–167, 186–97.

3. Note that the image of the serpent is not always hostile in the biblical tradition; see Num. 21:9 and John 3:14–5.

4. See Pritchard 1955:60–72, 129–42; on the dragon/serpent in Revelation, see Bauckham 1993:185–98. For a different reading of the mythological background to Revelation 12, in terms of ancient astrology and the zodiac, see Malina 1995:153–73.

5. Although a masculine noun, δράκων does not necessarily refer to gender; however, the personal pronoun αὐτοῦ (vv. 3, 4, 7, 9, 15, 16) suggests that the dragon is male.

6. Compare the preface of Augustus's *Res Gestae*, where his achievements are the means "by which he subjected the whole world [*orba terrarum*] to the empire [*imperium*] of the Roman people" (Brunt & Moore 1967: 18).

7. Compare the figure of Hagar in the Hebrew scriptures (Gen. 21:8–19), another mother sent out into the wilderness with its dangers. Hagar, however, is accompanied by her son; see Trible 1984:9–35.

8. The period of time here and at verse 14 is the same: three and a half years, which is the apocalyptic period of woes before the coming of the end (see Dan. 7:25, 12:7) and the earthly duration of the church's life (Harrington 1993:131).

9. Note that *Pantocrator* ("all-ruling/all-holding/all-embracing one") is a major title for God in Revelation (Rev. 1:8, 4:8, 11:17, 15:3, 16:7, 14, 19:6, 15, 21:22).

10. A contentious issue for the early church was that of the status of meat offered to idols in pagan temples (which, in the ancient world, acted also as abattoirs). Whereas Jezebel in Revelation seems to take a more lenient view—as does Paul, though in a qualified way (see 1 Cor 8, 10)—John the Seer regards any such conduct as idolatrous; see Garrett 1994: 378–9.

11. According to Iser, "convergence of text and reader brings the literary work into existence" (1978:275).

12. Against this, see Pippin (1994:119–20), who sees Revelation as irredeemably misogynist and therefore unliberating for women.

13. See also Rev. 17:13 where the whore is seated on a scarlet beast (ἐπὶ θηρίον κόκκινον) who has seven heads and ten horns, the seven here associated not with divine perfection but the seven hills of Rome (17:9). Note that the Lamb also has seven horns (5:6).

14. In Apuleius's *Metamorphoses* (11.5), Isis reveals herself to Lucius as *rerum naturae parens* (the Parent of the universe), *elementorum omnium domina* (Mistress of all the elements), governing *caeli luminosa culmina* (the shining heights of heaven) and bearing all divinity within herself. On the issue of whether the heavenly woman is a manifestation of a prehistoric, cosmic goddess, see Pippin 1994:117–19. For a different reading of Goddess religion, see Lee 1999.

15. Note that the verb *diwvkein* normally means "pursue," though here as elsewhere in the New Testament, it also carries the metaphorical sense of "persecute."

16. The closest parallel is Matthew's birth narrative, which tells the story of the threat from Herod the Great, the massacre of the innocents and the flight into Egypt-a narrative dominated by the figure of Joseph (Matt. 2). While Luke's account gives prominence to Mary, no parallel stories of danger and flight are found in his version; instead the mood is one of joy and praise (Luke 1–2).

17. For a definition of "icon" within a feminist theological context, see Lee 1998:249–64.

18. In Eastern Orthodoxy, this eschatological vision is understood as "deification," interpreted in christological terms; see Stavropoulos 1995:183–92. See also Trible on the restoration of Paradise and mutual relations between men and women in the Song of Songs (1978:144–65).

References

Apuleius 1989. *Metamorphoses*. 2 vols. Cambridge, Mass.: Loeb Classical Library.

Bauckham, Richard. 1993. *The Climax of Prophecy. Studies in the Book of Revelation*. Edinburgh: T. and T. Clark.

Bird, Phyllis A. 1989. The Harlot as Heroine: Narrative Art and Social Presupposition in Three Old Testament Texts. *Semeia* 46:119–39.

Boring, M. Eugene. 1989. *Revelation*. Louisville, Ky.: John Knox.

Brunt, P. A., and J. M. Moore (eds.). 1973. *Res Gestae Divi Augusti. The Achievements of the Divine Augustus*. Oxford: Oxford University Press.

Carmody, Denise L. 1996. *Mythological Woman. Contemporary Reflections on Ancient Religious Stories.* New York: Crossroad.

Carr, Anne. 1989. Mary: Model of Faith. In D. Donnelly (ed.), *Mary, Woman of Nazareth: Biblical and Theological Perspectives.* New York: Paulist Press: 7–24.

———. 1990. *Transforming Grace. Christian Tradition and Women's Experience.* San Francisco: Harper.

Christ, Carol. 1987. *Laughter of Aphrodite: Reflections on a Journey to the Goddess.* San Francisco: Harper and Row.

Collins, Adela Yarbro. 1976. *The Combat Myth in the Book of Revelation.* Missoula, Mont.: Scholars Press.

Collins, Adela Yarbro. 1984. *Crisis and Catharsis. The Power of the Apocalypse.* Philadelphia: Westminster.

———. 1993. Feminine Symbolism in the Book of Revelation. *Biblical Interpretation* 1:193–213.

———. 1987. Women's History and the Book of Revelation. *SBL Seminar Papers for 1987,* Missoula, Mont.: Scholars Press, 80–91.

Collins, John J. 1984a. *The Apocalyptic Imagination. An Introduction to the Jewish Matrix of Christianity.* New York: Crossroad.

———. 1984b. *Daniel: With an Introduction to Apocalyptic Literature.* New York: Crossroad.

Collins, John J., and Adela Yarbro Collins. 1992. Apocalypses and Apocalypticism. In *The Anchor Bible Dictionary.* Vol. 1. New York: Doubleday: 279–92.

Downing, Christine. 1988. *The Goddess. Mythological Images of the Feminine.* New York: Crossroad.

Frymer-Kensky, Tikva. 1989. Law and Philosophy: The Case of Sin in the Bible. *Semeia* 45:89–102.

Garrett, Susan. 1992. Revelation. In C. A. Newsom and S. H. Ringe (eds.), *The Women's Bible Commentary.* London: SPCK: 377–82.

Gimbutas, Maria. 1989. *The Language of the Goddess.* London: Thames and Hudson.

Harrington, Wilfrid J. 1993. *Revelation.* Minnesota: Liturgical Press.

Irigaray, Luce. 1993. Place, Interval: A Reading of Aristotle, *Physics* 4. In *An Ethics of Sexual Difference.* Ithaca, N.Y.: Cornell University Press: 34–55.

Iser, Wolfgang. 1978. *The Implied Reader: Patterns of Communication in Prose Fiction from Bunyan to Beckett.* Baltimore: John Hopkins University Press.

Johnson, Elizabeth A. 1993. *She Who Is. The Mystery of God in Feminist Theological Discourse.* New York: Crossroad.

LaCugna, Catherine Mowry. 1991. *God for Us. The Trinity and Christian Life.* San Francisco: HarperCollins.

Laws, Sophie. 1988. *In the Light of the Lamb. Imagery, Parody, and Theology in the Apocalypse of John.* Wilmington, Del.: Michael Glazier.

Lee, Dorothy A. 1996. Women as Sinners. Three Narratives of Salvation in Luke and John. *Australian Biblical Review* 44:1–15.

———. 1998. Touching the Sacred Text: The Bible as Icon in Feminist Reading. *Pacifica* 11:249–64.

————. 1999. Goddess Religion and Women's Spirituality: A Christian Feminist Response. *Theology* 102:19–28.

McFague, Sallie. 1982. *Metaphorical Theology. Models of God in Religious Language*. London: SCM Press.

McLean, A. 1989. *The Triple Goddess. An Exploration of the Archetypal Feminine*. Grand Rapids, Mich.: Phanes Press.

Malina, Bruce J. 1995. *On the Genre and Message of Revelation. Star Visions and Sky Journeys*. Peabody, M: Hendrickson.

Minear, Paul S. 1991. Far as the Curse Is Found: The Point of Revelation 12:15–16. *Novum Testamentum* 33:71–7.

Pippin, Tina. 1992a. Eros and the End: Reading for Gender in the Apocalypse of John. *Semeia* 60:67–82.

————. 1992b. The Heroine and the Whore: Fantasy and the Female in the Apocalypse of John. *Semeia* 59:211–17.

————. 1994. The Revelation to John. In E. Schüssler Fiorenza (ed.), *Searching the Scriptures*. Vol. 2. *A Feminist Commentary*. New York: Crossroad: 109–30.

Prévost, Jean-Pierre. 1993. *How to Read the Apocalypse*. New York: Crossroad.

Pritchard, J. B. (ed.). 1955. *Ancient Near Eastern Texts Relating to the Old Testament*. 2nd ed. Princeton: Princeton University Press.

Reddish, Mitchell G. (ed.). 1990. *Apocalyptic Literature. A Reader*. Nashville, Tenn.: Abingdon.

Ricoeur, Paul. 1967. *The Symbolism of Evil*. Boston: Beacon Press.

————. 1976. *Interpretation Theory: Discourse and the Surplus of Meaning*. Fort Worth, Tex.: Texas Christian University Press.

Roloff, Jürgen. 1993. *The Revelation of John*. Minneapolis: Fortress.

Rowland, Christopher. 1982. *The Open Heaven. A Study of Apocalyptic in Judaism and Christianity*. London: SPCK.

Schaberg, Jane. 1992. Response to Tina Pippin, "Eros and the End." *Semeia* 59:219–26.

Schneiders, Sandra M. 1993. The Bible and Feminism. In C. M. LaCugna (ed.), *Freeing Theology. The Essentials of Theology in Feminist Perspective*. San Francisco: Harper: 31–57.

Schüssler Fiorenza, Elisabeth. 1984. *Bread Not Stone. The Challenge of Feminist Biblical Interpretation*. Edinburgh: T. and T. Clark.

————. 1985. *The Book of Revelation. Justice and Judgment*. Philadelphia: Fortress.

————. 1991. *Revelation. Vision of a Just World*. Minneapolis: Fortress.

————. 1992. *But She Said. Feminist Practices of Biblical Interpretation*. Boston: Beacon Press.

————. 1998. *Sharing Her Word. Feminist Biblical Interpretation in Context*. Edinburgh: T. and T. Clark.

Spretnak, Charlene. 1984. *Lost Goddesses of Early Greece. A Collection of Pre-Hellenic Mythology*. Boston: Beacon Press.

Stavropoulos, C. 1995. Partakers of Divine Nature. In D. B. Clendenin (ed.), *Eastern Orthodox Theology. A Contemporary Reader*. Grand Rapids, Mich.: Baker Books: 183–92.

Sweet, John. 1990. *Revelation*. London: SCM Press.

Talbert, Charles H. 1994. *The Apocalypse. A Reading of the Revelation of John Louisville.* Westminster: John Knox.

Thompson, Leonard L. 1990. *The Book of Revelation. Apocalypse and Empire.* New York: Oxford University Press.

Thompson, Marianne Meye. 1992. Worship in the Book of Revelation. *Ex Auditu* 8:45–54.

Tolbert, M. A. 1990. Protestant Feminists and the Bible: On the Horns of a Dilemma. In A. Bach (ed.), *The Pleasure of her Text. Feminist Readings of Biblical and Historical Texts.* Philadelphia: Trinity Press International: 5–23.

Trible, Phyllis. 1978. *God and the Rhetoric of Sexuality.* Philadelphia: Fortress.

———. 1984. *Texts of Terror. Literary-Feminist Readings of Biblical Narratives.* Philadelphia: Fortress.

Wainwright, Elaine. 1995. What's in a Name? The Word Which Binds/the Word Which Frees. In M. Confoy, D. A. Lee, and J. Nowotny (eds.), *Freedom and Entrapment. Women Thinking Theology.* Melbourne, Australia: Dove: 100–119.

Working with Greek Mythology

A Journey through Images

Diane Fahey

My interest in Greek mythology began in the early 1980s and led to my writing two collections of poetry based on Greek mythology: *Metamorphoses* (1988), which centers on female figures in Greek myth, and *Listening to a Far Sea* (1998), which is mainly about male figures.

At the time I began, I was aware of the way myths could offer insight into some of the abiding patterns and themes in human experience—developmental issues, the quest for freedom and self-realization, finding a place and way of being in the world, the facing of death and suffering—and I soon became acquainted with the work of writers such as Christine Downing (1996) and Ginette Paris (1990) who were using myth as a tool of personal differentiation and cultural exploration with a specifically feminist focus.

The very substantial literature on the Mother Goddess offered an image that acted as a touchstone for the mystery of the cycle of birth, death, and rebirth that underpins all life, while presenting a foundation image of woman as life-source and creator. I experienced a powerful sense of freedom in imaginatively connecting with earlier layers of human culture where the Mother Goddess was honored. Indeed I remember thinking, on one occasion, that the only way I could leave patriarchy was by going out backward! However, having developed a stronger sense of the immanence of the Mother Goddess since then, I now have a more hopeful view on that subject.

In the process of negotiating with mythic images I became increasingly attuned to the way myths have been and can be shaped by power, so many of them having been dislocated and done violence to in the service of the patriarchal agenda. A radically revisionist approach seemed called for, and I worked archeologically as it were, accessing the earlier female-oriented layers of mythology, believing that if many myths had been changed away from earlier images that honored the strength, dignity, and complexity of women, they could be again changed in a way that retrieved those values, and told the story of their appropriation.

These were my beginnings, then, in what was to be a long and fruitful journey. It is one that has increasingly alerted me to the way myth is a great repository of stored human consciousness—at once personal and transpersonal—that one can interact with, both changing it and being changed by it. In the present, myth and mythological thinking can function as—and need to function as—instruments of personal and spiritual transformation, as well as, and in conjunction with, outer political change. In lieu of guidance and connectedness from genuine myths, human beings tend to be susceptible to all kinds of false mythologies that offer the lure of surrogate power to the disempowered. Such false mythologies can, as we know, be cleverly manipulated by tyrannies in the interests of expansionism and genocide and by global capitalists in the interest of taking the marketplace into the human psyche and co-opting it for its pleasure, power, and gain.

Myth as history, myth as psychology and spirituality, and myth as politics. Also, myth as autobiography . . . In writing *Metamorphoses* I explored some of the furthest and most difficult reaches of my experience as a woman, while connecting with the great collective movement to do with the owning, voicing, and redressing of damage to women in the patriarchal order. My critique focused on the outer and inner violence that is generated by and thrives on the continuing imbalance of power between men and women. In the process, I presented manifold images of the strength and creativity of women while also plumbing those crises of self-valuing and self-identity that are at the heart of women's experience in patriarchy.

Because of the fact that men are at the center of so many mythic narratives, in *Metamorphoses* I adopted a woman-centered approach, with most poems telling the story of a female figure; the rest deal with stories involving a couple, in which the woman's point of view is given its due—often against the grain of the original, as in the case of Penelope. This seemed to me a necessary part of reclaiming space and rightful power for women, as well as opening up imaginative and psychic space in which new perceptions and possibilities could emerge.

Subsequently, I changed from this woman-centered approach because I wanted to present something of the range of male figures in Greek mythology so as to avoid any counter-scapegoating of men on an individual level. I wanted my work to be about, and to be seen as, a further rebalancing process in which men and women were given equal attention. I was further exercised by the awareness of the psyche carrying both female and male images, which meant that critique of, and retrieval and renewal of, male images from mythology were part of the discriminating and energizing work of the individuation process—to employ Jung's term for the progressive accessing of wholeness and self-identity through the work of consciousness.

Listening to a Far Sea presented studies of creativity and suffering with regard to male figures (Arion, Orpheus, Philoctetes, Teiresias), as well as portraying folly, hubris, and the abuse of power (Midas, Bellerophon, Cinyras). In this book I traveled deeper into the hero myth, whose appropriation and diversion from a myth of inner journey to a tool of asserting "power over" (this process very much in evidence in the evolution of the figure of Heracles) seemed to me at the heart of the problem of patriarchy, and emblematic of it. I believed this new declension of the hero myth was born of a pathological fear and envy of women and their creativity. I saw in the traditional imaging of women as monster on the one hand and victim on the other the same combination of erasure from consciousness and psychological dumping that characterizes all scapegoating. Sexism, like other forms of oppression and imperialism, adds the act of theft (of resources, of sense of personal value) to this.

In what follows I will trace my treatment of the key themes I have enunciated through my work and the developing pattern of engagement that took me from investigating the culturally and politically created victim to celebrating women's ability to name and honor their own reality, to choose the freedom to exist in a fully human way within the universally inescapable toils of limitation and mortality. It was a journey through anger and despair to a holding in consciousness of the process of oppression, and from there to a celebration of creativity and spirituality as embodied in muse and oracle.

Of Victims and Pinups

Once, let's say it was in 1983, I was looking up the word "Philistine" in the dictionary—just double-checking. Nearby was an entry for "Phil-omela." Her story is an extreme one. She is raped by her brother-in-law, who then cuts her tongue out. But Philomela tells her story by means of a tapestry she weaves and sends this to her sister Procne—who devises a terrible revenge, serving her murdered son up to her husband at a feast. The gods interfere at the end—such interventions are usually after the fact—by transforming the three main characters into birds: swallow, nightingale, and hoopoe.

The poem I had written within ten minutes of reading the story was the beginning of *Metamorphoses*, and the image of the woven tapestry is to some extent an image of that book itself. It tells the story of the damage, allows the victim-self to speak. I should explain here that "victim-self" is for me a factual term—signifying that part of the self carrying actual damage against which one was powerless—and is not to be conflated with playing the victim on either a personal or a societal level, as does happen. (I note however that, under the ideological aegis of economic rationalism and global capitalism, victims of these ventures are often further scapegoated by a rhetoric that depicts imposed victim-hood as self-created victimhood.)

Victims' work, it seems to me, is to tell the truth of their experience and seek the resources needed for self-liberation. This cannot be pack-aged, may take more than a lifetime, and is full of traps, as the psy-chology of victimhood is complex: death wishes, a desire to return the scene of the damage—to convince oneself that it really happened; to prove that one really has survived it, or can ultimately survive it—and unassuageable rage. My poem "Philomela" holds the possibility of self-reconciliation and the transformation from speechlessness into speech, in tension with despair:

Philomela

In flight, but hardly
swift enough . . .
Her limbs splayed,
bruisings to the marrow.
As if in afterthought
he cuts her tongue—

this man of flesh,
this man of blood.

Days pass—shadows
flickering on a wall—

and then it comes:
the healing magic
she has waited for,
called in lost words for . . .
It has come—too late,
as it always does—

bringing transformation
to the defeated one.

So now she rises on wings,
feels—almost—peace,

then hears the song—her own,
that she could never sing—
and, yes, is reconciled:
in the song, free,
and in flight, always
swift enough.

The last poem I wrote for *Metamorphoses* was "Polyxena"—a return to the theme of victimhood that I arrived at after I thought the book was finished and its process completed. I remember encountering the story of Polyxena being sacrificed so that the ghost of Achilles (who covets her) could be appeased and the Greeks could set off for home after the Trojan war. I was as angry as I have ever been, on reading this story, because it constellated the sacrifice of women, and parts of their selves and lives—and of the feminine itself—in patriarchy. But I found in Polyxena an image of extraordinary strength, and I see this poem now as, while certainly an intensified expression of personal and transpersonal rage, also an exorcism of it. This is the final part:

Polyxena takes command of her execution, choosing
what has been chosen. Unpinioned, she steps
on to Achilles' grave, kneels, rends her garments.
When Achilles' son stands before her, she positions
his sword above her heart, leans forward—she is doing
it all for them, with so much more style than they.
Dying, she hears a moan high in the throats
of a multitude of men; this act of ritual pollution
seals their victory, clears their journey home.

For Polyxena, it is a translation from present slavery
into concubinage with a Very Important Shade.
She takes with her what she achieved in life:

> An adamantine possession of self;
> the brazen courage to take on death,
> to hold an entire army in her power
> and to defy her own powerlessness.

My representation of Polyxena raised the question of the victim being in a kind of complicity with the oppressor, albeit a complicity of
despair: in my rendering, she acts out her defiance by in effect murdering herself. In other words, what of the internalized oppressor—the
inner voice prompting one to live out the oppressor's worst intentions
for one? This was in the realm of the pathology of the victim, and this
poem is one of the places I have imaged the morbid and tragic possibilities of the way victims may respond to their plight. For me self-
liberation meant, along with achieving inner clarity about the forces of
oppression, facing my rage at myself for having believed and internalized the lie of inferiority, of lesser value.

In writing such an intense book as *Metamorphoses* I must confess to
eventually becoming a little lightheaded, especially in the poems of its
final section, which blend irony, humor, and burlesque—with a ven-
geance, one might say. This felt like a swing into an opposite—a desire
to let off steam after so unremitting an engagement. The following
poem was one of several in that last section, dealing with exploitative
aspects of the iconography of women in Western art.

Danaë

Pennies from heaven—
a celestial dew!

Artists show your garments
conveniently askew . . .

With immaculate conceptions
there's so little to do—

you just lie there pretending
you're looking at the view.

Not being raped but being rained on,
it's difficult to sue.
Should you sleep with an umbrella
in case he tries to renew

your acquaintance with a brief
shower or two?

In the end, it seems to me, to have seen the lie is to have seen the joke. To be held hostage to the primitive fantasies of others is—whatever else it may be as well, including terrifying—on one level, laughable. Many forms of oppression have a grotesque absurdity about them— they are acts of amoral compensatory behavior in which the tyranny of unboundaried primal emotions in the psyche of the oppressor has become monstrous and virulent, hungering to hold the world to ransom and to fashion it in its own nightmare image.

While reflecting on the way the nakedness of women in art is so often designed to empower the male viewer—by now a widely received insight—I became aware of the popularity of the myth of Andromeda and other female figures that take the theme of disempowerment further by placing the naked woman in the presence of an armored man. The dismaying spectacle of Perseus (returning from decapitating the Medusa with his trophy now added to and various other trappings of power, including Hermes-like winged sandals) seeking out Andromeda's parents and arranging the marriage settlement before he will save her from a sea-dragon did not endear him to me. The following poem was provoked by various Renaissance and nineteenth-century paintings of Andromeda by Titian, Tintoretto, and some other Renaissance painters, as well as by a scene in the British film *Poor Cow*, where a young girl is photographed almost naked by a pack of male photographers.

Andromeda

She was the first pin-up.
Naked and bejewelled,
she was chained to a rock
then thrown by heavy-breathing
winds into wild postures:
at each new angle, lightning
popped like a photographer's flash.

The gold circling her neck
matched her hair, the emeralds
her eyes, the rubies her nipples,
and the amethysts those bruises
covering her skin, once pearl-
white as for all princesses.

In lulls of wind, she pulled
against iron, stood almost straight.

The sky was a mouth swallowing her,
the sun a glimmering eye.
Lolling in the tide, a sea-dragon
slithered and gurgled like
some vast collective slob.

From afar, Perseus saw her first
as a creature writhing on a rock;
close-up, she was a whirlpool
of rage and terror and shame . . .
The dragon he changed to stone
with hardly a thought. But
his strength almost failed him
in unlocking those chains.

Looking away from her nakedness,
he smoothes her ankles, wrists.
She waits for the moment
when he will meet her eyes.

What kind of relationship can there be between the man who is buying even as he saves and the woman who has, at this moment, only the knowledge of her own suffering, the consciousness of her own truth, and the perception that a similar expression lurks in the eyes of Perseus to the one she saw in the eyes of the sea-dragon?

Of Pools and Mirrors

What does it mean, then, to be internalized within the male gaze? One man who cannot be blamed for the turning of women into visual objects is Narcissus. I imagined him—and the particular imaginative trigger for this poem was a chic, black-and-white television advertisement for Smirnoff vodka in the mid-1980s featuring an exercise bike by a pool—living in an opulent setting. His wife is Echo—the nymph rejected by him in Ovid's story in his *Metamorphoses* (1987). But while Narcissus lives on in one of the Greek myths with widest currency, Echo has been fated to live out the implications of her name: her story has been sidelined, she is a footnote. Thus this mythic tale seemed emblematic of the imbalance in kinds of attention given to men and women as they were represented in Greek myth, and subsequently. The following version of the story of Echo and Narcissus also works on an intrapsychic level, as I believe myths possessed of depth and power inevitably do—whatever they encode of social and political power relations, historical and contemporary, they hold a mirror up to the psyche itself: a mirroring pool for the individual to read his or her own psychological truth as well as those other undulating shadows crisscrossing that self-image.

The Pool

He has given her this room of mirrors, in which she is bored;
she may speak to him only when he speaks to her.
He spends most of his time by the pool. What is it he sees,
staring down at its tiled floor—some classical coin
with shimmering bronze face? He is as beautiful as a dolphin
but never swims. She often does. She likes the splashing cry
of the water as her long arms slice through vivid green.

Why does he never look at her? He is always looking down—
even into his glass as they sit in the evening by the pool.
"Have you had a nice day?" (he stirs and pokes his ice);
". . . a nice day?" she echoes, desolate.
Oh, but she loves him!
Once she swam the pool's whole length to surprise him,
curving up to where he gazed soulfully, teardrops pocking
the chlorine. At first he did not see her face, then,
when she was almost out of breath—but still smiling—
those clear eyes glazed with shock and he looked away.
She did not hear the slapping of her feet on concrete
as she walked inside then dripped up the long, soft stairs
to her room. "With only mirrors to keep me company
I shall waste away, waste away . . ." she thought,
but could not say—as usual, the words stuck in her throat.
And she curled into herself, hiding from all those faces.
Stretched out flat by the pool, he too loved and wasted,
had not even sensed her walking away, her stifled sigh.

Like many women who have written new versions of myths in this period, I have been concerned with reversals. For who, after all—given half a chance to change the situation—would want to hang around all those reflecting surfaces with multiple images of an anorexic self, starved of love and power, staring back at one as if at an undesirable stranger? Or yearn for a man whose eyes are starry with his own image.

Yet it seems to me that while the occasional dose of magical thinking may be salutary, there are traps in wait in the business of rewriting myth. A compensatory triumphalism is one trap: for instance, what I call the "I felt like Helen of Troy (or Medea or whoever) when I got up this morning" poem. If it helps you get through the day, fine, but such

poems are often a missed opportunity. What don't we know about Helen
of Troy? What has not been imagined about her? And what can't be
imagined about her? Poetry thrives on the tension provided by such
questions, which can lead one into interesting places—though these are
not necessarily places where one will have a nice day. Another trap is
a polarizing contempt—again, an understandable reflex or strategy in
extreme situations, of which there are many; but in the end a total
dismissal of men creates a sense of unreality and is a rehearsal of
stuckness, militating against the working-through of difficult experiences and burdensome attitudes.

It is not easy to win back ground, but once under one's feet, the
consciousness of cause and effect—of other people's choices radically
delimiting one's own—and the knowledge of one's innate freedom to
be is on some level incontrovertible. And the gaze of the person liberated
from internalized oppression, and working at gaining a true place in
the world, is powerful: can look back at predatory dominance and take
its measure.

In *Metamorphoses* I began a quest to find certain kinds of visionary
strength emerging in response to entrapment or imposed transformation. In "Arethusa," the nymph of that name who was changed into a
pool when escaping from a pursuing river god,

> bathed
> and mirrored those who came.
> All unlived longings sank like shadows
> through her, and rose fulfilled.
> She was still, with the power
> of a waterfall tumbling.

"Weaver" tells the story of Arachne, changed by (the patriarchal
version of) Athena into a spider. In her diminished state, a new mag-
nified awareness emerges:

> Now, ringed planet, nucleus
> of atom, she waits in a network of dew
> to catch and hold the sky, moves with every wind
> hovering close to earth. Trapped in that
> tiny globe her self is inexhaustible—
> it spins and spins and spins.

Ariadne, in a dialogue with her psychiatrist in "Ariadne: A Case
Study," insists on her own reality, answering her interrogator's in-

sinuations and accusations blow by blow. (His comments are inset in the text.) Theseus, who abandoned Ariadne on Naxos, looms large in the discourse, naturally enough. To the psychiatrist's charge that, through her role in giving Theseus the clue to the labyrinth, she was "controlling everything," indulging in "delusions of grandeur," she replies:

> I saw Theseus in the grip of them
> when he returned. Night after night,
> he shouted in his sleep,
>   "I am the Minotaur!"
> By day he swaggered with secret knowledge.
> In the end, he no longer saw me.
>
>   So he stopped loving you, or never did.
> Fulfilment lay, for him, in other things.
>
> In selfish power. He had no heed
> for my pain, or vulnerability.
>
>   Anger! You need to get in touch
> with it, own it, work it through.
> I should be able to help you to do that.
>
> So many mazes, so many minotaurs,
> she said, and shook her head.

The moment of taking possession of one's own body, self, destiny, is imaged in a poem about Helen, based—only partly, alas—on the figure of Marilyn Monroe. The poem begins, "For every spotlit myth / there are a million shadows." By the end, Helen, who knows that "their ultimately / embodied woman is a ghost," moves from icon to self-determining woman:

>   Each Dawn She Walks Alone
> to the sea, steps into flesh-pricking coolness.
> Breathing slowly, she wades against the tide,
> then, at her own moment, enters that flux,
> that tension, her body poised, moving freely,
> inside the wave.

In the final section of the sequence "Atalanta," there is again, as for Arethusa, a transformation into water. Here I further transformed this image into one expressive of a spiritual translucency, of a self-shaping principle coexisting with attunement to life as a process.

Waterfall

Before it falls,
The water is held
in a chalice of rock:
unshadowed, still.

As it falls,
it is a pure line,
a sound like breathing.
And so swift.

The water merges
with a pool masked
by tree shadows, etched
by the wind's light.

This is the place that,
partnered and alone,
knowing and unknowing,
she has learnt to see.

She is of this setting,

her spirit is rooted here
beyond all changing forms:
at home, singular.

Of Money and Dancing Horses

As signaled in my introduction, I hold the view that the evolution of
the hero myth within patriarchal society has, by virtue of being appropriated to serve the uses of power, been brutalized. The figure of Heracles is a key example of this. While he is a figure of some subtlety, and
moral as well as physical strength, in the story of Alcestis and Admetus
he ultimately represents the blindness of overinvested power to the sacredness and vulnerability of life itself. He becomes a polarized figure,
locked into endless stories of valor that are tied to territorial expansion
in Greece. In Euripides' *Heracles* (1963) he acts out his unconscious
devaluing of the nurturing dimension of life by murdering his children.
Another story—one of those to be found in the interstices of myth,
surviving almost in the unconscious margins, as it were—tells of his
slaughter of a youth who serves him the wrong portion of the beast at
a meal. In the following poem, one of a sequence on the violence of
Heracles, I conflate that tale with a similar one:

Heracles' Lunch

Disliking the drink set before him, he struck Cyathus, the cupbearer, with one finger only, but killed him none the less.

Robert Graves

A cup-bearer killed
for a disappointing sip.

The host's three sons slain
for serving the wrong
portion of the beast . . .

Lucky that only Heracles
behaves like a hero
at the table.

Four dead before
the meal is underway . . .

What's for dessert,
and who will serve it?

In wanting to further my engagement with critiquing the roots of violence, I turned to the figure of Ares, the god of war. He is a rather shadowy figure, and what drew me to write about him was not the idea of violence issuing from an excess of strength and lack of boundaries, as with Heracles, but the sense of a core of uncreation, of nullity—a passive refusal to do the work of relating and becoming, from which refusal a propensity to violence grows:

Ares

He has no memory,
and what he sees is that nothing is happening . . .

only life itself—pigeons on terraces,
hot dinners, urchins in a field.

He wants something, anything, to happen
that will change all this.

Walking, later, through the ruined village,
he says over and over, *This is real.*

But he doesn't believe that, either.
They are lying there, they are dead.

He just doesn't believe it.
He still wants something to happen.

One rumor about Ares, or trace element of his personality, is that he was a dancer as well as a warrior. This suggests the potential for turning the negative, recessive energy I have described, into an act of creative shaping—of both art and self. Dancing is opposed to warlike activities in another poem that resulted from my being beguiled by a story about the Sybarites.

Flute Music

The Sybarites taught some of their horses to dance to flute music. This sometimes led to embarrassment on the battlefield.

> More than the bracelet of
> massed shields, it was the light
> on the flanks of prancing
> horses that mesmerised
> the enemy . . . In pricked
> ears, the dulcet breath of
> wind in high trees as a
> blushing warrior broke
> rank, sashayed on his light-
> footed beast towards them,
> rupturing their line, their
> faces immobilised
> as they waited with clutched
> spears and ambivalent-
> ly poised hooves, watching man
> and horse frisk, whirl, go through
> their paces—disarmed by
> that errant sight as if
> by a centaur waltzing.

If this poem depicts (however momentarily) a nonviolent version of war, what, I wondered, would a nonviolent version of the hero be like? The one I imagined in the following poem (from a sequence called "Monsters Talk Back," which looks at monster images as parts of ourselves we refuse to own) may seem short on intelligence, but he is long on patience. He hopes to defeat the dragon by waiting until its scales fall off—as if this were somehow a similar process to scales falling from one's eyes. The dragon I imagined combines the two dominant aspects of dragons in Western mythology. The first, like Grendel, constellates Mother—she who must be overcome, then rejected. The second is a configuration of the hoarding and marauding ego sitting on its pile of gold—a repulsively anal-retentive image, which can also be read as the riches of the self being clutched by the ego rather than becoming the currency of exchange with other humans and the life of the earth itself that holds us in being. So this particular dragon is also very much alive among us now, residing in the cave of economic rationalism and associated fictions that act to reshape culture and society in the interests of economic privilege and global capitalism.

Dragon and Nonviolent Hero

The nonviolent hero is the one
who is waiting for the dragon's
scales to fall off,
though it has lived for a millenium
and will survive another.

The dragon watches the hero
  who has no scales,
  cannot breathe fire, or fly,
  and claims not to
  covet the treasure—
the dragon watches the hero
sleeping in a corner of its cave,
with curiosity, with tenderness . . .

It stirs the fire, thinking.

Here, the dragon is a presence in the hero's psyche, and in the collective psyche. It's the hero's task to get a handle on it, and so depotentiate its monstrousness—and so discover what lies beyond that, or is buried beneath it. We get a glimpse of this other side at the end of the poem, with the skeptical but companionable dragon stirring the fire, as if searching for new possibilities in its flickering images.

Eventually my thoughts turned to Midas. It seemed to me that a world in which gold (standing for monetary gain) was the prime value was a world turning in fact into lead—as Midas indeed came to experience it when unable to eat while surrounded by objects he had changed into gold. Midas, with his famed rose garden—a wonderful image of spirituality and nature in fusion (and speaking perhaps of an underdeveloped potential within Midas himself)—projects all value outward on to material gold rather than recognizing the gold yielded by inner search, the alchemy of wholeness that Jung spoke of.

Midas

Not just golden hair and golden wheatfields and golden wine,
  but golden spiderwebs, golden cornflowers, golden doves:

everything, anything at all, becoming bankable—even
the cockroach waiting in a finger of the royal glove:
   spy into scarab.

Gold-fleshed women flashed their million-dollar smiles—
so much brightness! He wore sunglasses which turned
opaque, glittered heavily. At night, clamped to chill
lumps, he felt his room, its very air, begin to shine
   through blackness.

Bread as inedible as stone! But still more punishing was
the brightness. In the stream's dark absolution he rests,
steps into an ordinary day, with the sun's radiance
reaching out from so far away: tentative, soft—
   a beggar's touch.

Another image of gold came to me when reading the story of Glaucus. I imagined the boy lifted up from the great jar of honey into which
he had fallen, the light of many candles turning the honey enclosing
his body, running back into the jar like an umbilical cord, into a living
gold talisman of rebirth.

Glaucus, Son of Minos

*As a child, Glaucus drowned in a storage jug of honey
while playing. He was found and revived by the seer
Polyeidus. Polyeidus taught the boy the art of divining, but
later caused him to forget his learning.*

Edward Tripp, Dictionary of Classical Mythology

His young son is lost—Minos orders the seer to find him.

The cellar flickers round his candle:
Polyeidus contemplates, as they close,

an owl's eyes, ochre and tawny,
points to the jar brimming with honey.

A serpent swirls, re-enters the jar,
as the body is raised aloft

into a circle of lamps, faces . . .
"Give him life," intones the king,

then as he breathes, "Teach him
your secrets—stay here till he learns."

When, at last, the seer may leave,
he has Glaucus spit in his mouth,

frees him from so much wisdom.
An image of coiling light

is all the boy retains—light,
gold and sinewy, connecting him

to that sweet, curved darkness.

Of Oracles and Dolphins

I remember visiting Delphi for three days, long ago. I walked around,
breathed the air, gazed at Mount Parnassus, and felt the earth under
my feet. I marveled at the great collection of fallen temples and sacked
treasure houses in the sanctuary of Apollo, but when I stood on the
road between that sanctuary and the temple of Artemis further down
the mountain, beneath the road I felt in the center of my body the
magnetic pull of the older, earth-based, woman-centered way of dwelling on this earth.

The Delphic oracle was supplanted, her function appropriated by
Apollo's priests for his purposes, but this circular temple preserves the
voice of woman speaking from the heart of earth. There was a point
somewhere there, on that winding road, where you could glimpse the
sea, and when I came to write a sequence "Oracle," in praise of female
wisdom, an image of listening to that far sea, as to the far sea of myth,
formed itself. This is the last section of that sequence:

> Though earth is my element,
> I can hear the sea beyond the mountains.
>
> It gives us word and chaos,
> shape and dissolution—rhythms reversing,
>
> flowing over us, as our ears echo
> with wavefall, wingbeat,
>
> and the almost audible
> song of the dolphin
>
> threading in half-moon arcs
> through crystal darkness.

The image of the dolphin has become very resonant for me, as it is
for many in this time of the death of nature. The dolphin configures
spiritual freedom, creativity, intelligence, relatedness; it is a creature that
is not only other but beyond: it follows pathways through the sea we

cannot map, it looks back at the human gaze with a reach of knowledge
we cannot access.

There is a link between the Greek words for dolphin and Delphi, as
J. C. Cooper (1978) points out:

> Delphi was regarded as an omphalos, the World Centre, with the
> Greek words *delphis* (dolphin) and *delphys* (womb) bringing in the
> symbolism of the masculine, solar Sun God and the feminine,
> watery power of the womb as the center of life. Also in line with
> their connection to Apollo dolphins were said to be music lovers;
> Aelion refers to "the music-loving dolphin, and in the aspect of
> music lovers and saviour dolphins rescued Arion from the sea: in
> Greek art, Arion is depicted riding on a dolphin." (76)

For the Greeks, the boy on the dolphin, and Arion on his dolphin,
were powerful icons, constellating a unity of human and nonhuman
creature, able to move as one through the power, mystery, and danger
of the sea—that primordial image of life itself. On revisiting the following poem, I find that, like "Glaucus, Son of Minos," it too offers an
image of rebirth:

Arion

*The crew of the vessel bearing him on his return journey
from Tarentum to Corinth determined to kill him for his
wealth. . . . They did, however, grant the bard's request that
he be allowed to sing once more before dying. Arion put on
his full minstrel's regalia and began to sing a hymn to
Apollo. Seeing that many dolphins, attracted by his song,
were playing about the ship, he leaped into the sea. One of
the dolphins took him on its back and carried him to the
shore at Taenarum.*

Edward Tripp

His chanted words were a sea they swam in—
dolphins wreathing the ship where Arion sang
to save his life. He sang without fear,
with ancient formality, dressed in the dignity
of his minstrel's robes. That set him free
to move through sounds like a dolphin—
to inhabit a sea of echoing pathways: his song
was a bright strand woven amongst them.
Then he leapt into water, his dolphin-voyage
a speeding through chill and sunlight—
each fragment of spray a drop of gold-

within-crystal. His homeland began where
that great line of energy broke on sand.
He walked through it, hearing a wordless singing.

The story of Arion seems very much a fable for our times. It dramatizes the value of creativity as against greed and shows the saving
power of a creature from the natural world—one rich with cultural and
spiritual associations.

I'm led to conclude this meditation on images with the final poem
from *Listening to a Far Sea*. I had begun this collection, as was fitting,
with a poem called "Muse," whose subject I characterize as "no re-
specter / of good intentions, pieties" but a guide through the unconscious:

> She is the keeper of the labyrinth
> who promises only one thing:
> if you are true to her,
> she will be true to you.

My last poem is a perversely complementing bookend. It is about
Circe, presented as a bemused transformer, searching—with an appropriate degree of circumspection, though in a rather unusual manner—
for eyes that might meet and answer her gaze.

Menagerie

Not all of them were changed to swine.
She kept experimenting,
intuiting their hidden selves,
unlived wishes:
> body of a lion; head of a horse;
> wolverine eyes; voice of nightingale.
Dignity had nothing to do with it:
they stood composed, liberated,
accepting their natures.

Once, she tried transforming one
into an image she might desire.
She concentrated. Would this work—
the most quixotic magic of all?
> A crinkly sound. Was that a dragonfly—
> out the window before she could blink,
> skywriting in silver across a rainbow?
The wrong page, the wrong potion—
why does she always get light-headed

> when it's been raining?
>   It's dusk:
> now she must mix their feed—
> for that she will need her wits about her.

In a sense this poem is a kind of signature to my work with masculine images in *Listening to a Far Sea*, where I refuse generalizations about men—as pigs, or whatever—and attend to the buried or denied or undiscovered self. By bringing consciousness to the dance of projections, we are both amplified and shriven—and so set free to become more connected to ourselves and life.

Circe is muse, artist, therapist, trickster. She is also the kind of contemporary woman who still looks to the possibility of relationship with men and with the masculine. As such she is using enchantment—if not to heal, then to ameliorate disenchantment. Both skepticism and playfulness, seasoned with knowledge and subversion, are at work in this poem. Circe is a grounded figure, in control on some levels, vulnerable on others. And her lapse of attention—could it be partly intentional?—is only temporary. Her focus will return to feed and nurture the images she has fashioned.

If this poem, and my work on Greek mythology as a whole, leaves the problem of what to do about patriarchy in a kind of suspended solution, it leaves little doubt about the problem of what to do about oneself. And holding that suspended solution with its strange floating forms up to the light is a salutary experience. For if, on one level, we become the images we contemplate—and are therefore in danger from the images by which we have been programmed, as I have shown—it is also true that the images we contemplate are changed by our contemplation of them. So it behooves us to view that which diminishes us with an unillusioned eye, and to create our own images of beauty, meaning, and hope—and then to contemplate them. In this venture, the store of images offered by mythology is, as I have suggested, sometimes a wellspring of fresh perspective and inspiration.

References

Cooper, J. C. 1978. *An Illustrated Encyclopedia of Traditional Symbols*. London: Thames and Hudson.

Downing, Christine. 1996. *The Goddess: Mythological Images of the Feminine*. New York: Continuum.

Euripides. 1963. *Heracles*. Trans. Philip Vellacott. Harmondsworth: Penguin Books.

Fahey, Diane, 1988. *Metamorphoses*. Marrickville, N.S.W.: Dangaroo Press.

―――. 1998. *Listening to a Far Sea*. Alexandria, N.S.W: Hale and Iremonges.

Ovid 1987. *Metamorphoses*. Trans. A. D. Melville Oxford: Oxford University Press.

Paris, Ginette. 1990. *Pagan Grace: Dionysius, Hermes and the Goddess in Daily Life*. Dallas, Tex.: Spring.

Conclusion

The Future of Feminist Spiritualities

Frances Devlin-Glass and Lyn McCredden

We hope that the essays in this book will awaken a desire in their readers to embrace the future, exploring new modes of understanding and practising spirituality. Or do they underline the fierce grip of centuries-old patriarchy on the lives, imaginations, and sacred insights of women? New insights come about from engagement of intellectual rigor *and* from broader cultural practices and experiences, both personal and communal. There is a clear range of new directions that find a voice in these essays, each one the result of contemporary women asking what it might mean to think and act with an awareness of the spiritual. The future-directed, intertwined areas that emerge in this book might be listed in the following way: critical utopic thinking; historical recuperation and remapping; earthed spirituality; engagement in the representational agenda; ecofeminism; redefining the liberal humanist agenda; poststructuralist interventions; psychoanalysis and redefinings of female identity; new modes of women's writing; performativity; postcoloniality.

Some of these new directions are intellectual and methodological. Some are part of current practices in dispersed sites. Many overlap and critique each other. But each has already begun to make a distinct contribution within the field of feminist spirituality. In particular, four conjunctions of thought and practice are offering ways forward and beyond current patriarchal boundaries: recuperative, critical utopics; earthed and politicized spiritualities; new female subjectivities; and new representational agendas.

Recuperative, Critical Utopics

The work of scholars such as Johanna Stuckey has uncovered a wealth of historical, archaeological, and mythological material crying out for critical reappraisal. It has also, interestingly, become an enabling basis for the current burgeoning of interest in the goddesses of the past. Some of this interest has not been critical but has arisen out of deep needs experienced by Goddess worshipers to write a future that embraces the female, and not merely the inevitably male, patriarchal figure—god/father, son, brotherhood—of monotheistic religions.

Stuckey is aware of the eclecticism of many such enterprises, their sometimes uncritical "borrowing" (appropriating?) of rituals and narratives from indigenous and African cultures, their tendency to rework older traditions (including mainstream and Jungian ones), and the political uses of their thealogy and practice. She defends their a-historicism on the grounds that Goddess worshipers do serve the psychic needs of modern women, and while they make gestures toward a romanticized past, they do not attempt to recreate the religious traditions of the remote cultures and do not treat their sacred stories as dogma (Stuckey 1998).

More important than their avoidance of traditions they find oppressive, these new spiritualities are at the very least in the process of constructing new versions of what it is to be a woman and sometimes looking to the past for indications of how this might be done or for legitimacy of their beliefs and practices. Some of the essays here in (Rigby, Stuckey, Devlin-Glass) stand as correctives to any simple utopics and problematize some of the impulses that drive such utopics. However, the utopic in and of itself is not merely romantic in nature. There are legitimate and pragmatic uses for the prophetic and utopic. Mc-Credden's essay has argued that Aboriginal Australian writer Oodgeroo uses a form of utopics that strategically mobilizes identity politics. The writing of this indigenous activist and poet makes a plea for a dialogic process of understanding between groups divided by racism; her blending of strident satire with hope for reconciliation mark a historically important postmodern, postcolonial, and feminist moment. The refusal of subaltern status is also part of the politics of postcolonial Ireland. Devlin-Glass's essay, for instance, has drawn attention to the different cultural purposes, often utopic in nature, that Irish myths have been made to serve since they were first put onto vellum by proselytizing monks. Representations of women have been both negatively and positively deployed in political, nationalist, and ecclesiastical games at different points in Ireland's troubled history. This is sometimes at the cost of effacing the actual bodies and lives of women, especially in the modern period. Hence the importance of recuperating earlier narratives of women's embodiment.

One of the major problems of those reading the texts of ancient cultures, especially those that have been patriarchalized, is the problem of the texts having been written by those who constitute the winning élites (Fontaine 1990:69). This is especially true of the Irish and Mesopotamian texts discussed by Stuckey and Devlin-Glass. Mesopotamian texts have often served as source documents for biblical studies rather than as texts in their own right (as the anthology *Ancient Near Eastern Texts Relating to the Old Testament* [Pritchard 1969] attests), and this epistemological purpose has inevitably skewed how they are read. Nor do the texts necessarily exist in coherent wholes, or in literary structures, that are familiar to the modern reader. As such they have already been subject to a systematic male hermeneutic and editing process, sometimes over many centuries. Because the texts are the products of patriarchalized cultures, and bear only traces of their origins in older oral cultures what is called for is a special kind of reading technology, that of reading, not just resistantly, but "slant"—a reading attentive to gaps and silences. To do so is to be committed to "indeterminacy of meanings," a refusal to suppress multiple meanings, a technique employed with some bravura on the Gospel of Mark by feminist exegete Susan Lochrie Graham (1992). In bringing marginal and silent women into central focus, she reveals their nonverbal behavior, their silences and physical actions: she sees such nonverbal elements as markers of the kind of intimacy that those men who debate and argue with Christ lack. She argues that this focus on sensuous contact is in marked contrast with the valorization of language in the writing of the sacred text (revelation to men) and contrasts markedly with the way men are represented in Mark as debaters and arguers in a way that is rarely the case with women characters. Her metanarrative, though, deconstructs itself even as it signifies in words what is implicit in the text.

Earthed and Embodied Spiritualities

We have already seen that Rosemary Radford Ruether, writing of an earthed spirituality and in a recuperative utopic vein, envisages a fem-

inist sacred as one that defines itself in opposition to patriarchal-
hierarchical society and in dynamic terms: she sees liberation as occurring through relationships, the healing of broken relations with our
bodies and with nature (1983), a radical theology of creation she was
to take to another level in *Gaia and God: An Ecofeminist Theology of Earth
Healing*. In the latter work, she argues that the view of the Bible as
being antinature is a legacy of nineteenth-century western European
Protestantism (1992:207). She contests the dualism in which a "Goddess" is identified with nature, immanence, and ecological well-being
whereas the God of the Semitic monotheism is aligned with transcendence and dominance (1992:247). In a radical maneuver, she rediscov-
ers covenantal and sacramental traditions within the Hebrew scriptures
and insists that "the biblical God and Gaia are not at odds; rightly
understood, they are on terms of amity, if not commingling" (1992:
240).

Not all the traditions that come under the banner of feminist spirituality are focused on history and historical reconstruction. What is
energizing about the practices that Kate Rigby has surveyed and cri-
tiqued in this volume and that she identifies as a new tradition—that
of ecofeminism—is its postmodern quality: its reaching back to secure
fragments from old traditions at the same time that it generates highly
interventionist political programs to reform millennia of earth-
destruction. Far from idealizing and homogenizing this tradition, she
has demonstrated how multivalent the multiple and sometimes contradictory agendas can be, and how fine the faultlines can be between
contesting groups within the tradition. She traces in some detail the
differences, for example, between black and white ecofeminist positions
and between cultural and socialist ecofeminists. However, what is most
striking about this new immanentist kind of spirituality is its political
thrust, its generation of a wide range of anticapitalist, anticonsumerist
projects—its real-world, situated politics.

Postcolonialism as an intellectual interdisciplinary set of practices
has made a tremendous impact on the ways women can think of their
bodies and subjectivities. The postcolonial revelation of women's bodies
as sites upon which racial, imperial, and patriarchal wars have been
waged has enabled a range of political responses to the past as well as
strategies for the future. Rather than a monolithic and mythologized
female body owned by masculinist power élites, the reality and useful-
ness of such notions as hybridity (see Bakhtin 1981, Bhabha 1994),
shifting and multiple cultural identities, and interactive models of subjectivity (see Lorde 1984; Anzaldúa 1987) have opened up the variety
of marginal positions of women in minority cultures. In the field of

feminist spirituality, this has allowed the other to speak and to offer forms of earthed, embodied spirituality, often ancient and indigenous and with tremendous potential for the future.

Contemporary postcolonial work by feminist and poststructural anthropologists has added considerably to the ways indigenous spiritualities might be approached and understood, both through a critiquing of anthropology's imperialist and patriarchal grounds and in a consideration of the gendered nature of religious practices and beliefs. Australian feminist Diane Bell's work on indigenous Australian spirituality has become a respected resource for many. Her most recent book, *Ngarrindjeri Wurruwarrin: A World That Is, Was and Will Be*, is a work of immense empirical and polemical scholarship, focusing mainly on the spiritual practices and stories of Ngarrindjeri women in South Australia, within the highly political context of urgent land rights issues in that state. While some critics argue that her position is utopic and partial, her work with and among the Ngarrindjeri and other Aboriginal women over several decades gives her great credibility among many indigenous and white Australians.

Of course, the work of Western feminist anthropologists is not always as culturally sensitive as it should be. The general ignorance in "the West" of Islamic religious and cultural practices has sometimes resulted in awful confrontations: the well-meaning Western feminist blundering into the complex negotiations of "Middle Eastern" women concerning their bodies and cultural and religious practices. A dramatic and increasingly highlighted practice is that of cliterodectomy. In her highly polemical essay "Feminism and Cliterodectomy," anthropologist Vicki Kirkby (1987) maps the complex issues surrounding this practice and examines the interweaving of religious with broader cultural considerations. Her final admonition to Western women, who believe they know the Islamic or Arabic woman and what she needs, is to take stock of the dark abyss of Western female sexuality, the ways Western women have been sexualized, fetishized, and subjected to extreme forms of violence. Who is to preach to whom, she asks. Amila Butrovic's essay in this book offers a rare insight into a different order of female spirituality and physicality, one with which Western feminist readers might find themselves struggling mightily.

Several essays in this book engage implicitly and explicitly with the notion of the embodied sacral female body (Raphael 1996) and either reread or re-create texts that image *the female body* as a vehicle for the divine, contesting vigorously the soul/body dualism of mainstream philosophy and religion. Divine generativity, imaged as female, remains controversial but is becoming a more familiar discourse. Nor is such embodiment necessarily limited by procreative notions of fecundity, though in some cases (notably Inanna), it is a foundational attribute. More significantly, the goddess is the principle of change, of liminality, a model perhaps of the *sujet en procès*. Of course not all the women discussed in this book are uncomplicated celebrators of their bodies. Some, indeed, like Margery or the Sufi mystic Fatima Umm Ali, are able to exploit the desacralization of women's bodies and to use their bodies as a form of control over merely mortal or flesh-focused men in pursuit of relationships they deemed erotic with God.

New Female Subjectivities

One of the major intellectual fields of research into female subjectivity has been within pyschoanalytic theory. Of course the history of feminist engagements with this theory is deeply ambivalent: neither completely accepting or rejecting its discourses, feminists put them to use only if they prove to be viable explanations, cues for constructing alternative narratives. Early criticism of biologism and misogyny (Millett 1970, Firestone 1970), gave way to more theorized readings of gender difference and identity (Mitchell 1974; Dinnerstein 1976; Chodorow 1978); and poststructuralists (notably Irigaray 1985a; 1985b; Kristeva 1982; Cixous 1975; Grosz 1989) have critically interpreted Lacan's neo-Freudian synthesis of linguistics and psychoanalysis, creatively reworking the tradition to revalorize and resignify the female body and its functions, especially its fertility function.

What is most curious, given the secular, scientific caste of psychoanalysis, is the extent to which its leading feminist practitioners, notably Kristeva (Kearns 1993) and Irigaray (Grosz 1993) are aware of the ways in which issues of female identity and the body are implicated in notions of the divine. Grosz claims that Irigaray sees the notion of the divine as part of a project of creating an ideal self-image for women, an ideal to which women may aspire and through which they make cultural artifacts, just as men have created abstract cultural artifacts in the form of ethics, religions, sciences, and philosophies of love rationalized by the authority of God (cited in Grosz 1993:202).

Such a confident, utopic assertion has a particular legitimacy in the mouth of a theorist who in *Speculum of the Other Woman* (Irigaray 1985a) not only systematically challenged Western philosophy and epistemology, as well as critiquing the mainstream religious tradition, but also enquired into the positive uses "a notion of divinity might play in the formation of a nonphallocentric [and female] subjectivity" (Jones

1993:122). It is perhaps worth stressing that for Irigaray, the notion of God is not a teleology but a becoming; the subject is always "in process." Such a stance also serves as a positive response to McCance's demeaning and derisive implication (in Hurtado 1990:171) that the "quest for the goddess" (or, one might add, more women-friendly definitions of the sacred) "is nothing more than a metaphor of the affirmation of female experience and female power." For our purposes in this collection, several key notions derived from psychoanalysis are invigorating. Psychoanalytic theory has been read by feminists as going some way to explain the problematic of the body and especially that of the female body and the role of religion defining the "clean and proper body." It is worth valuing a tradition, like the one that the Sumerian story of Inanna points to, that honors the deity's vulva and celebrates it when one is inheritor of cultural and religious systems that insist on the body's defilement and need for purification.

Julia Kristeva's theory of abjection (outlined in *Powers of Horror*, that drew on the work of Mary Douglas and Jacques Lacan) probes the psychopathology, that destabilizes the relationship between mother and child (in the educative process of distinguishing between the properly clean body and the excremental). Kristeva understands the maternal (by extension womanly?) body to be threateningly abject because of its innerness, the impossibility of clear borders between the clean and the unclean, between blood and menstrual blood, between mother's body and fetal child, in short, its materiality (Kristeva 1982:54; Grosz 1989: 71–8). In Kristeva's formulation, "[a]bjection accompanies all religious structurings," and the abject is what is written outside the sacred. Feminist exegetes, drawing on such insights, see religious texts as implicated in the process of subordinating maternal power to the symbolic order and "divine Law" (Kristeva 1982:91). Shields (1998), following Kristeva, for example, reads Ezekiel 16, exposing the body and gender rhetoric of the Old Testament writer who is an objectifier and nothing less than complicit in gang rape. Shield's methodology is to raise problems of translation, which construct the sense of woman's unclean body, which is integral to this tribal tale. While her sense of the pathologies that underlie patriarchy constitute helpful and profound understandings of the difficulties of women in history, there is a compensatory move in Kristeva's writings that sees ways out of the impasse, and these directions are the more valuable because she is antiseparatist in her thinking (see Kristeva 1981).

Feminist engagements with spirituality have found Kristeva's work on abjection a new source for thinking about the role of the female in religion. Pamela Sue Anderson (1998a, 1998b) uses the notion of abjection to deconstruct Ricoeur's work on the myth of Adam and Eve in *The Symbolism of Evil*. In her essay " 'Abjection . . . the Most Propitious Place for Communication': Celebrating the Death of the Unitary Subject," Anderson writes of the death of the unitary subject, and specifically the subject in religion, arguing that the "idealized unitary subject of traditional philosophy of religion has been found lacking precisely in what it has excluded" (1998a:211). She goes on to argue that the female exists in the place of abjection and that this is "potentially a site of intellectual privilege" (211).

Kristeva's defense of what she terms the *semiotic* is another potentially fruitful path for feminist spirituality. Whereas cultural feminists engage in social renegotiations of meanings, in rational ways, exposing and explaining, Kristeva describes the powers of the semiotic, that site, perhaps sacramental in nature, where the body, the associative, the unspeakable, the revolutionary are in play. She designates its strategies for expression as "analytic listening" and "aesthetic practice" and is not above practicing both, simultaneously, in her split essay "Stabat Mater," a rigorous analysis of the semiotics of maternity (1977).

A further useful strategy that derives from neo-Freudianism but that often designates itself postconstructivist (Diamond 1996) is the body of theory that draws on phenomenology and names itself performativist or queer (Butler 1990, 1993). Such theorists acknowledge the constructed nature of sexuality and the regimes of power that implement and control socially acceptable forms of sexual identity and behavior. They refuse essentialism and even deconstructive games in favor of a different metaphor: that of gender as performance, or rather successive performances, that enact and constitute gender. Putting aside the designation of Margery as a hysteric (a term used to denigrate her and deny her a place in history), one is spectator to a bewildering range of performances (actual and imaginary): she is the mother of many real children, and a mother to her Creator; she is the submissive daughter who must be so to avoid immolation as a heretic; she is also wife, and not-wife and lover of Christ; writer and not-writer; and a humble but effective legal advocate in courts where men are the main performers. She enacts a range of performances that exceed contemporary definitions of woman.

New Representational Agendas

Far from being concerned simply to denounce men's signification of women, the corresponding active impulse since the 1970s has been for women to explore and create meanings themselves and to enter into debate with masculinist representational agendas (Godard 1985:6; Wilshire 1992:108–12). Not only can narratives be made to resignify, for good or ill, but feminists concerned with defining spirituality have also been active in critiquing the use of symbols and engaged in renovating them, especially language associated with the female body (*cunt, crone, hysteric,* among many). Judy Chicago and her team of creative potters and embroiderers who created the *Dinner Party* would certainly understand the politics of Kramer and Wolkstein's celebratory translation of Inanna's hymn to her own vulva or the wonder that lies behind Medb's landscape-forming gush of blood. Margery's perverse insistence on wearing white (despite her nonvirginal status) at the point that she takes on radical celibacy is a more ambiguous act of resignification, and although it may not be consonant with some modern feminist agendas, it certainly represents an aggressive wresting of control over one's body from an institution that so often arrogated the right to define and order it.

Women need to continue to reinscribe themselves on the historical maps of what it is to be human, persons of spirit, and to do it in ways that are not merely wish-fulfilling. The methodologies in use—reversals of signification, drawing attention to characters on the margins, reviving and resuscitating lost or neglected texts to augment both writing and hermeneutic traditions, questioning the prejudice against female subject matter and problematizations of genre—are well-established and productive practices, in use for at least three decades. However, as with the gynocritical enterprise more generally (Moi 1985), this project is undoubtedly limited by its tendency to essentialism (and tendency to homogenize women's experience, especially in relation to race and class) and to separatism (e.g., goddesses tend to be privileged over male and female pairs) and by its failure to reckon with the systemic and institutionalized nature of sexism, and with race and class, which postmodernist theory addresses directly.

For example, deconstructionist notions of language as an unstable and decentered system consisting of webs of signifiers without ultimate terms to guarantee meaning represent a powerful set of opportunities for women in thinking about their spirituality, their participation as active agents, and their representation in discourses of the sacred. In Curkpatrick's essay, the protagonist struggles with the instability of meanings and what words cannot easily embrace, in mounting the metaphor of "wall-papered worlds." His excursus on categories is playful in tone but deeply serious in intent when the principle is applied to how to talk about *resurrection into life* (with its problematic coupling of discourses of transcendence and immanence) and how to understand and talk about a God understood to be always under erasure in the Derridean understanding of language.

Perhaps the most celebrated gift of feminist deconstructive study of sacred narratives is its method of destabilizing the binary oppositions that structure texts. Feminist theorists following Derrida (Moi 1985: 104–5; Ortner & Whitehead 1981) have long been aware that these oppositions are asymmetrical and biased against women. One strategy has been to proclaim writing methods (e.g., *écriture feminine, parler femme*) designed to deconstruct, in particular, the opposition between poetic and argumentative modes of discourse, blending them wittily, foregrounding the sensuality of language itself, its metaphoricity. Although such programs have been criticized for their essentialism, some scholars argue that these forms of discourse are better understood as poetic metaphors, analogies, and symbolic challenges to phallocentrism rather than biological essentialism (see Grosz 1989:110–3, Schor and Weed 1994; Whitford 1991a). However, the deconstructive analytic mode is not always as rhetorically flamboyant as it is in the hands of its celebrated French practitioners, Irigaray and Cixous, and, in the Anglophone tradition, Mary Daly.

Poetry and the development of specifically female rituals and liturgies have become a widespread practice in many places over the last decade. Kristeva's semiotic, with its challenge to the rigid categorizing and dichotomous thinking of the symbolic, has been inspirational, whether directly or diffusely, to a range of women writers and practitioners. Rituals celebrating female puberty, the menopause, old age, and mother–daughter relations have been developed in Jewish, Christian, Wicca, and other kinds of groups. While some of these rituals could be considered essentialist, in that they seek openly to celebrate universalized and biologically determined aspects of the feminine, they are most often written without any eye to posterity. That is, they enjoy a fluidity, transience, and freshness, being conceived and written for specific local groups with particular purposes (Ling 1999). This is also a practical, ongoing, and enabling example of Irigaray's female fluidity and her "sensible transcendental" (cited in Whitford 144b).

Some critics have identified the flamboyance and playfulness of *parler femme* and the various flowerings of women's writing *as merely* rhetorical, arguing that a broader, transpersonal perspective, one not simply based on a band-aid revalorization of what exists, would also be advantageous. In the field of feminist spirituality, the question of women as creatures of language—even if new language—is in tension with claims to move beyond *mere language*. This of course is a tension common to many inquiries into the spiritual. The contributors to this book share an acknowledgment of the power of language, specifically religious language, understanding its ability to distort and confine the spiritualities of women. This acknowledgment brings with it a double response: a drive to continue the processes of resignification and a desire to move, in ritual and communal experience, into a dynamic, lived understanding of spirituality in process, sometimes in silence, sometimes in the continuous changing of language. Such an understanding is not pleasing, or even comprehensible, to religious practitioners, if what they seek amounts to dogma, traditional fixities, hierarchy, and legalism. This book celebrates the women and men working and practicing within the field of feminist spirituality, all those who are moving into the future seeking to embrace "a *sensible transcendental* coming into being through us, of which *we would be* the mediators and bridges" (Irigaray cited in Whitford 1991b:144).

References

Anderson, Pamela Sue. 1998a. Abjection . . . the Most Propitious Place for Communication: Celebrating the Death of the Unitary Subject. In Kathleen O'Grady, Ann L. Gilroy, and Janette Gray (eds.), *Bodies, Lives, Voices: Gender in Theology*. Sheffield, England: Sheffield Academic Press.

———. 1998b. *A Feminist Philosophy of Religion: The Rationality and Myths of Religious Belief*. Oxford: Blackwell.

Anzaldúa, Gloria. 1987. *Borderlands/La Frontera: The New Mestiza*. San Francisco: Spinsters.

Bakhtin, M. M., 1981. *The Dialogic Imagination: Four Essays*. V Austin: University of Texas Press.

Bell, Diane. 1998. *Ngarrindjeri Wurruwarrin: A World That Is, Was and Will Be*. Melbourne, Australia: Spinifex Press. Trans. Carly Emerson and Michael Holquist.

Bhabha, Homi K. 1994. *The Location of Culture*. New York: Routledge.

Butler, Judith. 1990. *Gender Trouble: Feminism and the Subversion of Identity*. New York: Routledge.

———. 1993. *Bodies That Matter: On the Discursive Limits of "Sex."* New York: Routledge.

Chodorow, Nancy. 1978. *The Reproduction of Mothering: Psychoanalysis and the Sociology of Gender*. Berkeley: University of California Press.

Cixous, Hélène 1975. Sorties. Trans. Ann Liddle. In Elaine Marks and Isobelle de Courtivron (eds.), *New French Feminisms*. Brighton, Sussex, England: Harvester, 1980:90–8.

Diamond, Elin (ed.). 1996. *Performance and Cultural Politics*. London: Routledge.

Dinnerstein, Dorothy. 1976. *The Mermaid and the Minotaur: Sexual Arrangements and Human Malaise*. New York: Harper and Row.

Firestone, Shulamith. 1970. *The Dialectic of Sex: The Case for Feminist Revolution*. New York: Morrow.

Fontaine, Carole R. 1990. A Heifer from Thy Stable: Goddesses and the Status of Women in the Ancient Near East. In Alice Bach (ed.), *The Pleasure of Her Text: Feminist Readings of Biblical and Historical Texts*. Philadelphia: Trinity Press International: 69–95.

Godard, Barbara. 1985. Mapmaking: A Survey of Feminist Criticism. In Barbara Godard (ed.), *Gynocritics/La Gynocritique: Feminist Approaches to Writing by Canadian and Quebecoise Women*. Toronto: ECW Press: 1–30.

Graham, Susan Lochrie. 1992. Silent Voices: Women in the Gospel of Mark. *Semeia* 54:145–58.

Grosz, Elizabeth. 1989. *Sexual Subversions: Three French Feminists*. North Sydney: Allen and Unwin.

———. 1993. Irigaray and the Divine. In C. W. Maggie Kim et al. (eds.), *Transfigurations: Theology and the French Feminists*. Minneapolis: Fortress Press:199–214.

———. 1994. *Volatile Bodies: Toward a Corporeal Feminism*. St. Leonards, NSW, Australia: Allan & Unwin.

Irigaray, Luce. 1985a [1974]. *Speculum of the Other Woman*. Trans. Gillian C. Gill. Ithaca, N.Y.: Cornell University Press.

———. 1985b [1977]. *This Sex Which Is Not One*. Trans. Catherine Porter. Ithaca, N.Y.: Cornell University Press.

———. 1992. *Elemental Passions*. Trans. Joanne Collie and Judith Still. New York: Routledge.

Jaggar, Alison M., and Susan R. Bordo (eds.). 1992. *Gender/Body/Knowledge: Feminist Reconstructions of Being and Knowing*. New Brunswick, N.J.: Rutgers University Press.

Jones, Serene. 1993. This God Which Is Not One: Irigaray and Barth on the Divine. In C. W. Maggie Kim et al. (eds.), *Transfigurations: Theology and the French Feminists*. Minneapolis: Fortress Press: 109–41.

Kearns, Cleo McNelly. 1993. Kristeva and Feminist Theology. In C. W. Maggie Kim, Susan M. St. Ville, and Susan M. Simonaitis (eds.), *Transfigurations: Theology and the French Feminists*. Minneapolis: Fortress Press: 49–79.

Kirkby, Vicki. 1987. On the Cutting Edge: Feminism and Clitoridectomy. *Australian Feminist Studies* 5:35–55.

Kristeva, Julia. 1977. Stabat Mater. Trans. Arthur Goldhammer. In Dan Latimer (ed.), *Contemporary Critical Theory*. San Diego: Harcourt Brace Jovanovich.

———. 1981. Women's Time. Trans. Alice Jardine and Harry Blake. In Robyn R. Warhol and Diane Price Herndl (eds.), *Feminisms: An Anthology of Literary Theory and Criticism*. Houndmills, England: Macmillan, 1997 (rev ed.): 860–77.

———. 1982. *Powers of Horror: An Essay on Abjection*. Trans. Leon S. Roudiez. New York: Columbia University Press.

Ling, Coralie. 1999. *Creative Rituals: Celebrating Women's Experiences in an Australian Feminist Context*. Ph.D. diss., San Francisco Theological Seminary.

Lorde, Audre. 1984. *Sister Outsider*. Trumansberg, N.Y.: Crossing Press.

McCance, Dawne. 1990. Understandings of "The Goddess" in Contemporary Feminist Scholarship. In Larry Hurtado (ed.). *Goddesses in Religions and Modern Debate*. Atlanta, Georgia: Scholars Press: 165–178.

Millett, Kate. 1970. *Sexual Politics.* New York: Doubleday.

Mitchell, Juliet. 1974. *Psychoanalysis and Feminism.* Harmondsworth: Penguin Books.

Moi, Toril. 1985. *Sexual/Textual Politics: Feminist Literary Theory.* New York: Methuen.

Ortner, Sherry, and Harriet Whitehead (eds.). 1981. *Sexual Meanings: The Cultural Construction of Gender and Sexuality.* Cambridge, England: Cambridge University Press.

Pattel-Gray, Anne. 1998. 1995. Not Yet Tiddas: An Aboriginal Womanist Critique of Australian Church Feminism. In M. Confroy, D. Lee, and J. Nowotny (eds.), *Freedom and Entrapment: Women Thinking Theology.* Melbourne, Australia: Dove:165–92.

———. *The Great White Flood: Racism in Australia.* Atlanta: Scholars Press.

Pritchard, James B.(ed.). 1969. *The Ancient Near East; Supplementary Texts and Pictures Relating to the Old Testament.* Princeton: Princeton University Press.

Raphael, Melissa. 1996. *Thealogy and Embodiment.* Sheffield, England: Sheffield Academic Press.

Ruether, Rosemary Radford. 1983. *Sexism and God-Talk: Towards a Feminist Theology.* London: SCM Press.

———. 1992. *Gaia and God: An Ecofeminist Theology of Earth Healing.* San Francisco: HarperCollins.

Sacks, Karen. 1979. *Sisters and Wives: The Past and Future of Sexual Equality.* Westport, Conn.: Greenwood Press.

Schor, Naomi, and Elizabeth Weed (eds.). 1994. *The Essential Difference.* Bloomington: Indiana University Press.

Shields, Mary. 1998. Multiple Exposures: Body Rhetoric and Gender Characterization in Ezekiel 16. *Journal of Feminist Studies in Religion* 14 (1): 5–18.

Stuckey, Johanna H. 1998. *Feminist Spirituality: An Introduction to Feminist Theology in Judaism, Christianity, Islam and Feminist Goddess Worship.* Toronto: Center for Feminist Research, York University.

Whitford, Margaret. 1991a. *Luce Irigaray: Philosophy in the Feminine.* London: Routledge.

———. (ed.). 1991b. *The Irigaray Reader.* Oxford: Blackwell.

Wilshire, Donna. 1992. The Uses of Myth, Image, and the Female Body in Re-Visioning Knowledge. In Jaggar and Bordo 1992:92–114.

Wolkstein, Diane, and Samuel Noah Kramer. 1983. *Inanna, Queen of Heaven and Earth.* New York: Harper and Row.

Index